'Are the economic imperatives for employment and growth reconcilable with those for transformation and redress? What are the tough choices confronting a developing economy to lift itself out of poverty into a globally competitive player? Read more from Herbst and Mills to find out the answers.'

— SIPHO PITYANA, Chairperson, AngloGold Ashanti

'South Africa 20 years after transition is a complex and multidimensional country. Competing alliances and juxtapositions have changed the dynamics of the "new South Africa". *How South Africa Works* helps to understand the evolving paradigm and provides potential solutions. It is a welcome and unemotional addition to the debate – a worthwhile read!'

— GARETH ACKERMAN, Chairperson, Pick n Pay

'As we enter the third decade of our democracy, the disjuncture between South Africa's potential and its performance has never been as stark. *How South Africa Works* is an urgent call to all South African leaders to revisit yesterday's assumptions and to abandon the politics, policies and practices that are stifling growth and with it, for millions, the hope of a better tomorrow.'

— MARK LAMBERTI, Group CEO, Imperial Holdings Limited

'South Africa is a complicated place. Held back by its history, it is challenged to break out of a motionless present to build a brighter future for the generation still to be born. This is an enormous task that all South Africans must debate and embrace. *How South Africa Works* is a courageous and timely contribution to that debate and ne action.'

— MOE SHAIK, Development Bank of South Africa

'The great strength of this book is that the analysis is su wealth of in-depth interviews: Herbst and Mills illustrat Africa could work so much better if its considerable hum were to be liberated by economic reform.'

— MIKE SPICER, Wesgro

'Jeffrey Herbst and Greg Mills present intriguing findings about how South African businesses are squaring up to local and global challenges, putting a vivid, human face to South African entrepreneurship. Their proposals provoke much-needed debate on how to improve South Africa's economic performance.'

— KENNETH CREAMER, economist, University of the Witwatersrand

'Jeffrey Herbst and Greg Mills have written an exceptionally timely book. Notwithstanding the country's significant political and economic advances, high rates of unemployment threaten those gains and, indeed, the freshly woven social fabric of the "Rainbow Nation" itself. The volume meticulously examines this crisis and thoughtfully engages virtually everyone in a position to either contribute to its resolution, or obstruct that progress. Even those who will find themselves disagreeing with the remedies prescribed in *How South Africa Works* will nevertheless need to grapple with the comprehensive case made by the authors.'

— J. PETER PHAM, Director, Africa Center, Atlantic Council, and Editor-in-Chief, *Journal of the Middle East and Africa*

'A brilliant book that lays out the problems and solutions for the South African economy with clarity.'

— RAY HARTLEY, Editor, *Rand Daily Mail*

'Jeffrey Herbst and Greg Mills succinctly argue in *How South Africa Works* that economic decline is not inevitable and that South Africa can compete on the world stage. This book is a must-read for those concerned about South Africa's economic future and how it may develop.'

— ALEX VINES OBE, Head, Africa Programme, Chatham House, London

HOW
SOUTH AFRICA
WORKS

HOW SOUTH AFRICA WORKS

And Must Do Better

Jeffrey Herbst and Greg Mills

HURST & COMPANY, LONDON

First published in 2015 by Pan Macmillan South Africa

First published in the United Kingdom in 2016 by
C. Hurst & Co. (Publishers) Ltd.,
41 Great Russell Street, London, WC1B 3PL
© Jeffrey Herbst and Greg Mills 2016
All rights reserved.

Printed in India

Distributed in the United States, Canada and Latin
America by Oxford University Press, 198 Madison Avenue,
New York, NY 10016, United States of America.

A Cataloguing-in-Publication data record for this book
is available from the British Library.

978-1-84904-656-5 paperback

This book is printed using paper from registered
sustainable and managed sources.

www.hurstpublishers.com

Editing by Sally Hines
Proofreading by Sean Fraser
Indexing by Ethné Clarke
Design and typesetting by Triple M Design, Johannesburg

South Africa's economy has enormous potential. But to realise this, we need the efforts and leadership of all. This cannot just come from one person. All of us occupying positions of leadership have responsibility to put the interests of tomorrow ahead of today.

— LESETJA KGANYAGO, Governor of the South African Reserve Bank

Contents

Foreword

Nicky Oppenheimer

Countries should never waste a crisis. Moments of great urgency provide opportunities to usher in reforms that otherwise might be too politically unpalatable.

To have a good crisis, however, governments first need to recognise the problem. In South Africa's case, our rates of economic and employment growth have been too low to meet the aspirations of our citizenry, particularly the burgeoning numbers of young people, where unemployment runs at almost 70 per cent. While we are still a young country, other nations have done more over two decades than we have accomplished since the transition to non-racial rule in 1994.

The reason for low growth is that we have too little public and private investment in the economy, nearer 20 per cent of gross domestic product compared to over 30 per cent for much of Asia and nearly 80 per cent in the case of China. This is a reflection of both a lack of opportunity and a shortage of confidence. Business craves stability and policy predictability, but too many variables are constantly introduced in this milieu for its comfort. Moreover, the rates of return do not justify the risk for many, reflecting, too, our relative uncompetitiveness, the difficulty of doing business, especially for smaller companies, and overall lack of productivity. If we are to develop our economy and create jobs on the scale required, we need to attract businesses that can invest anywhere in the world, and not just in what lies beneath our soil.

A little panic can be a good thing; it is a call to action and does not allow the option of doing nothing because the question is too difficult. A little panic will stimulate a sense of urgency for government to change direction. As this book points out, South Africa has had no shortage of plans for development. It is the political will and leadership, at every level, in business, government and labour, that has been lacking. The history of successful global reform tells us that to take advantage of a crisis, leaders also have to act toughly, not sparing their own privileged constituencies.

We have to conquer the legacy and mistrust of South Africa's divided past to go forward. With the depth of engineering talent and financial resources we have available, for example, we should easily be able to resolve the electricity crisis, the record of chronic disappointment in education and the poor performance of many government agencies. However, these actions require a national and not an intrinsically narrow, political response. It requires acknowledging failures of governance and delivery, and acting on them. It demands breaking the stand-off between government, labour and business, which fuels misperception, isolationism and poor performance.

If we are to grow South Africa's economy and to live up to our promises to our future generations, we need to set priorities and act on them. In this, there is no room for 'them' or 'us', only 'all of us'.

I am proud that this study by members of The Brenthurst Foundation shows exactly how South Africa can work better. It illustrates that there are a great many South Africans who are poised to make significant innovations and investments that could change the fundamental trajectory of the economy. Many countries lack the basic entrepreneurial talent that resides in South Africa. The task now is to create a political and economic milieu that will encourage new investment and thereby address the fundamental issue of employment.

Foreword
Johnny Clegg

As someone who lived through the struggle for a free, democratic, non-racial and non-sexist South Africa in the 1970s, 1980s and early 1990s, I am wary of prophets of doom, and have a long view of history. In 1994, South Africa beat the predictions of a 'race war', 'economic collapse', and 'tribal and ethnic cleansing'. We found a way to negotiate ourselves to a new start, a fresh promise of an all-inclusive South Africa, and laid the constitutional foundations for this.

All things considered, we have done reasonably well over the past 21 years. The post-1994 period has been framed by the immense historical weight and consequences of both segregation during British colonial rule and then apartheid, and the terrible damage this wrought on the majority of South Africa's people.

Since 1994, we have seen the provision of three million homes, potable water and health clinics in rural areas, the widespread electrification of townships, the development of local and national infrastructure, the introduction of free health care, the opening of schooling and tertiary education for all, and the creation of an efficient and capable taxation system among many other achievements. Although not without their challenges, these accomplishments should be lauded, reminding us of the scale of the inherited challenge and offering a sense of progress.

However, like all societies undergoing fundamental transformation, South Africa has reached a point where the policy solutions developed over the last two decades are finding less traction and are even in some cases retarding progress and undermining the ability of the economy to deliver the dividend that our new democracy promised. We have entered a treacherous period of rising inequality, entrenched levels of poverty and structural unemployment.

Many of our economic woes derive from the almost impossible task of trying to rectify the racially structured economic imbalances that were created by the previous political system. Various interventions were attempted that were designed to redistribute wealth as quickly and widespread as possible as the majority of South Africans cried out for distributive justice. This is well and good if the economy is at the same time growing and creating the wealth to sustain such a radical economic realignment. Unaccompanied by growth, redistribution sets South Africa up for failure.

A more equitable South African economy depends principally not on redistributing the existing cake, but expanding it at a fast pace, and on job creation. This demands competing on a global stage, requiring all of: education, skills, leadership and a supportive environment, from labour agreements and predictable policy to reliable energy and efficient infrastructure. Although the right to industrial action is an important part of the negotiating process in any normal society, and an essential aspect of the functioning of a market economy, countries with an unrelenting focus on economic development do not have five-month-long strikes such as South Africa has experienced in the mining industry.

Jeffrey Herbst and Greg Mills illustrate how we have gone from an apartheid society divided by race to one where individual futures are determined by access to jobs. Higher rates of economic growth, which, in turn, depend on increased volumes of local and foreign investment, will make the tragic legacy of the past much easier to transform.

So far South Africa's growth record lags when compared to the first 21 years of independence of other newly democratic nations.

To achieve higher rates of growth and inclusion, the authors illustrate that South Africa should not hesitate in following an agenda for competitiveness, requiring all three parties to more closely co-operate: business, government and labour.

South Africa already has one critical component waiting to burst through – entrepreneurship. It only has to be given the opportunity to flourish. The benchmark for success should not only be in the way we plan but also in the way we implement our policies and the number of new small- and medium-sized enterprises that establish themselves, and in the volume of investment flows and jobs created.

In their extensive survey of a range of businesses far and wide across the country, big and small, Herbst and Mills spell out clearly the importance of practical actions to productivity, from regimes for skills creation on the one hand to allowing parastatals to fail on the other hand. This requires tough choices, and owning our problems and their solutions.

As I write, the rand has hit 12.63 to the US dollar, a 13-year low. The country is gripped by power outages due to bad planning, skill shortage and supply chain abuse at the state-owned electricity utility Eskom and the unfortunate choices in the practice of cadre deployment in the selection of executives and board members across all parastatals. The wider social framework is characterised by an increase in crime, a bloated civil service, municipalities that have become numbed by the thousands of service delivery protests countrywide, and the near-collapse of health services in certain provinces.

Cadre deployment and corruption not only impinge on the efficient functioning of the state, but erode that most precious of all commodities: confidence, and the general morale of the ordinary citizens and their faith in their country.

Official statistics put unemployment at a conservative level of 26 per cent. But there is a more persistent, human face to these circumstances. The traffic intersections in Johannesburg, among many other cities and towns, are now begging sites for unemployed youth, signalling also their minimal stake in the future.

I have faith that we can resolve these shortcomings and pull ourselves out of this dark moment in our development and political history. With strong doses of critical self-reflection, political will and openness to new ways of thinking, South Africans should easily overcome many of the self-imposed obstacles we have laid on the road in front of us. This challenge will either kill us or make us stronger, and hopefully we will look back in 10 years and be proud of our versatility, entrepreneurship and will to win.

There is, therefore, an imperative for a debate, a national conversation, to be developed around how South Africa *really works* and why it is struggling to meet the expectations of its people. This book is a timely and vivid demonstration that the need for dialogue in South Africa did not end with the transition from apartheid to democracy 21 years ago. We have to do better.

Everyone interested in South Africa's future should read Herbst and Mills on *How South Africa Works*.

About the Authors

Jeffrey Herbst is President of Colgate University, a leading liberal arts college in the United States. Holding a PhD from Yale University, previously he was Provost at Miami University. Dr Herbst started his career as a professor of politics and international affairs at Princeton University where he taught for 18 years. He is the author of *States and Power in Africa: Comparative Lessons in Authority and Control* (Princeton University Press) and several other books and articles. He has also taught at the University of Zimbabwe, the University of Ghana, the University of Cape Town and the University of the Western Cape. He has advised governments and international organisations, and regularly travels to Africa to conduct research, write and teach. A member of the Council on Foreign Relations, he has served on the Advisory Board of The Brenthurst Foundation since its inception in 2005.

Greg Mills directs the Johannesburg-based Brenthurst Foundation, and is the author of the best-selling books *Why Africa is Poor: And What Africans Can Do about It* (Penguin, 2010) and, with Jeffrey Herbst, *Africa's Third Liberation* (Penguin, 2012). In 2008 he was deployed as Strategy Adviser to the president of Rwanda, has directed advisory groups in Malawi, Mozambique and Afghanistan, and has worked for governments in Liberia, Lesotho, Kenya, Zambia and Zimbabwe. He holds a PhD from Lancaster University and an Honours degree in African Studies from the University of Cape Town. A member of Chatham House, and on the Advisory Board of the Royal United Services Institute, in 2013 he was appointed to the African Development Bank's High-Level Panel on Fragile States. His most recent book, *Why States Recover: Changing Walking Societies into Winning Nations – From Afghanistan to Zimbabwe* (Picador Africa and C. Hurst and Co.) was launched in July 2014.

Abbreviations

APDP	Automotive Production Development Programme
AGOA	African Growth and Opportunity Act
AMCU	Association of Mineworkers and Construction Union
ANC	African National Congress
ASGISA	Accelerated and Shared Growth Initiative for South Africa
BBBEE	Broad-Based Black Economic Empowerment
BEE	Black Economic Empowerment
COSATU	Congress of South African Trade Unions
EFF	Economic Freedom Fighters
GDP	gross domestic product
GEAR	Growth, Employment and Redistribution
IDZ	Industrial Development Zone
IPAP	Industrial Policy Action Plan
MIDP	Motor Industry Development Programme
MPRDA	Mineral and Petroleum Resources Development Act
NDP	National Development Plan
NEDLAC	National Economic Development and Labour Council
NGP	New Growth Path
NUM	National Union of Mineworkers
OECD	Organisation for Economic Co-operation and Development
PBF	Programa Bolsa Família
PIC	Public Investment Corporation
RDP	Reconstruction and Development Programme
SAA	South African Airways
SAAF	South African Air Force
SACP	South African Communist Party
SACTWU	South African Clothing and Textile Workers' Union

SETA	Sector Education Training Authority
SEZ	Special Economic Zone
SMME	small-, medium- and micro-sized enterprises
SOE	state-owned enterprise
UCTA	United Clothing and Textile Association
US	United States

Introduction

A Post-Heroic Future

'Nelson Mandela is dead. Long live the struggle,' might have read the epitaph to the first 20 years of non-racial democracy in South Africa. While the end of apartheid in April 1994 brought about political rights for the excluded black majority, their economic enfranchisement over the subsequent two decades has proven to be exceptionally difficult.

The fundamental claim of this book is that the overwhelming challenge that South Africa faces, and has to date failed to address, is unemployment. The current unemployment statistics are appalling and fall especially on young African youths who were promised a better future in 1994. As the premier of KwaZulu-Natal, Senzo Mchunu, put it to us, 'The pain in our stomachs is the rate of unemployment, the pain of poverty, the pain of the gap between the rural and urban areas, the pain of underdevelopment.'[1] This challenge, he said, 'is threatening our future'.

If the unemployment crisis is not addressed, it will be impossible to lift many millions of people out of poverty. Especially in light of the Arab Spring – fuelled in good part by youths who believed that they had no future – the stability of South Africa cannot be assured given compounding issues of insecurity, unemployment and lack of investment. The prospects of the African National Congress (ANC) will also be challenged if it cannot deliver jobs to the 'born-free' generation. Equally, the ANC's trade union partner, the Congress of South African Trade Unions (COSATU), with an ageing cohort of members, requires economic and employment growth to refresh their membership.

Government has long recognised the need to create jobs. President Nelson Mandela said at the opening of Parliament in 1996, 'Despite the welcome rate of growth, very few jobs have been created. In fact, against the backdrop of new entrants into the job market, there has been a shrinkage of opportunities.'[2] Yet, two decades on, the crisis remains. This situation has made many business and other leaders we have spoken to 'nervous' about South Africa's direction of change and growth, especially when compared to the positive changes elsewhere in sub-Saharan Africa. Yet, as we will demonstrate throughout this book, many firms have succeeded in becoming competitive and generating jobs despite all the barriers to commerce in today's South Africa. However, much more could be done if business' and government's interests and actions were better aligned.

Two decades and five 'new' strategic economic plans into its democratic transition, South Africa does not have the luxury of too many more chances.

We also do not believe that South Africa can solve the unemployment problem solely through redistribution. The most dramatic redistributive steps that South Africa has taken are Broad-Based Black Economic Empowerment (BBBEE) and the social grant. BBBEE, like its predecessor, Black Economic Empowerment (BEE), has succeeded in creating a small class of African business people who have wealth on the same order of magnitude as very rich whites – 10 per cent of the Top 100 companies on the Johannesburg Stock Exchange are held directly by black investors largely through BEE schemes[3] – but it has had, as will be shown, no perceptible impact on unemployment. As a project of elite transformation, BEE has been successful, but it is, as will be discussed below, more a burden for employers than a transformative agent for the unemployed. The social grant has been a great success in keeping an increasing number of people out of absolute poverty, but it pays far less than the salaries of even those with unskilled jobs. Simply put, South Africa is not sufficiently rich to redistribute enough resources to address unemployment. It must expand the economic pie and increase the number of jobs if the poorest are to benefit.

Black and white cats

As we have observed throughout the course of this study, constraints on growth and business cut across racial boundaries in South Africa. Equally their success will ensure job creation across the economy – or as Deng Xiaoping famously observed: 'It doesn't matter whether a *cat* is *black* or *white*, so long as it catches mice.'[4]

This retrospective of the experience of the first 20 years of the 'new' South Africa began with Mandela's death in December 2013 given how the statesman had personally come to symbolise both the struggle against institutionalised racism and the promise of South African democracy. We have deliberately chosen to write this book after the spasm of remembrance because there is little need to produce another report card on how South Africa has done, but rather to understand the choices it faces in what could be called, especially after the passing of Mandela, the 'post-heroic' future.

The book also differs from many other retrospectives in that it digs deep into South Africa's economic workings through extensive interviews with a broad spectrum of business managers, government leaders, unionists, entrepreneurs, taxi drivers and farmers, among many others. The country's future is being built daily on the shop floor, on the farm, down in the mine and in corporate boardrooms where South Africans are making millions of uncoordinated decisions that cumulatively will determine the country's future. These decisions are made in contexts that are established by major policy documents, but also by how legislation and regulation are understood and executed by officials at every level of government. Sometimes, the results are far different than imagined by government or apparent from simply reading the national newspapers. This book shows that how government actually works often hinders job creation. It highlights the actions of some entrepreneurs who have created world-class businesses despite the challenges of the current economy. And it shows how important it is for South African business to transform along with government and labour.

This book shows how South Africa *really* works.

The importance of history

No country, not least South Africa, can ignore its history and we will not minimise the burdens of the past. However, as South Africa becomes a 'normal' country – where politics centres around jobs, growth and who gets what – rather than be obsessed with existential questions about the future of the country, it is important to have an intentionally forward-looking and pragmatic perspective.

We are concerned with why South Africa has settled on its particular growth path and if the political dynamics in the country will promote or enable – if the rulers are so willing – a change in a policy direction that garners higher growth, more jobs and further significant reductions in poverty. We know from considerable work in other countries[5] that once growth paths are launched, they develop great inertia – for the benefit of those who are growing quickly and to the detriment of those failing – because winning coalitions reify around the status quo, institutions are developed to point to a particular future and governments gain confidence in taking further steps along the same road.

Successful countries have demonstrated that it is possible to jump to a higher growth path, especially at a time when a record number of people globally are being lifted out of poverty and when so much is known about what promotes development. South Africa is in some important ways a late developer because it only focused on how to enrich its entire citizenry after 1994. It therefore can benefit particularly from the lessons of other countries, if its leaders are so amenable.

We begin this book with a review of South Africa's major economic challenges and then describe what might be reasonable to expect after 20 years given the experience of other countries. It focuses on specific sectors – agriculture, manufacturing, services and mining – that are both critical to the country's future and illustrative of the policy challenges that leaders face. The sector studies emphasise the incentives and choice sets that government, business and labour face and why these actors make the decisions that they do. The social grant and education systems are examined to understand whether South Africa has established mechanisms where people can not only escape destitution, but also be ready to be employed.

We describe steps that some of South Africa's most exciting entrepreneurs have taken to build world-class enterprises, both to highlight success in current circumstances and to learn from these efforts. In the conclusion, we identify what must be done so that South Africa can work better.

Acknowledging progress

In examining the general and specific records, there are certainly many accomplishments to note since the advent of non-racial rule. However, our emphasis is on what more can be done given that few in South Africa are satisfied with the overall economic performance. Indeed, the country seems to be at a clear inflection point, especially regarding dismal job performance and the knowledge that a wave of young people will be entering the job market soon.

We do not believe that the inability to develop new policies will lead to South Africa becoming a 'failed state' in the near future, despite the debate around this status.[6] The country has considerable resources that will allow it to go down its current path for many years. Indeed, that is part of the problem. However, Eskom's travails in supplying South Africans with regular and sufficient power and the chronic failure of the education system to deliver requisite skills are signs of state dysfunction and the corrosive effect of political mismanagement. These are serious in and of themselves, but the longer the repair, the more daunting the challenge South Africa will face.

Accordingly, the most likely scenario, as one observer remarked to us, is of a 'slow puncture' rather than a sharp decline.

In such a future, South Africa will continue to resemble the status quo, but with ever-more unemployed and impoverished people, a government budget increasingly devoted to transfers and less investment for growth. South Africa will not, if these trends continue, be able to meet its enviable ambitions for its population. When the degree of decline finally becomes blatantly obvious – much like the frog that is finally boiled – it may be too late. What is at stake is literally the life chances of tens of millions of people who now benefit from the freedoms wrought by the struggle, but still await many of the economic benefits that were assumed to come with liberation.

This new generation will inevitably ask if enough has changed in the new South Africa.

This book is directed at policy-makers and citizens in South Africa concerned about the future of the great task of peaceful transition from non-racial rule. We do not underestimate, especially from the perspective of South Africa's leaders, the degree of difficulty in changing the country's path given that South Africa has such limited history of growth for all. It is precisely because the stakes are so high that the time to investigate these issues and to act is now.

1

South Africa's Development Story

> We should lay the scourge of racism to rest. This requires strong
> democratic institutions and a culture of compassion. None of this is
> possible without a strong economy.
>
> — Nelson Mandela, Davos, 1999

Nelson Mandela was not only a man of great moral principle. He was also pragmatic, making decisions about how to move his country forward and embrace the future, on questions of reconciliation and nation-building as well as economic policy.

When Mandela emerged, finally, from prison on 11 February 1990, he held economic views that were derived from the then 35-year-old Freedom Charter and his socialist past. There had been no real impetus for the ANC to change and Mandela had, economically speaking, seemingly been frozen in time. In January 1990 he wrote to his supporters: 'The nationalisation of the mines, banks and monopoly industries is the policy of the ANC, and a change or modification of our views in this regard is inconceivable.'[1] No doubt this rhetoric was in part a political calculation designed to keep his more radical colleagues in leadership on board, leading Mandela on other occasions and matters 'to engage in rhetoric and defend positions he did not really believe in', explaining 'that a leader who lost the support of his followers would have nothing better to do than write his memoirs'.[2]

Confronting and conferring with the international captains of industry, Mandela had what bordered on a Damascene conversion in Davos in 1992. He attended the World Economic Forum summit with the intention of explaining to those present why nationalisation was the right approach for South Africa. But things did not go as planned. Referring to Davos business delegates, he said: 'They had a dinner where they listened to me very politely, before explaining to me exactly what would happen if we carried out the plans we made in prison. I went to bed thinking while I had been out of the real world for 27 years, things had changed. Nobody told me I was stupid. But I could see that they thought I was not very clever. I woke up the next day and realised nationalisation would be the wrong policy for my country.'[3]

Mandela showed what is possible with a long-term vision, political courage and if pragmatism trumps ideology. It is time for a similar brand of leadership and pragmatism in today's South Africa.

■ ■ ■

Since Mandela's ANC was elected in 1994, the South African government has delivered many socio-economic benefits, particularly to poor citizens. There have been huge improvements in the social wage underpinned by scaling up welfare payments to the poor. The number of such welfare recipients has increased from two million in 1994 to over 16 million 20 years later. There has also been a notable increase in those with access to education, to public health clinics, and to electricity and clean, piped water. All of these efforts are reflected in absolute poverty levels: only 11 per cent of South Africans experienced hunger in 2011, down from a quarter of the population just 10 years earlier.[4]

South Africa is not only a much better country than it was before 1994, but the scale of the challenges of change it has faced often have been underappreciated. South Africa had to integrate seven armies and five different (homeland and South African) administrations, while attempting to make the system fairer, more efficient and meet very high expectations. It also had to develop its economy in an era of openness, of globalisation, rather than nationalistic protectionism.

For all of the above progress, things have not gone as well as they might have. The greatest problem facing South Africa, as the ANC itself has recognised, is unemployment. Joblessness remains stubbornly high, as much as 36 per cent of the labour force.[5]

Since 1994 South Africa has created jobs, just not enough for its growing population. Figure 1.1[6] highlights South Africa's continuing employment challenge. Between 1994 and 2014 South Africa almost doubled the number of employed from 8 million to 15.1 million. Despite this growth, the number of unemployed (as defined broadly) increased even faster from 3.7 million to 8.3 million. In 1994, there were 2.2 people employed for every unemployed person, a rate that varied over time and rose to as high as 2.4 in 2008. With the increase in unemployment since then, by 2014, the ratio has fallen to only 1.8 employed people for every one without a job. As a result, unemployment, using the expanded definition, has actually risen from the 31.5 per cent recorded in 1994 to almost 36 per cent in 2014.[7]

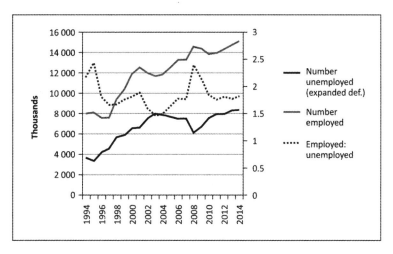

Figure 1.1: South Africa's employed and unemployed, and the ratio between, 1994–2014.

South Africa will have to create a significant number of jobs in the next few years, especially considering the country's demographic profile. For many years, South Africa will have a large number of young people. The government's National Development Plan (NDP), a development vision for 2030 released in 2011, estimates that people between 15 and 29 will make up at least a quarter of the population until 2030.

As Figure 1.2 indicates,[8] however, the burden of inadequate job creation is carried by the youth. Many young South Africans, especially if they are low-skilled, have almost no prospect of being employed. The life chances of this generation of South Africans will inevitably be greatly compromised by their failure to find a job and, accordingly, their families' dependence on social grants and informal sector subsistence.

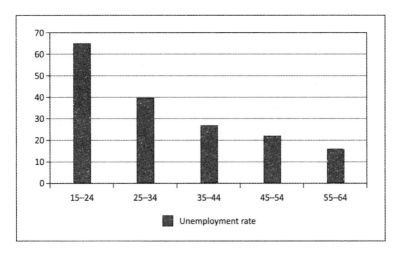

Figure 1.2: Unemployment rate by South Africa's age groups.

The NDP notes the problem starkly: 'If youths fail to get a job by 24, they are unlikely ever to get formal employment. Unresolved, this trend poses the single greatest threat to social stability.' In return, if South Africa is able to change its economy to employ a large number of young people, it will benefit from a significant youth dividend as these young people will bring tremendous verve and dynamism to the country.[9]

The NDP projects that 11 million jobs will be able to be created to support a South African population that is predicted to increase from 51 million to between 58.5 and 60 million in 2030. However, others believe that the population could grow as high as 69 million given variations in the rate of inward migration.[10]

The stakes are extremely high for South Africa.

The situation is especially concerning because some of the policies that have worked to ameliorate unemployment in recent years cannot be repeated. For instance, South Africa is reaching the end of its ability to borrow. While it entered the post-apartheid period with relatively little debt because few banks would lend in the 1980s, in recent years it developed what risks becoming an unsustainable dependence on borrowing, not least because of the spending on grants, burgeoning public sector numbers and salaries, and large infrastructure projects including power generation.[11] As then Finance Minister Pravin Gordhan warned in 2013 about the pace of South Africa's economic recovery and its substantial deficits, 'high levels of government debt put upward pressure on interest rates and can have other effects that undermine growth and investment in the economy.'[12] In June 2014, the ratings agency Standard & Poors gave South African debt its lowest investment grade – just one notch above 'junk' status.[13] Such changes will make the option of future government borrowing more expensive, though the demands to source international finance remain high.

This challenge is highlighted by the projections, as in Figure 1.3, presented by Finance Minister Nhlanhla Nene in his 2015 budget speech, of a government debt gross domestic product (GDP) ratio of 44 per cent by 2017, a projected six percentage points higher than the 'peak' set by his predecessor Gordhan in 2012.[14] The failure of the economy to grow caused the threefold rise in government debt. Accordingly, the solution is accelerated economic activity and better management of borrowing.

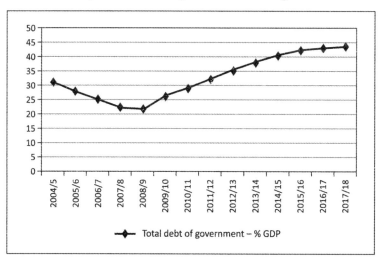

Figure 1.3: The government debt trajectory.

The challenging unemployment problem drives the fundamental inequality in South Africa: between the unemployed and those with jobs. As the minister responsible for the National Planning Commission (which produced the NDP) Trevor Manuel noted in 2014, 'The trends over the past 20 years are actually quite disturbing. In 1995, the poorest 40 per cent of the population received about 6 per cent of national income. Today, that figure is slightly below 6 per cent, notwithstanding a massive expansion of social grants. In 1995, the top 20 per cent of income earners earned about 72 per cent of national income. That figure today stands at about 70 per cent. For the top 10 per cent, however, the figure has actually gone up. More starkly, the unemployment rate for young, black South Africans stands at over 50 per cent. The comparable figure for white South Africans is below 10 per cent. Notwithstanding significant social change, the chasms remain unbearably large.'[15]

Indeed, South Africa has the highest Gini coefficient worldwide, as measured by the World Bank, the calculation that measures the difference in wealth between the richest and poorest segments of society.[16] A major cause of inequality in recent years has been the growing disparity of income within the majority black population, which is divided depending on whether they are employed. Black South Africans with the skills and education to enter the formal economy have done well while the unskilled and semi-skilled South Africans, according to labour market economist Mike Schussler, 'nearly have the highest unemployment numbers in the world'.[17]

The most damaging aspects of this unemployment situation have been addressed by a combination of the social welfare payments and the informal sector. While the government estimates the latter to be two-million strong, other estimates put this figure as high as between 'six to eight million'.[18]

While welfare and informal employment may reduce the worst impacts of racial, apartheid-induced poverty, they are not going to be enough. Indeed, poverty levels slightly increased to 21.5 per cent of the population in the five years since 2010.[19] At the same time, South African formal sector employees are in the top 20 per cent of income earners in all countries. As a result, the 'wage' gap between an unskilled employee and someone who receives a child welfare grant (and is unemployed) is 19 times.[20]

Employment is the most sustainable and broadest-based form of empowerment there is.

The health of South Africa, and its economy, can be measured to an extent in the tensions within its society, and the succour it provides to outsiders. The record is concerning. In May 2008, riots left 62 people dead, two-thirds of them foreigners, in what were billed as xenophobic attacks. Hundreds of foreigners fled the townships. The shocking murder of Ernesto Alfabeto Nhamuave, a 35-year-old Mozambican who was set on fire by a mob at the Ramaphosa township on the East Rand, was emblematic of the events. In the week in early 2015 when we interviewed taxi drivers in central Johannesburg, notable for their virulent anti-immigrant sentiments, a spree of attacks on foreign-owned shops was sparked when a 14-year-old boy was killed by a Somali shopkeeper in Soweto. Within a few days, more than 100 'Pakistani' shops had been looted, and Somalis, Bangladeshis, Ethiopians and Pakistanis, among others, had once more fled the townships. 'I'm not safe in Somalia. I'm not safe here. We've got too many problems,' said Faisel Ali, a shopkeeper in Matholesville, a tiny township outside Bram Fischerville.[21] The same violence broke out again, this time to greater international opprobrium, in April 2015, fuelled it seemed by Zulu King Goodwill Zwelithini's reported comments that immigrants should 'take their bags and go'.[22] Xenophobia appears to thrive amidst a combination of poor leadership and a suffering economy.[23] Ironically, those being attacked were entrepreneurs who had demonstrated that it was possible to build businesses in South Africa's poorest townships without government assistance and amidst very trying circumstances.

South Africa's widening wealth gap has occurred at a time when the world is fascinated by the cause and impact of inequality. Thomas Piketty's much-lauded *Capital in the Twenty-First Century*,[24] for example, sees the concentration of capital in a few hands and the related tendency of returns on capital to exceed the rate of economic growth as the main drivers of inequality – a fundamental flaw, he argues, of the capitalist system. Hence his call for a global tax to redistribute wealth. In South Africa's case, however, it is not the rate of return but the rate of joblessness that is the main driver of inequality. Just as Piketty highlights the need for political will as the core solution, ending unemployment in South Africa will require similarly large dollops of will and a laser-like focus on development above all else. But Piketty is correct to focus on the need to ensure the conditions that encourage commercial risk-taking and productive activity, rather than business-government collusion that raises prices and reduces competitiveness.

This situation is not entirely of the ANC government's making. One of the legacies of apartheid is that South Africa has always had an extremely low rate of participation in the workforce. Harvard's Ricardo Hausmann notes, for example, that if South Africa had the same employment levels as Latin America, employment would be higher by an astonishing 66 per cent.[25]

Little wonder that some South Africans advocate more radical redistributive solutions to the country's plight, with a greater role for the state over the private sector, not for the first time in South Africa's contemporary political history. There is much that business should be ashamed of in terms of the way in which capital made its profits in South Africa and the exploitation of workers in the process. The reinforcing patterns of racial and wealth divisions and opportunities, including education, have left both a bitter legacy and deep antipathy towards the still white-dominated private sector.

Nonetheless, while there is little doubt that historical injustices have contributed to this environment, it is unclear what advantage this rearward obsession offers government, especially in finding the means to deal with contemporary problems. The memories and legacies from the still visible past have constantly constrained ruling party debates over the past two decades.

The road behind

When Mandela was inaugurated as president of South Africa on 10 May 1994, he and the members of the ruling coalition – the ANC, COSATU and the South African Communist Party (SACP) – faced innumerable challenges. Inevitably, high on the list was how to begin to address the deliberate impoverishment of the majority, which was caused by institutionalised racism. Mandela noted in his 1994 inaugural speech, 'We have, at last, achieved our political emancipation. We pledge ourselves to liberate all our people from the continuing bondage of poverty, deprivation, suffering, gender and other discrimination.'[26] Expectations were very high that, after such a long road, tens of millions of black South Africans would be able to participate and benefit from what was still Africa's most dynamic economy.

The problem, of course, was that no one knew quite how this was to be achieved. In particular, there was no obvious model available to South African leaders that would produce significant gains in growth, employment and reductions in racial inequality. The economic model of apartheid – whereby the economy was deliberately distorted to privilege whites and prevent blacks from competing – seemed to have little to offer. Indeed, what the Afrikaners had developed, especially after they came to power in 1948, was actually more than inappropriate to the new South Africa. It was actually deceiving. To address the 'poor-white' problem, the Afrikaners had distorted the economy by government regulation and the establishment of economic institutions such as Sanlam, Iscor and Gencor. They were able to do so because the whites represented only a small portion of the population and economic resources could be diverted to them relatively easily. Far from capitalism, apartheid was a kind of racial socialism dedicated to enriching a small portion of the population that could not be reproduced on a nationwide basis for the benefit of all.

The ANC did not, in fact, devote much attention to the post-apartheid economy for most of the time that it was struggling for power. Accession to power seemed too distant and there were more important tasks that demanded attention. In addition, specification of economic policy would only hurt the ANC's 'broad-tent' approach whereby it sought to develop the largest possible constituency to oppose white rule. From 1955 onwards, the words of the Freedom Charter, adopted in Kliptown that year, were enough to suffice for the ANC's economic policy. The famous economic portion of the Charter is well known:

> The People Shall Share in the Country's Wealth!
> The national wealth of our country, the heritage of South Africans, shall be restored to the people;
> The mineral wealth beneath the soil, the Banks and monopoly industry shall be transferred to the ownership of the people as a whole;

All other industry and trade shall be controlled to assist the wellbeing
of the people;
All people shall have equal rights to trade where they choose, to manufacture and to enter all trades, crafts and professions.[27]

Less well known, but also found in the document, is a strong commitment
to unions and to regulation of employment conditions that would prefig-
ure policy decades later:

There Shall be Work and Security!
All who work shall be free to form trade unions, to elect their officers
and to make wage agreements with their employers;
The state shall recognise the right and duty of all to work, and to draw
full unemployment benefits;
Men and women of all races shall receive equal pay for equal work;
There shall be a forty-hour working week, a national minimum wage,
paid annual leave, and sick leave for all workers, and maternity leave
on full pay for all working mothers;
Miners, domestic workers, farm workers and civil servants shall have
the same rights as all others who work;
Child labour, compound labour, the tot [dop] system and contract
labour shall be abolished.[28]

Of course, during the struggle years, there was also a broad inclination
within the ANC towards socialist policies that favoured strong state intervention. This orientation was due, in part, because the allies that the ANC
counted upon while in the wilderness – most notably the Soviet Union
and the Eastern bloc countries – worked hard on the ideological indoctri-
nation of South Africans, and lent the liberation movement matériel and
financial succour. However, South Africa also had a home-grown communist party that, while never very significant in terms of popular support,
wielded an intellectual heft that was completely out of proportion to the
votes it might attract.[29]

The simple rhetoric of redistribution and a commitment to the protection of union workers would suffice for the ANC until the late 1980s when

the prospect of a transition to power became real. The ANC started to produce papers and hold workshops on future economic policy, but this was still a secondary concern given the need to confront the white state. In addition, of course, many ANC leaders were still in prison and therefore not able to participate in these debates.

An economic policy for the new South Africa

As soon as it was legalised in February 1990, the ANC began to engage in conversations with South African business leaders, diplomats and officials from international organisations to learn about modern economic policy and thinking. Inevitably, they began to confront the reality – in a world where the Berlin Wall had recently fallen and where their erstwhile allies were in a full-blown flight away from socialism – that the rhetoric of the 1950s and the ideology of the 1960s would not suffice as economic policy.

An early turning point for the ANC came in the aforementioned, now famous, 1992 visit that Mandela made to the World Economic Forum in Davos.

As Mandela put it to Anthony Sampson, his friend and the author of *Mandela: The Authorised Biography*, 'They changed my views altogether. I came home to say: "Chaps, we have to choose. We either keep nationalisation and get no investment, or we modify our own attitude and get investment."'[30] One senior ANC official told us that 'Davos threw all the cards up into the air' because Mandela, as he had done several times while in prison, had publicly changed his mind on an important policy issue, but had not communicated in advance to the ANC or its allies.

The very real challenges and contradictions faced by the ANC in formulating an economic policy for a post-apartheid South Africa were therefore clear by the early 1990s, before the transition from apartheid would even commence. The ANC's initial response was found in the document 'Ready to Govern' adopted at its National Conference in May 1992. The ANC reasonably highlighted at the very start its goals for the economy: 'eliminating the poverty and the extreme inequalities generated by the apartheid system' and 'democratising the economy and empowering the historically oppressed'.[31]

The ANC saw the state as responsible for the delivery of local services and as a provider of infrastructure with business 'making a major contribution to the provision of good quality, attractive and competitively priced goods and services for all South Africans'. The ANC did not go as far as saying that the private sector should drive growth, but it was still quite a distance from the traditional stance. There were certainly indications of a statist approach, notably: 'The democratic state will have ultimate responsibility – in co-operation with the trade union movement, business and other organs of civil society – for co-ordinating, planning and guiding the development of the economy towards a sustainable economic growth pattern.'

At the same time, the approach towards macroeconomics was arguably neoliberal: 'Emphasis will be placed on macroeconomic balance, including price stability and balance of payments equilibrium. The policy surroundings will be characterised by the principles of transparency, consistency, predictability and accountability.' Overall, the major pre-election document indicated that the ANC policy, while certainly statist and including a privileged place for civil society groups such as the trade unions, was also in flux and capable of absorbing ideas that only a few years before would have been considered reactionary.

However, the development of an economic stance that might have moved beyond the vague socialist constructs of the past was subsumed to the ANC's vital need to decisively win the 1994 election. The major problem that the ANC faced was that while it (and especially Mandela) was popular nationally, the recently legalised movement, not surprisingly, had no domestic party structure. As Ray Hartley, the author of *Ragged Glory: The Rainbow Nation in Black and White*, has noted, 'The ANC lacked the organisational capacity to run a major national election on its own.' The solution was to turn to the unions, which had managed to organise under apartheid: 'COSATU offered both a national infrastructure reaching into every community and an experienced core of organisers. It was in a strong position to bargain, and bargain it did.'[32] In particular, the ANC agreed to accept COSATU's 'proposed Reconstruction and Development Programme (RDP), a combination of fiscal measures to boost government social spending on the neglected majority alongside a major effort to right the wrongs of apartheid infrastructure. The RDP became the ANC's 1994 election rallying point.'[33] The tensions in 20 years of post-apartheid economic policy were therefore baked into the ANC's outlook at the very beginning: it had handed the unions considerable power in designing economic policy in exchange for political and electoral support even though, paradoxically, the unions did not represent the poorest segments of South African society because those without jobs are the most impoverished.

Alliance tensions: RDP to GEAR

At the point of transition in 1994, the ANC formally adopted the RDP as the actual programme for government and it was endorsed by Nelson Mandela. Certainly, the document suggested an understanding that there had to be a balance between the state and the market: 'We are convinced that neither a *commandist* central planning system nor an unfettered free market system can provide adequate solutions to the problems confronting us. Reconstruction and development will be achieved through the leading and enabling role of the state, a thriving private sector, and active involvement by all sectors of civil society which in combination will lead to sustainable growth.'[34] At the same time, a strong role for the state was envisioned: 'The democratic government must play a leading and enabling role in guiding the economy and the market towards reconstruction and development. Legislative and institutional reform will be effected to enable the implementation of the RDP. We aim to achieve a dynamic balance between government intervention, the private sector and the participation of civil society. There must be a significant role for public sector investment to complement the role of the private sector and community participation in stimulating reconstruction and development.'[35]

Ultimately, despite the contending rhetoric, it was clear in this document, issued right before the 1994 election, that labour had succeeded in entrenching its perspective: 'Central to building the economy is the question of worker rights. Past policies of labour exploitation and repression must be redressed and the imbalances of power between employers and workers corrected. The basic rights to organise and to strike must be entrenched. And negotiations and participative structures at national, industry and workplace level must be created to ensure that labour plays an effective role in the reconstruction and development of our country.[36] The RDP would set the stage for 20 years of economic debate: there was often intellectual diversity within the ANC (perhaps more than is usually recognised). However, at the end of the day, on the almost existential issue of the labour market, the unions were able to win, if not always in rhetoric but certainly in execution. COSATU's hold on the electoral fortunes and ideological core of the ANC appeared simply too great.

After the historic 1994 election, the ANC's economic honeymoon was relatively short as problems soon became apparent and the alliance between the ANC and the unions was shaken. The basic problem, soon to be obvious within parts of the ANC, was that they would not be able to redistribute enough, due to economic realities and the restrictions it had agreed to in the constitution, to assure a peaceful transition from apartheid that would satisfy its major constituencies.

South Africa would, therefore, have to grow the pie for job creation to be assured and poverty accordingly reduced. This view was driven by a realisation that the country would never repair historical injustices without investing more, moving the country's trade stance from protectionist to open, and by stabilising the macroeconomic environment. The hero of this period was Trevor Manuel, first as Minister of Trade and Industry from 1994, and, from 1996, Minister of Finance, who put in place a strategy enabling South Africa to enjoy a boom growth period in the 2000s until the global financial crisis of 2008.

As a first step, in 1996, the Department of Finance launched its GEAR strategy: Growth, Employment and Redistribution. While hardly a repudiation of the RDP, GEAR's initial premise was striking: the growth trajectory of about 3 per cent per annum 'fails to reverse the unemployment crisis in the labour market [and] provides inadequate resources for the necessary expansion in social service delivery; and ... yields insufficient progress toward an equitable distribution of income and wealth'.[37]

The formulation of GEAR signalled the start of public tensions between the Treasury and other government departments. It was the first initiative, too, in a series of government plans aimed at answering the tensions – growth or redistribution, public or private emphasis – that were running through the ruling Tripartite Alliance of the ANC, COSATU and the SACP. By their own admission, it was difficult for some ANC members to live with a market-based economy with 'the profit motive of business' at its core, 'especially in a highly unequal society such as South Africa's'.[38] This issue was viewed to be at the heart of their uneasiness about the compromise that Mandela had led them to after his Davos conversion.

However, the Mandela administration did not so much try to change minds with GEAR as to force it through. Famously, GEAR was introduced without the traditional elaborate consultation that was a hallmark of the Alliance, presumably because the government knew that the unions would never agree to it.[39] This was a critical opportunity lost to try to change minds and develop a consensus about the economic way forward very early in the country's non-racial history.

Under GEAR, the Treasury argued that South Africa had to have a growth rate of 6 per cent and create 400 000 jobs per annum. To do this, the government proposed some significant reforms that were a direct threat to the position of labour, including 'a brisk expansion' in private sector capital formation; 'improvement in the employment intensity of investment and output growth' that could presumably be garnered by decreases in wages; and, most tellingly, 'greater labour market flexibility'.

However, while GEAR contained many prescient critiques of the South African economy and its rhetoric enraged the unions, publication of the document did not yield major reforms. As Hartley notes, '[F]ollowing the strong political challenge to GEAR from within the ANC and its Alliance partners, government wilted. Despite many public pronouncements and plans to do so, no changes to the labour markets would ever be implemented.'[40]

Alec Erwin, the Minister of Trade and Industry and, later, Public Enterprises in Mbeki's government, says, 'The issue of labour market flexibility was always a contentious issue … many (myself included) have never really bought the argument in the South African context as we don't in fact have as organised a labour market as is contended by capital … As it was it was a red rag to the bull for the unions and in my view rightly so.'

Erwin identifies several constraints to the South African economy *circa* 1994: a low rate of saving; low wages for the lower echelons of the civil service; inflated and excessive wage bills inherited from the homelands; too high wages as a proportion of total state expenditure; that public sector capital expenditure had largely ground to a halt; and no access to capital markets.

As a result, 'In the main GEAR was a macroeconomic stabilisation programme designed to give South Africa access to capital markets and to prevent a rapid rise in inflation. We needed the former as our saving rate has been low for a long time due to a range of structural reasons,' he says. '[W]e had a basic structural problem in that we were borrowing for consumption – a problem for growth.'[41]

Sipho Pityana was the director-general in the Department of Labour during the Mandela presidency. Over the issue of the failure to implement GEAR's precepts on labour market flexibility, he recalls that at the time 'Treasury and Labour were in different places, as you can imagine, on labour reform. There was a strong feeling from Treasury that what we were doing would result in a too rigid labour market, with negative consequences for employment and growth.' The outcome for GEAR, he notes, 'was a reflection and function of the balance of forces in the political arena at the time, where labour was a major constituency, and of the prevailing policy thinking around redress towards labour in meeting its demands.'[42]

GEAR was thus more a rhetorical than policy loss for COSATU, but it set the stage for profound tensions within in the Tripartite Alliance over the following years: labour, a formal member of the electoral alliance, was able to assert its interests in high wages and a regulated employment market that made it hard to fire workers. However, it was recognised in some parts of the government and even the ANC that a high-wage policy in a low-skill economy would prevent the country from adding jobs at the rate that it needed. There was a fundamental contradiction between the relatively few number of employed who were unionised, relatively highly paid and with job security – enforced by government regulations that made it extremely difficult to shed workers due to business circumstances or to fire them for cause – and the unemployed who had none of the above.

A legacy of distrust with business

The ANC itself recognised that the almost reflexive distrust of business in what would inevitably be a largely market-based economy was a problem. And it was also widely acknowledged across South Africa that after 1994 there was, in fact, much still to be discussed because the architects of the transition had wisely left some critical economic issues – including a roadmap for land redistribution, targets for reduction in inequality and the modalities of income redistribution – unresolved simply because to address them might have derailed the march to the April 1994 non-racial election.

Various attempts were therefore made to create dialogue between government and business. However, those efforts – including the National Economic Development and Labour Council (NEDLAC),[43] involving labour, Business Leadership South Africa, Business Unity South Africa, Big Business Working Group and so on – have had limited results. They have failed partly because the ANC and the government it controls sees white-dominated firms increasingly, in the words of one white business person, as 'little more than an impediment to the Nirvana of a black-owned economy'.[44] In turn, business has felt no compulsion to move beyond immediate commercial interests to embrace the ANC agenda, and has inevitably struggled to speak with a single, unified voice.

A key business-led attempt to advance the debate around jobs and growth was in the form of the 'Growth for All' economic strategy prepared for the South Africa Foundation in February 1996. The document called for a 'comprehensive reform programme' in dealing with what it saw as South Africa's biggest challenge of unemployment. Noting that if the 'economic challenges are not met, and economic policy is not transformed, then the world will forget about the political miracle before long, because its economy would have failed'.[45] 'Growth for All' argued that South Africa's economic growth rate was too low to address steadily rising unemployment. Instead the country needed a 'development strategy 1996–2015', it said, to enable 'rapid and sustained growth (5–6 per cent per annum) and job growth rapid enough (3.5–4 per cent per annum) to cut unemployment markedly'. It called for greater labour flexibility in creating a zone of entry for outsiders, in the form of a dual labour market rather than overall deregulation.

Despite the plea in the document that '[g]overnment should work with business, not against it', 'Growth for All' was expressly rejected publicly by government. Even though some of its tenets, for example those on sound macroeconomic policy and limits on government spending, found policy expression soon after in GEAR, and despite its overall orthodoxy and government apparently accepting the value of the document in private, in the words of one of its authors 'government viewed the business establishment prescribing what economic policy should be'.[46] 'The last thing in the world the government wanted,' in the words of a business delegate who attended the briefing of then Deputy President Mbeki and his team in Cape Town, 'was to be marching to tune of business, especially given the imminence of GEAR.'[47] The fundamental problem with 'Growth for All' was thus less the message, given GEAR's ultimate similarity, than the messenger.

It was perhaps therefore not surprising that when South Africa began to grow, the uptick in economic performance did not lead to concomitant employment gains.

Growth, but not enough jobs

Figure 1.4[48] illustrates South Africa's growth history since the beginning of non-racial rule. The post-1994 economic environment has certainly been better than the waning days of apartheid. For instance, the increase in GDP between 1984 and 1994 was 0.8 per cent, but rose to 3 per cent between 1995 and 2005.[49] The 'golden period' seems to have been between 2004 and 2007 when GDP increased each year by more than 4.5 per cent. Since the recession in 2008, growth has resumed, but at a lower rate.

Yet, even South Africa's greater growth has not created jobs in the volume required. While GEAR reinforced the government's commitment to macroeconomic balance and therefore promoted growth, it and subsequent programmes have set South Africa down the path of growth without adequate jobs because employers were incentivised to hire as few workers as possible

The poor performance can be directly tied to the high cost of labour, and the difficulties presented by government protection of existing workers.

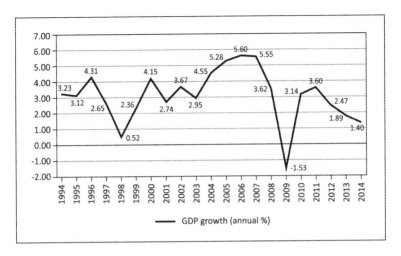

Figure 1.4: South Africa's GDP growth since 1994.

The minimum wage helps structure the cost of labour. Writing in 2012, Mike Cohen and Andres Martinez noted, '[T]he minimum monthly wage paid to a 19-year-old apprentice in South Africa is $543.00. In China, where unemployment is at 4.1 per cent, the minimum wage is $183.00, while it's $300.00 in Brazil and $30.00 in India. Brazil's jobless rate is 5.8 per cent, while in India it's 9.8 per cent.'[50] South African starting salaries are just 4 per cent below gross OECD (Organisation for Economic Co-operation and Development, a group[51] of 34 developed countries) salaries, and may be higher after the deduction of taxes. South African teachers, for example, start about 11.5 per cent higher than the simple average of all these countries on a purchasing power parity basis.[52] As Figure 1.5 demonstrates, South African labour costs have risen at a faster rate than OECD countries throughout the first 15 years of the post-apartheid period, explaining rather clearly why it seems to become ever-more difficult to employ workers. The wage disparities have continued in recent years. As Schussler notes, 'A South African miner earns more than twice the per capita GDP income share compared to miners in India or Brazil, while the minimum wage for government employees is six times the ratio of Russia's minimum wage.'[53]

The high wages of the employed South Africans are driven in significant part by the power of unions. At a time when unions across much of the world have become less influential, over the last 20 years, South African unions have been able to confront business, construct a high minimum wage, help design the high-wage policies of state-owned business and influence government policy because they are themselves part of the ruling Alliance and because they are critical to the ANC's electoral success. Few unions in other countries have recently had that much leverage.

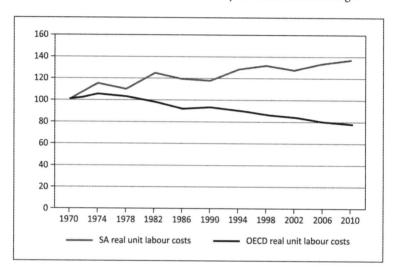

Figure 1.5: OECD and South African real unit labour costs.

It is not only that South African wages are high in themselves, but compared to the output per worker in the competition, they are expensive. For example, in coal mining, Australian workers are paid five times more, but produce 10 times as much per employee than their South African counterpart. A similar point was made to us about apple farming, 'The minimum wage in the South Tyrol region of Europe is ten times than it is in South Africa, but their productivity is ten times what it is in South Africa.'[54] According to the World Economic Forum, South Africa rates 136th in the world in terms of the relationship of pay to productivity, a strikingly bad performance.[55]

The South African government has also created, partially by design but sometimes perhaps inadvertently, a regulatory system that is often highly discouraging to employers. Early on, the unions were able to pass legislation highly favourable to workers. The Labour Relations Act continued previous labour legislation and required compulsory arbitration when there was an allegation of unfair dismissal. The Basic Conditions of Employment Act 'provides a minimum protective floor for workers' rights by proscribing minimum standards and conditions of employment, including minimum wages in individual economic sectors, and by regulating matters such as hours of work, overtime payments, leave, and severance pay.'[56] And the Employment Equity Act of 1998 inter alia stipulates that, through affirmative action, 'suitably qualified employees from designated groups have equal employment opportunity and are equitably represented in all occupational categories and levels of the workforce.'[57]

The current labour regime is particularly costly to smaller businesses that demand labour flexibility given acute variations in commercial demand. As will be seen in Chapter 5 on manufacturing, government and bigger business have devised a structure of wage negotiations through sectoral Bargaining Councils, which can be extended to non-signatories in the sector. As a result, small- and medium-sized businesses are often hurt because they have different cost structures. Also, dissimilar companies (for example, steel producers and light manufacturers) are frequently lumped together despite real differences in how they operate.

Rather than improve labour flexibility, encouraging employers to employ more workers, government has attempted to clamp down on labour brokering (which has sought to increase such flexibility by outsourcing casual labour) and even on the informal sector. With unemployment at some 6.6 million people, comprising the unemployed (4.4 million) and discouraged (2.2 million), the informal sector offers some options to the jobless and social grants provide limited benefits to some families. Yet, mooted business licensing regulations and the threat to clamp down on street hawkers, both apparently driven by a need to control and to prevent tax leakage, is harsh and unjust given the absence of alternatives.[58]

Overall, South African labour regulations have created what is in many ways a notoriously inflexible labour market. The World Economic Forum rates South Africa 113th in the world in overall labour market efficiency, including sub-ranks of 131st for flexibility, 144th for co-operation in labour-employer relations, 139th in flexibility of wage determination and 143rd in hiring and firing practices.[59]

Business has not necessarily fought the unions very hard over wages because firms recognise the political realities and because they have other options. Companies have chosen not to invest at all, placing capital elsewhere where labour is less expensive, or spending heavily on machines that are becoming relatively more economical and do not strike. Indeed, we document in later chapters that a high wage/low employment future is fine for many companies.

The unions vociferously defend their position as not only helping their own members but also all South Africans. They note the very high dependency ratio in South Africa: each union member, according to Dumisani Dakile, Gauteng provincial secretary of COSATU, supports 10 family members, including the young, elderly and the unemployed.[60] Unions also note that the structural challenges in the South African economy inherited from colonialism and apartheid – including gross inequality, a poorly educated workforce and a spatial distribution of housing that makes it very expensive for blacks to set up businesses and travel to work – are more important than the wage demands of workers in determining how the economy generates jobs. The ANC, they argue, has done some work to redress these structural imbalances, but not enough. Until the apartheid inheritances are addressed, the unions view it as cynical to claim that they are the chief villains in the unemployment crisis.

While the economy – or at least some aspects of it – moved forward, the ANC government recognised in the 2000s that growth was still not fast enough. Therefore, another economic policy statement – the Accelerated and Shared Growth Initiative for South Africa (ASGISA) – was developed in 2006. ASGISA saw a major role for government and, thus, the trade unions, perhaps as a sop by President Thabo Mbeki to the left after he had fired Jacob Zuma as deputy president in June 2005.[61] Although the left was lukewarm about the document, there was even less hope that it would lead to labour market restructuring than GEAR.

Eventually, President Mbeki's attempts to make policy formulation the exclusive domain of the ruling party, and not the Alliance, ended in failure. Rather than support the government policy, the unions threw their support behind Zuma, who was elected ANC president in December 2007 at the Polokwane party conference, in what has been described as a victory by a political 'alliance of the wounded'.[62] The ANC's internal policy and decision-making dynamics and its inability to execute against its professed developmental path (and vision) have made it possible for COSATU to protect the relatively privileged position of those already employed against the interests of the poor. Mbeki shortly thereafter lost the South African presidency and Kgalema Motlanthe became interim president before Zuma was elected outright in May 2009.

Polokwane's double whammy

Polokwane was a turning point, not only because it was an outright repudiation of Mbeki and his stress on macroeconomic stability, but also because of the deliberate hard left turn on economic policy driven by the unions. A resolution on economic transformation noted, 'The changes we seek will not emerge spontaneously from the "invisible hand" of the market ... [t]he state must play a central and strategic role, by directly investing in underdeveloped areas and directing private sector investment.'[63] The government had hardly made the kind of reforms necessary to promote significant employment growth, but now, with the unions among the clear backers of Zuma, even the possibility of change was foreclosed. Once again, COSATU, at that point just over two million strong,[64] was a power broker for the ANC.

After Polokwane there was an inward turn, away from the markets and a mixed economy towards the 'developmental state'.

But not everything changed for the worst after Polokwane. Some of the policy missteps were made under Mbeki, not least the failure to invest in Eskom, by the former president's own subsequent admission.[65] Public investment levels (as a percentage of GDP) fell considerably from the mid-1970s and only rose again during the ASGISA period, though this still remains, around the 20 per cent levels, too low for the growth rate required (see Figure 1.6).[66] While the Mbeki era was lauded for its fiscal conservatism, this rectitude has proven costly to the health of long-term infrastructure requirements. Figure 1.6 also highlights the comparative consistency in private sector investment levels in the economy, contrary to the notion that the reason for a failure of post-apartheid transformation is the investment 'strike' by business.

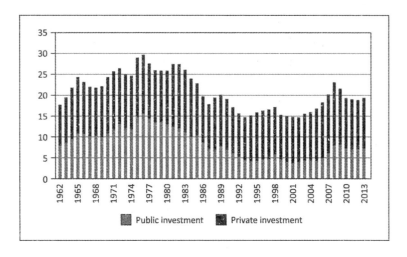

Figure 1.6: South African private and public investment as a percentage of GDP.

The reason for the low level of public investment during the GEAR years has been explained by government members at the time as partly down to the overwhelming focus on macroeconomic stability – 'we wanted to perform our own structural adjustment programme', says President Mbeki's strategy adviser Joel Netshitenzhe – and in 'not wishing to borrow'. Likewise the failure to focus on the labour flexibility component advanced in GEAR (termed an 'appropriately structured flexibility within the collective bargaining system') was down to, as he puts it, 'not wishing to be distracted from the primary task of macroeconomic stability'.[67] Alan Hirsch, the economic adviser in Mbeki's office, notes, too, that 'GEAR was about cutting the deficit more than anything else'. In the process, 'it went too far and undermined the investment processes both by cutting resources and weakening the implementation structures'. This, he says, was a mistake, and an accidental by-product of the overzealous implementation of budget cutting to reduce the deficit. When the budgetary pressure eased, the first beneficiaries were social transfers (the expanded child support grant, etc.).

'This wasn't deliberate Treasury policy, but it had the impact of delaying the recommitment to investment,' he says. This was compounded by the events of the Asian and other financial crises of 1997–8, which 'heightened fears and fiscal conservatism'.[68]

Erwin says 'that there was not a decision to curtail capital expenditure; it was rather we were trying to sort things out so that we could get the level to rise. The later ASGISA programme had this as its key focus because by that time we were starting to run primary surpluses and had good access to capital markets. Then came 2007!'[69]

As Erwin indicates, a combination of Mbeki's 'recall' from the presidency at the ANC's Polokwane conference in September 2008 and the simultaneous global financial crisis marked, however, the end of the relatively high growth that South Africa had experienced. Between 2009 and 2014, South Africa's GDP growth averaged 1.7 per cent per year, compared to 3.5 per cent between 1994 and 2008. Private sector profitability grew an average of 5.9 per cent compared to 12.6 per cent over the same periods, while private sector employment swung from an average annual growth of 4.2 per cent in 1994–2008 to –1 per cent in 2009–14.[70]

The low growth reflected a failure to invest, even though South African business was, at the end of 2014, sitting on a R760-billion 'cash pile'. The government has preferred to label this in terms of an 'investment strike', but it is in effect a reflection of a lack of confidence and absence of opportunity.

Of course, the 2008 global recession had a major impact on the country. However, when the rest of the world began to recover, South Africa's growth rates remained low. Part of the low growth was because the relative boom of the mid-2000s was not sustainable. That growth was derived from domestic demand and high commodity prices rather than from South Africa becoming more competitive on the global market.[71] As one of our interviewees noted, 'Since 2008, unemployment in South Africa is up while in rest of the world it is down. South Africa gets twice the debt with half the growth.'[72]

Figure 1.7: Ratio of South Africa to sub-Saharan Africa per capita incomes.

Indeed, the South African growth rate has been well below the *African* continental rate, indicating that South Africa has not been able to take advantage of a relatively benign international economy since the 2008 crash. As Figure 1.7 indicates,[73] South Africa is still richer than the African continent, but the countries north of the Limpopo, which certainly have their own structural problems, are catching up.

In part, ironically, Africa's growth surge is due to those South African businesses that have preferred to invest across the continent – an investment stake averaging $1 billion per year since 1994. The 2013/14 annual report of Shoprite Holdings noted,[74] for example, South Africa's economy was 'falling behind other African countries where we trade'. While the turnover of their South African stores during 2013 increased 7.6 per cent, in other African markets this was 28.1 per cent; and profits 5.4 per cent and 26.5 per cent respectively.

Responding to the 2008 crisis

Inevitably, in the face of these economic troubles, the Zuma government has formulated a new economic strategy – three in fact: the New Growth

Path (NGP); the Industrial Policy Action Plan (IPAP) of the Department of Trade and Industry; and the National Development Plan (NDP). If nothing else, there has been no shortage of development plans since the end of apartheid.

The NGP is the product of the Economic Development Department. Released in November 2010, the aim of the NGP is to increase economic growth to sustainable rates of between 6 and 7 per cent annually in order to create five million jobs by 2020, thereby reducing the unemployment rate to 15 per cent.[75] The difference with the NDP, announced a year later, is in terms of the diagnostic of the problems and where the jobs will be created. Whereas the NGP sees jobs coming from investments in infrastructure (2.5 million), agriculture and agro-processing (nearly 500 000), the green economy (300 000), the public service (260 000) and mining (140 000), the NDP foresees that most of its nearly 11 million planned new jobs (by 2030) will be created in small firms servicing the domestic market.

While the NDP emphasises the removal of barriers and constraints to entry, the NGP (like the annual, rolling IPAP,[76] which aims to create 2.45 million jobs by 2020) places much of the low growth blame on an overvalued local currency. The NGP proposes 'an elaborate and controversial social pact to moderate growth in wages and prices lest inflation offset the competitiveness boost derived from a cheaper rand'.[77]

Additionally, the NDP trenchantly recognises an important central problem facing South Africa: '[T]oo few people work and the quality of education available to the majority is poor. While all nine [central] challenges [listed in the document] must be tackled in an integrated manner, increasing employment and improving the quality of education must be the highest priorities. Failure to raise employment and improve the quality of education would signal failure.'[78] There is broad agreement on the central importance of unemployment, including from the trade unions. However, the diagnosis of the problem differs, the NDP highlighting systemic weak capacity and the role of patronage and nepotism,[79] and COSATU preferring to pinpoint the lack of resources and nature of the apartheid inheritance.[80]

Across its 430 pages, the NDP – the document that has emerged as the central policy statement of the Zuma administration – has literally dozens of policy measures flowing from its comprehensive diagnostic designed to induce employment. At times, it swerves close to a critique about the South African labour market but then moves away. For instance, in a section on 'A Responsive Labour Market' (exactly what South Africa needs) the authors note all the usual problems of an inflexible labour market that does not generate employment, but they are satisfied with relatively minor measures such as 'clarifying' dismissal and retrenchment policies, 'reviewing' regulation for small- and medium-sized enterprises, and 'addressing' public employment labour relations.[81] There is nothing wrong with these ideas, but they only vaguely hint at the problems of regulation of the labour market and say nothing about South Africa's uncompetitive wage rate as a key factor of productivity. The NDP largely repeated the sentiments of past documents (although not as bluntly as GEAR published 15 years earlier) that highlight the unemployment problem.

It appears that those who authored the NDP understood what actually needed to be done (increase labour market flexibility and bring down real wages to increase employment) but they lacked the ability to counter the unions' strength. The unions were able to continue to exert their power in part because they had systemically infiltrated the ANC by placing stalwarts in key ANC positions, thereby entrenching their influence. The ANC, even after 20 years in power, also lacked the confidence in its own electoral prowess to try to shed some of the unions in order to be able to have a more flexible labour policy.

It is highly unlikely that the NDP can differ from past documents in changing the fundamental trajectory of the economy, and of unemployment in particular, without altering South Africa's competitiveness, a project that must involve labour, business and government. As one of our interviewees noted with brutal candour about the Zuma administration, 'New slogans and songs do not change economic realities.'[82]

As concern about the effects of joblessness has increased since Polokwane, government performance has deteriorated. Table 1.1 compares several international indicators that seek to measure corruption and government regulation in the late 1990s – roughly at the end of the Mandela administration – and in 2014.[83] Corruption is increasingly spoken about and referred to, including by one senior South African ruling party politician, 'as the elephant in the room'. Yet the corruption endemic may be worsened by government rhetoric acknowledging the scourge on the one hand, but failing to act against it on the other hand, thereby undermining institutional credibility.

Corruption may have been fuelled by the destitute circumstances in which many ANC and other cadres found themselves back in South Africa once the armed struggle ended. The need to enter a capitalist society with little or no assets, and against high expectations of family, may have compelled some to seek short cuts to personal enrichment and financial security.

Nonetheless, at precisely the moment that South Africa is desperate for investment to improve employment, it is becoming a less attractive destination compared to many other countries that seem determined to improve their economy. Corruption is worsening perceptions of South Africa, and in so doing, is raising the cost of doing business. This is not only a question of capturing foreign investment, but of convincing South Africans to invest in their own country.

Table 1.1: South African governance and competitive indicators.

Indicator	Year	Rank/score	Year	Rank/score
Corruption Perception Index – Transparency International	2001	Rank = 38 (out of 91 countries) Above Costa Rica	2013	Rank = 72 (177) Above Bulgaria
Index of Economic Freedom – Heritage Foundation	1999	Rank = 58 (161)	2014	Rank = 75 (178) Above Kuwait
Global Competitive Report – World Economic Forum	2008	Rank = 45 (134) Above Slovakia	2014	Rank = 56 (144) Above Brazil
Freedom of the World – Fraser Institute	2000	Rank = 47 (123) Above Bolivia	2012	Rank = 93 (152) Above Tanzania

There are several reasons for this marked governance decline. Certainly, one important reason is government bloat. While the number of government employees (excluding parastatals and those on short-term public works programmes) remained steady between 1994 (1.6 million) and 2006 (1.6 million), the figure increased to 2.2 million in 2014.[84] In 2014, 3.1 million people were employed by the state if parastatals were included. Public sector labour costs are rising quickly, more than 80 per cent in 10

years, an annual growth rate 6 per cent above inflation, a trajectory that
the National Treasury's Head of Budget Office Michael Sachs calls 'unsustainable'. Indeed, public sector wages rose in the wake of the post-2008
financial crisis, in contrast to other economies, and civil servants now are
part of the 'richest 30 per cent' of all South Africans.[85]

As Figure 1.8 indicates, the rise in the number of South Africa's civil
servants contrasts starkly with the situation of private sector employment.[86] By the end of the 2000s, state employment was growing four times
faster than total employment.[87] In the first quarter of 2013, government
employees increased to 22.6 per cent of total employed persons, the state
in the process becoming South Africa's single biggest employer.[88] This situation is inherently unsustainable as public sector wages are paid for by
private sector taxes.

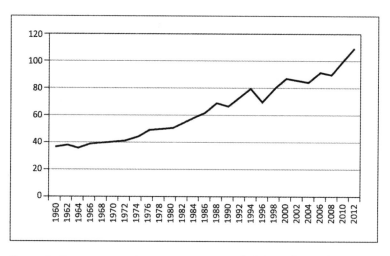

Figure 1.8: Government employees as a percentage of mining and manufacturing
employees.

Critical portions of the South African public sector are performing poorly,
including Eskom, Transnet, the Post Office, South African Airways (SAA)
and the South African Broadcasting Corporation. For instance, Eskom has
introduced uncertainty, if not outright chaos, into the economy through
poor service delivery, including load shedding. Thus, Ford, the kind of

industrialist that South Africa would like to have more of, suffered 90 power outages over the preceding 12 months at its engine plant in Port Elizabeth. Given that the plant was a high-speed machining process, each unplanned shutdown costs a few hours as technicians have to repair equipment damaged by the outages. Similarly, the Post Office experienced a devastating strike in 2014, which encouraged many South Africans who had the funds to privatise their mail service, much as they have previously done with security and education. SAA appears to be perpetually tottering on the brink of bankruptcy.

The problems of SAA reflect many of the challenges faced by other parastatals and the government itself. There has been 'state capture' – by which key state institutions become tools of a small ruling clique to entrench power and distribute favours, including contracts and jobs.[89] More practically, these problems illustrate how far-fetched the notion of a 'developmental state' – with strong state intervention, planning and regulation of the economy, as in Northeast Asia – appears against the South African reality of weak state capacity. Such 'capacity' problems reflect 'the overarching elephant in the room', says a prominent banker: 'cadre deployment. This is not universal,' he notes, 'given the excellence which exists in the Treasury, Reserve Bank and Revenue Service. But it is about skills and qualifications, the result of putting some incompetent and some inexperienced people in government, the first reaction of whom is generally to delay decisions.'[90] The effects have been exacerbated by the high turnover of senior management of crucial departments in the civil service.

While any one indicator can be criticised as problematic, the weight of the evidence is that the Zuma administration has created a far more corrupt economy with regulations that will impede, rather than create, jobs. The poor governance performance is especially notable as the South African public sector has sought to take on even more tasks in its guise as a 'developmental state' from the private sector. As one South African economist noted to us, 'South Africa has a developmental state mentality without a state that has capacity.'[91]

The South Africa public itself is now well aware of the numerous problems caused by poor governance. Afrobarometer – the service that has conducted groundbreaking public opinion work across the continent

– asked 'respondents to name the three most important problems facing the country that government should address'. It found: 'Corruption has risen on the public agenda during the past ten years. In 2002, 13 per cent of respondents thought corruption was one of the most important problems facing the country. The 2011 survey, however, shows a dramatic increase, with 25 per cent of respondents mentioning corruption as a priority issue for government to address. Moreover, this is the first time since 2002 that corruption has appeared in the top five priority issues. In all previous years, the top five issues were: unemployment; crime; poverty; housing; and HIV/AIDS. In 2011, for the first time, corruption was rated as more important than both HIV/AIDS and poverty, putting it in fourth place.'[92]

The road ahead

As we acknowledged in the Introduction, post-apartheid governments have enjoyed many successes.

However, these hard-earned triumphs are at risk unless, as the authors of the NDP rightly note, employment generation (and education) improves. The fundamental challenge facing South Africa is how it can stimulate economic growth that generates jobs, given that the governing political alliance is heavily dependent on unions that are opposed to the very reforms – lower real wages and greater flexibility for employers in hiring and firing – that would make it possible for employment to increase.

This book is dedicated to understanding how South Africa can get on a different growth path before it is too late. Historian C.W. de Kiewiet reminds us that in the past South Africa 'has advanced politically by disasters and economically by windfall'.[93] Yet, we do not believe that a simple windfall from resources will save the country this time. The lands have been exploited, it is difficult to harness resource-led growth in today's world economy, and the population as a whole, as opposed to a small minority, must now be employed. Rather, a holistic view of the country's challenges and opportunities must be developed.

2

Expectations of a New Country

Like slavery and apartheid, poverty is not natural. It is man-made
and it can be overcome and eradicated by the actions of human
beings.

— Nelson Mandela, London, 2005

The new South Africa is 21 years old. Given the modern expectation
that countries should last forever, that is still very young. However,
especially considering the power of compounding growth, two decades is enough time for some countries to have seen profound changes in
their economy if their government has created an enabling environment
and can execute stated policies. What could reasonably have been accomplished and what needs to be done in the future are therefore extremely
relevant questions for South Africa. As the 'born-free' generation matures,
meeting and managing expectations will only become more important.

Of course, the burden of the past continues to weigh on South Africa.
In this chapter, we describe what some countries, which also faced significant burdens from the past, have nonetheless achieved in two decades.
No country can follow the same path as any other, but these examples
show the great potential of South Africa if the entrepreneurial energy lurk-
ing (and described in future chapters) is unleashed. At the same time, the
record of the last 20 years serves as a warning of how little economic gain
will be achieved if an enabling environment is not established. As Sipho
Nkosi, a foremost South African mining entrepreneur, observes: 'More
than anything, government needs to create a good climate for investors,
giving us hope, and creating the necessary space for us to operate.'[1]

What can be done in 21 years?

Table 2.1 shows what some countries have done in 21 years after political transition (in South Africa's case) or after independence for Botswana, Malaysia, Namibia, Zimbabwe and Singapore. The same time span is used for Vietnam, starting in 1984 because that is the first year for which data is available after the chaos of the war and communist rule. The indicator is GDP per capita in constant 2005 US dollars, a basic measure of how fast the economy has grown, accounting for population growth.[2]

Table 2.1: The 21 years of progress: select GDP per capita (2005 US dollars).

	Per capita income at start	21 years later	% change
South Africa*	4 520	5 917	31
Malaysia (1965–86)	1 173	2 565	119
Singapore (1965–86)	2 915	12 367	324
Vietnam (1984–2005)	263	700	166
Botswana (1967–88)	482	3 282	581
Namibia (1990–2011)	2 813	4 290	53
Zimbabwe (1980–2001)	633	681	8

* The South Africa data uses 1992–2013 as more recent data is not available. As recent growth performance has been poor, the inclusion of more recent official data would not significantly change the results.

South Africa has had, at best, mediocre results in terms of growing its economy since Nelson Mandela became president, expanding the pie by about 30 per cent over 20 years. As a result, there has to be a significant reliance on redistribution for the African majority to benefit, a difficult exercise given the constraints of how economies work in the real world, in addition to the self-imposed restrictions on economic agency that the ANC agreed to as part of negotiating the peaceful transfer of power. South Africa has done better than Zimbabwe did in its first 21 years, suggesting that the pressures to engage in the kind of radical, self-destructive behaviour of the Mugabe regime are not yet present in South Africa.

Still, it is telling that other countries have done so much better and that the results after two decades, given the power of compounding, begin to have real implications for national futures and for the possibilities of individual citizens. Namibia, during its first 21 years, increased its economy per person by about 50 per cent and therefore has made considerable gains on South Africa, even though Windhoek also had to confront weighty challenges of reconstruction and ecology after independence in 1990. Botswana's experience of growing its economy more than five-fold when at independence it had essentially nothing, including almost no paved roads, shows the transformative power of sustained effort over time.

The Southeast Asian examples are even more dramatic. Despite Vietnam emerging from a highly destructive war and strict communist rule, it managed to increase its economy, even accounting for population growth more than one-and-a-half times. Singapore, despite being little more than a swamp and having been expelled from Malaysia in 1965, managed nothing short of an economic miracle in its first two decades. Malaysia also significantly increased its economy in the first 21 years, establishing the foundations for its rise in the international economy. This performance was despite being an economic backwater, which had decided that expelling Singapore was part of a rational economic policy.

What is it that these countries have done that has allowed them to improve their economies so quickly? We examine the lessons of two of Southeast Asia's most impressive and influential reformers: Singapore and Malaysia.

Singapore

It was not inevitable that Singapore would be rich. Independence was a tough time, reflects S.R. Nathan, the sixth president of Singapore, who served nearly a dozen years before retiring from his post in 2011. 'We had our backs to the wall.'[3] Like many Singaporean officials he has worn a variety of other hats during his long career: intelligence chief, permanent secretary of the Ministry of Home Affairs, several stints in the Ministry of Foreign Affairs and various directorships, including that of Mitsubishi Heavy Industries Singapore, an industrial and ship-building concern. He was involved in many of the early Non-Aligned Movement conferences where he made friends among the African group.

Nathan notes, 'We had no money, no skills and no resources. But we had a group of leaders with a common purpose and a common vision.'

Singaporeans soon learnt that even then they had skills that could be used more productively, such as 'those who welded or those who fixed bicycles. Our challenge was creating the environment to make use of these skills.' Each challenge was met with, as Table 2.1 suggests, outstanding success. 'We got steel from ship-breaking, and that formed the basis of the National Iron and Steel Mills,' recalls Nathan. 'Then we went to Japan to get help in building up our ship-repair industry. From Australia we acquired the know-how to make ammunition, and from this developed ST Engineering.' Singapore encouraged investors to improve skills by setting up bespoke training academies.

One of the critical first steps was to get the unions to play a productive role, he emphasises. 'The unions made demands meant for another world. Organised labour is a vote block,' he says, 'in a democratic society; this creates a certain dependence. But your problem is beyond this small group; it's instead to provide for the multitudes.' He had a special interest and role in labour matters. Ninety years old in 2014, Nathan cut his teeth in government as a medical social worker in the mid-1950s before being seconded to the Labour Movement ultimately as director of the Labour Research Unit during the 1965 divorce from Malaysia. 'We were faced with an international labour movement, which had laudable aims but an ulterior [political] motive.' But the government was faced with little choice. 'If you ask for European wages, they will employ Europeans not Asians. There would be no point in employing Asians.'

On a building site near Singapore's Marina Bay Formula One Grand Prix track is a sign 'Goodbye Yesterday, Hello Tomorrow'. It is a metaphor for Singapore's success. Nathan puts it this way: 'Our first generation of leaders, who set us on our path, was educated in Britain. Whatever their failings, we benefited from the British. There is no point,' he adds, 'in harping on the evils of colonialism – no point at all. It's over, you're in charge now. By talking about it, injustices will not become justices. This is in our hands. Instead, get on and go ahead with the job you have to do, and put money in the pocket of your people.' He adds: 'Until you solve your problems yourself, they will not be solved.'

Malaysia

Next to Penang's Protestant Cemetery is a Lexus dealership, a metaphor for the island's, and Malaysia's, contemporary rise.

Manufacturing today employs around one-third of the island's labour force, more than 130 000 people, generating an annual export income of over $6 billion. Despite being the smallest of Malaysia's 13 states, Penang contributes more than 20 per cent of the country's GDP.

This is no sweatshop economy.

Near the toll on the mainland for the second bridge to the island is a spanking new Bose facility – its first big venture in Asia. The factory has rapidly ramped up its operations since opening in 2013 so that it now employs 10 per cent of the $2.5-billion speaker giant's 10 000-strong global workforce. On the island, clustered in four industrial parks, is a plethora of high-tech giants from Plexus to Bosch, Motorola to Intel. The latter led the way in opening operations, establishing a $1.6-million plant, in Intel's words, 'in a paddy field' in 1972. The new plant was Intel's first offshore operation and second-ever factory.[4] This was 17 years after Malaysia's independence and radically different from the kind of investment that South Africa has seen since 1994. Then Intel president, Gordon Moore, the author of Moore's law positing the doubling of computer power every two years with dramatic development implications, laid the cornerstone of the next Penang facility in 1978.

The same exponential growth has applied, it seems, to Intel's other Malaysian investments. With an investment totalling more than $4 billion, today the world's biggest chipmaker employs more than 8 000 Malaysians across its 12 plants in Penang and on the mainland in Kulim, many of them the sons and daughters of the original 100-strong, batik-clad workforce. The Penang Development Corporation was established in 1969 specifically to drive economic growth, urban renewal and development of new townships, focusing its activities around the establishment of a free trade zone, the first created in 1972 on the southern side of Penang. The Corporation can provide subsidised land or, in the case of start-ups, factory space for small- and medium-sized enterprises, and works with investPenang and the Malaysian Investment Development Authority, the latter offering tax and training incentives 'especially for high-tech, strategic industries.'[5] Fiscal incentives include tax holidays for up to 15 years, and deferments of 'up to 60–70 per cent of tax losses against future profits.'

Monthly salaries have risen in Penang as skills have increased and global demands changed, now averaging $500–$800. Despite competition from lower-wage regional rivals in Vietnam, Cambodia and China, the reasons for businesses situating in Penang remain: widespread proficiency in English, the free industrial zones (which have superseded the free trade zone), good international logistics (one side of the airport, opposite the passenger terminal, is dominated by operations for TNT, UPS, Fedex and DHL, dedicated to moving out high-value electronics), and unions that are present but generally intent on working with rather than confronting business. Industry security specialists cannot recall the last time there was a strike.

As wages have increased, business has moved up the technological rungs. Firms in Malaysia are no longer assembly operations relying solely on cheap and bountiful labour. The upper end of the electronics industry is increasingly dominant across Penang. For example, Penang houses Intel's Design Embedded Center, a crucial design and development facility for the company.[6] This high-end shift has drawn a workforce from other states in Malaysia, some travelling two hours each day on company buses to work on the island.

Electronics today makes up two-thirds of Penang's manufacturing output, ahead of equally high-tech medical devices, pharmaceuticals and food processing. There are unusual spin-offs. More than 70 000 medical tourists visit Penang hospitals annually for complex procedures, including open-heart surgery, at prices about 10 per cent of similar operations in the US. All of these initiatives contribute to an impressive national achievement: with revenue of over $60 billion annually, digital electronics comprise a third of Malaysia's total exports.[7]

Lessons for South Africa

Our point is not that South Africa should or even can emulate the great economic successes of Singapore or Malaysia. Those countries developed strategies that may or may not be relevant to South Africa given differences in society, history and the nature of the global economy today compared to the 1960s. Rather, the Southeast Asian examples highlight what it possible even in economies that, in their formative stages, were seen as having very little potential. What can be taken from these cases is that leaders in both countries had a laser beam-like focus on promoting economic development and that they were willing, in some instances, to end failed policies or to adjust their perspective as their economies evolved. Labour unions were also part of the economic success, did not disrupt the nascent industrialisation and clearly also prospered as their countries grew.

Our Introduction described the evolution of South African economic policy at national level since 1994. It demonstrated that the South African political economy has a set of features – inequality, structural unemployment, high labour costs – that have, to some degree, become worse. At the same time, government does not apparently possess the necessary laser-like determination that would be needed to overcome these obstacles and realise opportunities, as Malaysia and Singapore had in their formative years.

One manifestation of the current economic policy challenge, despite numerous policy statements, has been that the South African government does not appear to own up to the responsibility for economic growth as was characteristic of Southeast Asian countries. On the ANC's 103rd anniversary, President Jacob Zuma stated at a party fund-raiser that 'all the trouble began' in 1652 when Jan van Riebeeck landed in the Cape, creating a howl of protest about 'hate speech' from predominantly Afrikaner movements. Polemic aside, President Zuma also used the occasion to blame apartheid for the power crisis that the country was experiencing. 'The energy problem is not our problem today,' he said. 'It is a problem of apartheid we are resolving.' But as journalist Hilary Joffe points out,[8] the drive to electrify South Africa's black townships began during apartheid in the 1980s. By the early 1990s, the number of households with access to electricity had tripled to about three million, with about 200 000 connections being installed each year. The electrification programme did accelerate significantly after 1994, adding another eight million households in the following 20 years. As Joffe notes, '[I]n advancing the "blame apartheid" argument, Zuma seems ... to be blaming the millions of poor households that now have enough to power a couple of light bulbs and a stove for using more electricity than the system could supply.' It also attempts to shift blame away from the 'obvious question': why did the ANC government not ensure new capacity was built to meet increasing demand, when the electricity experts forecast that the country would need new power stations by 2007 at the latest?

There have also been consistent problems with policy implementation partially due to unavoidable capacity issues, but also due to a lack of determination. Matt Andrews, a Harvard economist, returned to South Africa, the country of his birth, in 2006 as part of the university's team that was assisting the National Treasury. GEAR 'was fairly successful', he believes, because 'it relied on five or six macro-interventions around strengthening the budget process and controlling spending which could be implemented by small cadres in the central bank and the Treasury'. The strategy required only 'limited inputs' and 'limited successes' without widespread internecine policy and thus political battles. It also 'fed into the things that the elite wanted, principally stability'.

By comparison, he argues, ASGISA failed and the NDP was stillborn because they 'required co-ordination and agreement between government departments. Whole of government,' he says, 'too often becomes the hole of government.' Problems of co-ordination are acute because there is unresolved policy contestation, while unconvinced government departments can simply slow things down to a standstill.

Also 'anything that requires contracting runs into trouble around corruption, leading to lags in implementation and increased costs. At the end,' recalls Andrews, 'we did not think that the government was that committed to economic growth and job creation. There were other things that seemed to be more important, such as BEE. But you could "push for growth or push for BEE at the top of the economy". You could not pursue both objectives at once.'

Another reason 'why there was no good conclusion to the Harvard work', recalls Andrews, 'is that the welfare state concept was getting a lot of support. Harvard's focus was on making it easier for people to enter the labour market, and for growth to be the engine of job creation. Yet this came up against the ideological divides within the ANC, against those who wanted to pursue a statist, socialist agenda rather than one favouring greater market influence. And leadership preferred to appease the left wing, though there was no long-term sense to the creation of the welfare state. It could only buy them time.'

Perhaps, he suggests, 'the NDP was never intended to deliver. Nothing happened as a result of it. It generated nothing. But was it only [President] Zuma's intention to create an ambiguous policy space, saying one thing, but doing another?' he asks. This hints at what Andrews sees as a core constraint within South Africa's political economy. 'The gigantic problem is around implementation, and it's not only about capacity. There are institutional and personal bad habits about hard work and delivery which also may be impossible to unlearn', operating in an 'extremely messy' environment, 'a strange sort of controlled combat within government, riven by schisms, dysfunctional and unresponsive to policy ideas'. In this way 'the country is a product of its past, reflecting the complexity of the country and of the ANC itself'.[9]

Constituencies for growth and the unemployed?

It does not appear that there is a pro-growth/pro-employment constituency within the ANC. Ideas to champion economic growth are still freighted with concerns about promoting capitalism and a disquiet with what ANC cadres refer to as 'the profit motive' in a country ruled by a party with strong socialist inclinations. There is also a continuing fear that most of the benefits of economic growth will be captured by whites in a society where all debates are viewed through racialised lenses.

Business, of course, wants exactly those policies that promote growth and profits.

However, business does not have a particular stake in promoting employment. Indeed, many companies have been content to collude with labour unions in high-wage/low-employment contracts that promote the interest of firms in stability and that of the unions in supporting their membership. The unemployed, at the moment, do not have the ability to highlight the urgency of the situation in a way that fundamentally alters the national debate, much less government policy. The unions certainly do not represent their well-being; indeed, in many ways, the unions' interests are diametrically opposed to the plight of the unemployed for whom a low wage is better than nothing.

This orientation can be seen in the policies favoured by COSATU, urging further leftward moves. Polokwane was just a start. As Tony Ehrenreich, COSATU's Western Cape head, argues, the labour movement would prefer 'decent wages so that workers become consumers and drive up aggregate levels of demand' and a 'Proudly South Africa buying campaign' to raise 'levels of demand of domestically produced products [to] create more jobs and further spur on economic growth'. The unions also, he says, would like to see beneficiation 'add more value before exporting raw materials', a 'reconsideration' of tariffs to 'balance protection for infant industries to expand industrial capacity', the review of the 'tax to GDP ratio ... to generate more money in the state coffers for targeted investment, like equalising education facilities and resources in all schools'. Finally, they favour the 'transformation of the economy to break up monopolies that artificially drive up prices through legalised theft', and a 'reduction in interest rates to make access to finance more easy and to drive investment'.[10]

In addition, COSATU would like to close the legal loopholes that allow labour brokers, those whose intermediation facilitates working for contract rather than full-time workers. An estimated four million such contract workers are in South Africa, one-quarter of whom are 'intermediated' by these brokers. COSATU and the government argue that these workers are in precarious situations, vulnerable and exploited. 'But', says Richard Pike, CEO of South Africa's largest such brokerage ADCORP, which has 110 000 workers on its books, 'you have to ask "why" labour brokers exist. The answer is that the more complexity there is in labour regulations, the more outsourcing there is, and the less full-time employment'.[11] Such strains are compounded by a militant, politicised workforce, where union interests are increasingly geriatric and institutionalised. By 2012 only one in seven of COSATU's 2.2 million members was under 30, compared to one in three of all South African workers. Where just 7 per cent of its members were in the public sector in 1991, 20 years later this had jumped to 39 per cent.[12] With the expulsion of the 300 000 members of the National Union of Metalworkers from COSATU in November 2014 and the haemorrhage of an estimated 50 000 workers from the National Union of Mineworkers to the Association of Mineworkers and Construction Union, the percentage of COSATU members employed in the public and private sectors is near even. Increasingly, even COSATU's interests should over time move to higher growth of the economy and employment so as to refresh its declining, ageing membership.

Politics in hard times

In contrast to the determined Asian approach that forged national consensus around economic policy, the most notable result of the policy gyrations described above has been scepticism about where South Africa is heading.

A caustic view of South Africa's future can be fuelled, no doubt, by the utterances of government officials when they say that they 'did not join the struggle to be poor', as Smuts Ngonyama, the ANC's official spokesperson in Parliament, put it in 2007.[13] This sentiment is a long way from that expressed by former President Kgalema Motlanthe who observed of his fellow Robben Islanders: 'We did not join the ANC to become rich; we joined it to go to jail.'[14]

Even South Africans who are deeply sympathetic to the ANC, and who served under Mbeki, now express their open fears about where government is heading. For instance, Alec Erwin, a minister during the Mbeki presidency who resigned with his leader's 'recall' in September 2008, has said, 'Our economy is in a cul-de-sac.'[15] As a result, he believes, 'It's in need of serious review. We need a determination to do so, for a sustained period of time. We had such leadership during the Mandela and Mbeki periods, and ASGISA was the first attempt to change the nature of the state, which we had inherited. But things are now more fractured, where power is focused on more immediate ends, often more perverse ones. We have no vision, and no plan. We have unions protecting their membership, but the reality is that their numbers depend on growth in the long term. We need to rethink our old ways.'

Perhaps most dramatically, even South African elder statesman and Nobel laureate Desmond Tutu in May 2013 said that he would no longer vote for the ruling ANC.[16] 'The ANC was very good at leading us in the struggle to be free from oppression,' he wrote, 'but it doesn't seem to me now that a freedom-fighting unit can easily make the transition to becoming a political party.' Describing South Africa as 'the most unequal society in the world', he pinpointed corruption, unaccountability and weaknesses in the constitution as key issues that needed to be addressed.

Despite these sentiments, there is little indication of a dynamic within the political system that will force change, much less the focus on economic growth that has propelled many Asian countries. In one South African political party's internal poll in August 2013, 72 per cent of blacks interviewed said that it was getting harder to find a job; 48 per cent said that jobs and unemployment should be one of the two top priorities; and 54 per cent said that the country was going in the wrong direction. Still, 68 per cent said that they would vote for the ANC. Importantly, 39 per cent said that the ANC needed more time to address unemployment while somewhat fewer (35 per cent) said that it was not doing enough. The afterglow of liberation is still too great, the opposition parties still too suspect and alternative paths still too unclear for the ANC to be fundamentally threatened by an increasingly jobless population right now. In addition, the explosion of social grants, discussed later in this book, provides a cushion for some of the families of those without work to avoid absolute destitution.

Whether these forces are enough for the ANC to avoid electoral challenge before it is too late to reform the economy is unclear. The evidence so far suggests that the ANC's constituents will opt out of electoral politics and engage, instead, in informal means of protest against government if at all. The rash of service delivery protests and the organic resistance to e-tolls is one measure of this trend; as is South Africa's low voter turnout.

Making progress in transforming South Africa's economy is difficult given the inheritance from the past and the complex politics of a country hungry for the fruits of liberation. There does not, however, appear to be a sense of urgency in actually transforming the South African economy, a fundamental feature of Singapore and Malaysia's successes during their first two decades. Rather, the forces that seem inimical to increased employment are on the ascendance in South Africa. As a result, despite the achievements that we celebrated earlier in the book, there is rightly a sense that more could have been done during the last two decades and that time is not on South Africa's side. Still, the new South Africa is a young country and it can deliver much in a relatively short time if it makes the necessary changes. The next 20 years can be transformative, but will not be so unless there are intentional policy changes.

It is in this policy and political context that we examine next how South Africa has, or has not, managed to grow the most important sectors of the economy. These efforts will determine if the scepticism about the future is justified.

3

Agriculture
More than Land

In business, if you are not growing, you are shrinking.

— Eddie Keizan, co-founder, Tiger Wheels

At the start of 2013, unrest hit the area of De Doorns, about 150 kilometres north-east of Cape Town, where agricultural workers had been on strike to demand a rise in the minimum wage from R70 to R150 per day. Two people died in various protests and rioters burnt vineyards and sheds, causing damage estimated at R120 million.

The strike was eventually settled by agreement on a nationwide minimum agriculture wage of R105, which the government said would 'spur the overhaul of farming'. South Africa's Minister of Labour, Mildred Oliphant, is said to have based the new minimum wage on research, which showed that many farms would be unable to cover their operating expenses if wages were to rise any higher than R105 a day. The new wage was supposed to herald the beginning of a transition away from a dependence 'on cheap, unskilled labour' to a more efficient production system in which more skilled, younger workers would be employed. COSATU's Tony Ehrenreich said that 'restructuring would now start', and responded to claims by farmers that they could not pay the new minimum wage by suggesting that they could lose their land: 'If they can't use it, they must lose it. This is a country that has shown it cares about farm workers. Bad farmers will lose their land in favour of good farmers who choose to work with us as a country.'[1]

However, the director of AgriSA (a body representing commercial farmers), Hans van der Merwe, said the new minimum wage was unaffordable to small- and medium-sized businesses and would 'lead to major structural adjustment, which will mean more capital intensity and bigger units, which will in time take over from small and medium farmers. Tough decisions will have to be made on each farm.'[2]

The minimum wage dispute was, in microcosm, reflective of the fundamental disputes between the ANC government and white farmers. These conflicts have occurred at a time of great change in farming. There have been substantive global shifts in the structure of agriculture and methods of agricultural production. Average farm size has grown, and worker numbers have fallen per hectare as higher yields have been achieved and production has increasingly emphasised higher value commodities.

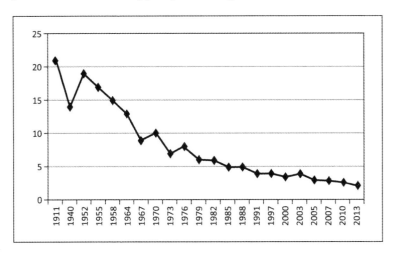

Figure 3.1: Agriculture's share of South African GDP.

South Africa's real agricultural output grew steadily, by 2.6 per cent per year between 1910 and 1980, though growth slowed thereafter to just 0.19 per cent per year from 1980 to 2008.[3] As Figure 3.1 indicates, overall farming has declined in importance as a percentage of GDP. Employment in agriculture has also declined 31 per cent between 2001 (969 000 workers) and 2014 (670 000), though it remains an important employer, behind only government, manufacturing and services.[4] Moreover, the National Development Plan (NDP) foresees a potential of one million extra jobs in the sector by 2030.

Land injustices

Political commentator Max du Preez has argued that land reform is about more than agriculture. It includes questions of history, notably, 'the restoration of pride and about a sense of justice'.[5] Land is at the heart of injustice against black South Africans, and centuries of poverty, even though agricultural output in South Africa is not simply related to land distribution.

The 1913 Natives Land Act drove scores of peasant farmers off their land, ensuring their lives as a subordinate labour force. Sol Plaatje records how he found bands of African peasants travelling all over the Orange Free State from farm to farm in the hope of finding shelter. 'It was heartrending,' he wrote, 'to listen to the tales of their cruel experiences derived from the rigour of the Natives' Land Act. Some of their cattle had perished on the journey, from poverty and lack of fodder, and the native owners ran a serious risk of imprisonment for travelling with dying stock. The experience of one of these evicted tenants is typical of the rest, and illustrates the cases of several we met in other parts of the country.'[6] In *Native Life in South Africa*, he noted, 'It looks as if these people were so many fugitives escaping from a war.'[7]

The 1911 South African Census recorded a 'native' population of 4 019 006 in the Union of South Africa, 67.3 per cent of the total population of 5 973 394, of which whites made up 1 276 242 (or 21.4 per cent). According to the findings of the Beaumont Commission, which was established in terms of the Natives Land Act, farms owned by whites constituted 74 per cent of the total at that time, native reserves and native-owned farms 8.9 per cent and Crown (state) lands some 12.4 per cent.[8] The dangers of the Act were, even then, self-evident. John X. Merriman, member of Parliament for Victoria West, said of the Act in the debate on the second reading of the Bill in the House of Assembly on 15 May 1913: 'A policy more foredoomed to failure in South Africa could not be initiated. It was a policy that would keep South Africa back, perhaps for ever.'[9]

As a result, from 1913 to 1991, black South Africans were denied the right to acquire land in most of South Africa. As Harvey Feinberg notes, the effects of this Act were 'worse than anyone anticipated. Rapid population growth among Africans and soil erosion in the reserves (partly due to over-grazing) seriously undermined African agriculture. And, after 1948, the reserves became the cornerstone of a key part of the apartheid system, the homelands.'[10]

And so the stage was set for the next 80 years of racial separation, economic marginalisation and political unrest – a bitterness that understandably continues, but one, as Zimbabwe illustrates, that will cost South Africa unless leadership aims at commercial transformation rather than only restorative justice. Yet, the government's plans are pointing in the opposite direction.

The ANC response

Speaking at the opening of the National House of Traditional Leaders in Cape Town in February 2014, President Zuma said that the laws governing land reform and restitution were biased in favour of land owners. The president called on members of the House to assemble a team of 'good lawyers' to take advantage of the recently passed Restitution of Land Rights Amendment Bill. This bill reopens the land restitution process with a new 31 December 2018 deadline for land claims. Zuma said 'history was made' with the passing of this legislation. Many who were excluded by the previous cut-off date of 31 December 1998 now stood a chance of regaining their land. A 'critical problem' was that while the process of seizing land from South Africa's inhabitants had taken centuries, 'when we are supposed to address this matter, we are only given a few years to deal with it'. The president said government had spent about R20 billion since May 2009 in acquiring about 1.8 million hectares of land for restitution and redistribution purposes. 'Work continues to acquire more land, and to improve the ownership patterns of land in our country, to correct the historical injustice of 1913.'[11] In his 2015 State of the Nation Address, President Zuma further announced that foreigners no longer would be allowed to own land in South Africa and that the state would have a 'right of first refusal' to buy land that non-South Africans wanted to sell. The likely effect of such a policy should it be adopted would be to significantly decrease the value of the land held by foreigners since there would be no competition amongst buyers for their land.

The government's approach, not surprisingly, has been criticised by farmers. Hans van der Merwe has said that land reform is critical given that land is in itself the most valuable asset of any farmer. 'Ownership in a market economy,' he says, together with security of tenure, 'are absolutely critical for investor confidence and basically for entrepreneurs to be confident about what they are doing.' The re-opening of restitution plans, he says, 'puts investment possibilities in the freezer for many years because of the insecurity that goes with such policy decisions.'[12]

The government and the farming community, therefore, seem to be at loggerheads on a set of fundamental issues. The ANC and the unions, driven by a profound sense of injustice, want to see transformative change in the area of agriculture. This issue is not only substantively important to those who might farm the land, but also highly symbolic given the history of South Africa. The farming community sees the need for transformation, but most have not agreed to anything close to what the ANC views as necessary. How this set of conflicts is eventually resolved will determine the future of agriculture and especially how many jobs the sector can contribute to the new South Africa.

The farming status quo

It is often claimed that white South Africans, who comprise less than 10 per cent of the 52-million population, possess 87 per cent of the land. Therefore, it is suggested that the 'solution' is simple restitution. For example, the Economic Freedom Fighters' Mbuyiseni Quintin Ndlozi has stated, 'So almost 80 per cent of the land is owned by less than 50 000 white households and trusts. This is a known fact ... Only a clear and unapologetic process of land expropriation without compensation can solve the land problem in our country to end the landlessness of the majority. The EFF is totally committed to returning the stolen land to end racism.'[13]

On closer examination, this shorthand for historical injustice, while a sweeping portrayal of apartheid inequities, is factually incorrect. Still more importantly, simply restating the 87 per cent figure obscures the real challenges facing farming.[14]

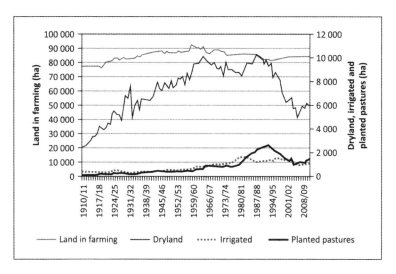

Figure 3.2: Land use in South Africa.

As of March 2011, 25 per cent of South Africa's surface area of 122 million hectares – 31 million hectares – was held by the state. The balance of state and privately owned land varies between provinces. For example, in both the Western Cape and Gauteng, 55 per cent was owned by the state, while in the Free State and the Northern Cape private owners possess 89 per cent and 91 per cent respectively. If state-owned land was previously regarded as part of the white-owned 87 per cent bloc (as is implicit in the argument), today this land should be regarded as black-owned. As the South African Institute of Race Relations' Frans Cronjé has noted, 'There is nothing preventing the state from handing title to much of that land to black people.'[15]

Since 1995, 2.6 million hectares have been distributed via land *restitution* programmes. A further 3.1 million hectares have been handed to black South Africans through the land *redistribution* programme by 2010. Additionally, more than R5 billion has been paid out to restitution claimants who accepted cash payments instead of land, equivalent to another 2.6 million hectares. Together, these efforts have increased the share of black-owned land to at least 32.5 per cent. Furthermore, there has been significant land trade between white and black South Africans. Of course, these figures say little about the value of land in terms of geography and the investments made. Finally, the bulk of all land is in the hands of commercial growers, averaging 1 500 hectares per farming unit for the 30 000 such farmers. Indeed, the doubling in the average size of a South African farming unit since 1994 points to an important trend: 'that farmers have found it necessary to expand their operations considerably in order to benefit from economies of scale that allow them to remain productive'. All the while, the number of urban dwellers has been increasing, from 52 per cent of the population in 1990 to 62 per cent 20 years later. More and more South Africans are thus dependent on a smaller pool of commercial farmers, which in turn reflects the imperative for higher yields to remain competitive and solvent.[16]

To date, the requirement of higher yields from a declining farming community has been realised. For example, the total tonnage of commercial wheat production countrywide has remained at two million tonnes, though the area under cultivation has fallen from 1.5 million hectares to half a million between 1990 and 2014. With maize, the area under cultivation has fallen from a peak in the 1990s of 4.5 million hectares that produced 12.5 million tonnes to 2.7 million hectares in 2013 that yielded 12 million tonnes.[17]

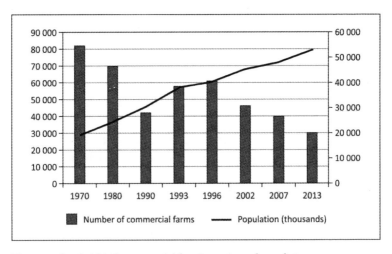

Figure 3.3: South Africa's commercial farming units and population.

However, improved yields have been achieved through greater mechanisation and, as noted before, an absolute drop in employment. As one benchmark, tractor sales have increased from under 5 000 units in 1990 to 7 500 in 2013. This reflects an overall increase in the levels of (fixed and machinery) investment in farms, from R4 billion in 2000 to R15 billion in 2013.

Overall, the farmers who remain appear to have made the right economic choices. Exports and imports also have increased substantially since deregulation in the early 1990s, with exports up from R20 billion in 2000 to R70 billion in 2013; and imports from a shade under R10 billion to R57 billion during this time. Farm revenue increased dramatically from 2000, from under R5 billion to R56 billion in 2013. These changes reflect, too, improved profitability, as net income as a percentage of turnover has doubled from 15 per cent to 30 per cent between 1999 and 2013.

Today, with only 12 per cent of South Africa's landmass considered arable and just 3 per cent 'truly fertile', the trend towards increased economies of scale continues. Just one-fifth of farmers produce 80 per cent of output. In turn, the number of farms has dropped from a peak of 120 000 in the mid-1950s to around 34 000 by 2014.[18] Only 1.5 per cent of South Africa's land is under irrigation, and that land produces 30 per cent of the country's crops.

Thus, improving the yields, and not simply the distribution of land, will likely increase the contribution of agriculture to the economy. Given the global trends towards increasing mechanisation and intensification, which also are apparent in South Africa, and considering shortages of water and the labour regime, the prospects for widespread job creation along the lines suggested by the NDP are improbable. This much is clear from the stories of farmers, old and new, which follow, and that document the shifts in production, the impact of global supply chains and the consequences of government policies. The South African people seem to understand this. One poll found that 0 per cent (!) of South Africans regard land as the most important issue to them personally. In contrast, 47 per cent see unemployment as the most important issue.[19]

Against the odds

The Ubongwa Cotton Development had all the necessary ingredients for success. The nearby Jozini Dam provided a giant irrigation source to feed the rich Hutton soils. A local ginnery is in place, under the control of Phineas Gumede and 31 other farmers who have experience and know-how to make cotton growing work. But it was not succeeding. Three of the centre pivot irrigation systems on Gumede's land in the Makhathini Flats in KwaZulu-Natal lay broken. The result: he was forced to replant cotton with yellow maize on 90 hectares. Despite many approaches to the Mjindi Farming parastatal responsible for the maintenance of infrastructure, to which Gumede had paid his rent for the centre pivots in the form of water rates, little action was forthcoming.[20]

Gumede has been involved with cotton since he finished school in 1984. After a period as a clerk with STK, a state company that ran the irrigated land, he joined the local farmers' association before taking over a piece of dry (unirrigated) land his father had farmed. The Makhathini ginnery was established on the flats in 2000. Things were looking up.

The revenue derived from cotton is slight compared to sugar, around one-third, or R9 000 per hectare on irrigated land in this area of South Africa. But the costs are much less, especially considering transport of the sugar cane. And importantly, not only can cotton be grown successfully on 'dry land', but it is also a labour-intensive crop, with better prices for hand-picked types. There are not many alternatives for work in a region with endemic unemployment.

Having borrowed heavily, in 2007 the Makhathini ginnery went bust. At that time there were 2 700 farmers supplying 10 000 tonnes of cotton. Seven years later this had fallen to 1 000 tonnes from fewer than 600 farmers. There is potential, maintains Gumede, for 4 000 hectares of irrigated cotton, plus a significant chunk of the 2.5 million hectares of Ingonyama Trust land in the area.

On the surface, the lessons from Ubongwa are clear. Logistics costs are high, and climbing, leading to a need for farmers to achieve economies of scale. Without a private sector hub to provide inputs and to guarantee a price to the farmer, smallholder schemes are largely at the mercy of government agencies for funding and capital upkeep. At the current time, however, these agencies cannot be relied on because of a lack of capacity and knowledge. Further, there are apparently reasons for government's obduracy beyond capacity and money. The farming hierarchy is seen as overwhelmingly Inkatha Freedom Party-aligned; while the executive of the Mjindi parastatal responsible for supplying the infrastructure is overwhelmingly ANC-aligned. And there is pressure for farmers to switch from cotton to sugar cane to justify a new mill nearby. As Gumede points out, 'Once government can support those farming organisations like ours, perhaps it can realise its dream of creating one million agriculture jobs by 2030.' He adds: 'If it does not engage the local community and ensure supply, the value chain will not work either, as it is not structured around commercial requirements.' This explains, he says, 'the failure of the fruit and vegetable cold room at Makhathini, which has stood empty for three years'. Makhathini is locked in a low-tech and low-yield past because of the political context in which farmers operate.

The next example shows what might be possible through improved collaboration in another area of KwaZulu-Natal.

A skewed picture

The caricature of a reluctantly reforming racist white farmer out of touch with the times is seldom accurate, no matter how politically convenient.[21]

Dick Muir gained four Currie Cup medals in the 1990s for the Natal Sharks rugby team at centre, and won five test caps for the Springboks, a team for which he also served as the assistant and backline coach. Muir teamed up with former Queens College school friend Lex Campbell to start an agro-processing business, Just Veggies, in northern KwaZulu-Natal near Vryheid. It is supplied by black farmers, and financially supported by the parastatal Public Investment Corporation (PIC) on behalf of the Government Employee Pension Fund.

The duo bought the plant in 2012 from the liquidators of the Swiss company BioSwiss. It had farmed, processed and exported organic vegetables in the area since 2003, leasing land that was transferred to blacks by the government. The enterprise collapsed when the owner died in 2010. Eighteen months later, Muir and Campbell secured R100 million in PIC funding after they had the local community on board. The PIC took 15 per cent, and also bought a 15 per cent shareholding in the R90-million factory on behalf of the local community.

This is a welcome turnaround in the Abaqulusi area, where agriculture has shrunk by 66 per cent from 1995. Of the 244 000 people living in the area, about 150 000 are impoverished. An estimated 85 per cent are unemployed. One reason for the extent of poverty is that farms transferred from white owners through land restitution often go from commercial production to subsistence farming or no production at all due to a lack of finance or skills. In the Abaqulusi area, about 50 farms have been transferred. The area has suffered economically from the 1995 closure of Anglo American's Coronation coal mine, on which a community of no fewer than 20 000 depended. The local municipality and Anglo both contributed to building and supplying the original factory with electricity.

By the start of 2015, Just Veggies was processing and freezing 20 tonnes of vegetables a day on site. Most of the product ends up under the McCain label, which has 70 per cent of the South African market, with Just Veggies supplying 10 per cent of the food multinational's requirements. 'Freezing', says Muir pointing to the giant coolers running at −23 degrees Celsius, 'gives us a market' while growing far from South Africa's urban centres.

Just Veggies' beans, cauliflowers, sweetcorn, broccoli, carrots, peppers and Brussel sprouts are sourced from two different types of farms: three of which were joint ventures with the local community, where the rehabilitation of the farm was funded by government; and six farms leased directly from the community. The joint ventures include a profit-sharing arrangement above agreed production targets.

Campbell says that faster expansion would be possible if government could respond more rapidly to community requests for assistance, based on an understanding with Just Veggies. According to Mandla Ngcobo, who deals with the local communities, two problems stand out. First, the challenge in convincing the locals of a commercial rationale in terms of pricing and productivity; second, 'getting the Eskom connection' to the farms.[22]

There is an unmistakable passion in Campbell's voice when he explains how Just Veggies might offer a different model to the depressingly familiar one of rural decline and confrontation in contemporary South Africa. As Muir puts it, 'It's all about embracing change.' With 1 000 seasonal and 200 permanent workers, Just Veggies shows what is possible with tripartite co-operation among the government, private sector and community.

There is no shortage of land in KwaZulu-Natal, rather a lack of finance and skills. The opposite is true for the Cape, even though the results may be similar.

The core of the challenge

Paul Cluver speaks in the measured tones one expects of a neurosurgeon. But he is obviously passionate about agriculture and the community around Grabouw where, since 1896, his family has farmed grapes, pears and apples.[23]

The grandson of Monrovian missionaries, he went into farming on his retirement from surgery 'around the time of the fall of the Berlin Wall', he smiles. But it is a difficult way to make money, he says. 'If you come from a socialist orientation, you might believe that wealth is connected with owning the means and mode of production, in manufacturing and land. But wealth has moved on all over the world, and the returns on farming are poorer than virtually any other sector.' The government's idea of small, successful farming units is an obstacle, he believes, to the expansion of farming in South Africa. 'The idea of the small farm runs counter to the global trend, especially in South Africa, where you have a harsh climate and need significant interventions in terms of investment in dams and land.

'There is a major difference between African-style farming and that of Europe or Southeast Asia. We cannot, in South Africa, farm on smallholdings. There is a lack of rainfall across much of the country, which lends itself thus to larger and larger units to make farming an economic proposition the farther west you go across the continent.'

The regulatory role of government has served to make increasing production more, not less, difficult. 'Currently we have 220 hectares under irrigation. We could expand by 100 hectares, but we need more water. We have had six years of discussion with the government about building a dam, which would create more jobs and income, and have completed a very expensive environmental impact study, and yet this project is so far not going anywhere.'

A similar situation exists elsewhere in the Western Cape. 'Currently,' he said in December 2014, 'there are proposals to open up another 6 000 hectares between Ceres and Grabouw. The investment required per hectare, if irrigation piping already exists, is R350 000, and perhaps twice that if it does not, and one can work on a ratio of 2 hectares per job created, excluding those in packaging.' There are few other options for expanding the deciduous fruit industry. While citrus production has increased from 40 million cartons annually in 1994 to over 100 million 20 years later, with the expansion of production particularly in Mpumalanga, there has been only 'marginal growth' in apple, pear and peach production, which remain around 40 million cartons annually. 'The government's role,' reflects Cluver, 'is not about incompetence; it's just that they don't seem to understand why we would want to expand our business, they don't seem to appreciate entrepreneurship.'

The trends in farming are moving rapidly towards mechanisation, in other words, fewer workers per hectare. So to expand the number of workers, an abovementioned goal of the NDP, it follows that more land (and thus more water) has to be found to farm commercially or farmers must employ more workers to increase yields. However, current policy points against using more workers. As salaries in South Africa rise, global competition will therefore drive economies of scale and greater mechanisation. Employment growth will depend on increasing the area under cultivation. The most labour-intensive sector within agriculture is that of horticulture, but that is also water intensive. 'With greater water being made available, the investment will flow,' believes Cluver.

The government should also, he says, help address input costs. 'Rail used to take most of our produce to Cape Town and the port. Now it takes zero,' he exclaims, holding his thumb and forefinger together. 'Road is 12 times cheaper, and much more reliable. This reflects,' he contends, 'the Portnet/Transnet monopoly.'

Cluver has a wider role than just a wine and apple farmer. The De Rust village on the farm is the site of the Thandi project, promoting and supporting community empowerment. The local school has 800 pupils from around the area. He is also involved in a variety of conservation projects, and was chairperson of Capespan for several years, the result of the amalgamation of Outspan and Unifruco, the citrus and deciduous fruit single-channel marketing boards.

Capespan was formed in response to the belief that 'you needed collective power to negotiate with supermarkets, rather than as individual producers, and to compete against other large multinationals such as Del Monte or Chiquita'. Previously the supply chain, he notes, 'went from producer to exporter to importer to wholesale distributor to service provider who packaged it, then the supermarket and finally the consumer. Now production and packaging have become linked, while containerisation has enabled smaller producers to get space for shipping directly without having to go via an exporter or importer. So Kromco,' he gestures, 'packages for farmers directly to Sainsbury's, complete with the pricing and sell-by dating.'

The complexities and challenges now facing the small-scale farmer are exacerbated by 'the collapse of South Africa's state extension services and research functions', and by the inexorable global move to increasing mechanisation. 'Technology means you can constantly use less people even though there are constantly more people available.' Even low-tech changes, such as multi-level picking platforms, electric shears and night-time picking, have a dramatic impact on productivity, while doing away with jobs. Thus it follows that 'to create jobs', he notes, 'you have to fundamentally grow the industry faster than you can grow productivity'.

The experience with bananas is similar to that of citrus and stone fruit.

When the Banana Board, on which he sat, was dismantled in 1993, Ian Lourens got together with a group of farmers to create a new marketing group, Lebombo. 'We realised there would be chaos in a free market system with no organisation, so we established a base in Komatipoort to market our bananas.'[24]

Twenty years later Lebombo supplies around one-quarter of the

12 000 hectares of bananas produced in South Africa. Lourens has moved quickly with the times. He sold his first farm 'for restitution' to the local community, which he then farmed for them on a 55/45 per cent share basis. 'After three years, they asked to change this system as apparently they did not enjoy the variations in profit, and preferred a straight and consistent lease income. So we changed it over to a 20-year lease.' Two of his three farms, some 1 000 hectares, are now managed according to this model.

'But ours is a business currently in trouble,' he warns. 'It's not a level playing field, which is why there are many people pulling out of bananas, which demand one labourer per hectare, and planting sugar cane, which has one person for every 10 hectares.' The cost of labour determines farmer decisions. 'The minimum wage in Mozambique is R750, while in South Africa this is now R2 500. I accept,' says Lourens, 'that living in South Africa is very expensive, and that we have to make a living, but you cannot compete with our margins. Before the salary rose, I was spending R150 000 per hectare to make R40 000; the wage increase pushed up costs to R165 000 and reduced the profit to R25 000. The government does not believe the farmer. They instead seem to think that they are super wealthy and can continue to accept a reduction in profit. That is just stupid.

'Getting involved in community projects,' as he has done, he says, 'offers some possibilities, particularly if the government asked them to work with those farms that lie unused, but it is a challenge. At the level of the farmer, they rarely know how to work with these communities. You can only make it work,' he says, 'with the patience of Job and with a government willing to do its share of the work. If you don't have political backing, you are farting against thunder. And the communities themselves are seldom well organised and stable. Instead they are riven with disagreements and jealousies, and are a very unpredictable partner to work with.'

The positive role to be played by government as a willing partner is emphasised by what has happened in the Kalahari. Yet these operations profit commercially because of their position in international markets.

Oasis in the desert

The 1897 date on the gate post of Kakamas' NG Kerk and the ubiquitous concrete slabs outside homesteads in the area in the Northern Cape province hint at the history of the country's most important table grape export region. They are the raisin-drying tables of an industry that started with the founding of Kakamas at the turn of the nineteenth century as a settlement 'colony' for white farmers who had lost everything as a result of a severe drought and rinderpest, circumstances worsened by the scorched earth tactics of the British forces in the second South African War, which saw the destruction of 30 000 farms.

Located between the equally bleak-sounding Pofadder and Keimoes on the N14 route, Kakamas is a Korana word meaning 'poor pasture'. That it may once have been, but today the area is the source of the bulk of South Africa's 225 000 tonnes of table grape exports and 65 000 tonnes of raisins, placing the country in the world's top 10 exporters of both products.[25] The region's grape business started in the early 1990s. Within two decades, the area had almost 5 000 hectares under production, employing 13 000 people. The weather allows all-year-round production. Within three days of picking and cooling, the grapes are at the port in Cape Town 850 kilometres away, and three weeks later on the shelves of Tesco, Sainsbury's or Waitrose in the United Kingdom. At R180 per carton, and with the country exporting 50 million cartons annually, it is an important source, too, of foreign exchange.

Kakamas is also a place of great contrast, where the summer heat rages at more than 50 degrees Celsius but where the Orange River feeds a green swath of grape vines and fruit trees in the orange soil. The river was tapped in the nineteenth century by a system of two dry-packed irrigation canals and tunnels that are still employed today. By 1908, the hand-dug 35-kilometre left (southern) bank furrow was completed, followed four years later by the 43-kilometre right (northern) circuit. All tools, dynamite and other materials and supplies had to be transported by wagon more than 400 kilometres away from the nearest railway at De Aar. Spirit levels attached to rifles were used to determine the level of decline.

Such innovation and forward-thinking continues a century later.

Less than 10 kilometres to Kakamas' north, on the road to Namibia, is a startling new R260-million agriculture development. Berekisanang Empowerment Farm is testament to the possibilities of collaboration between the local community and private entrepreneurs, with government playing its part by granting water rights and providing some finance.

It started with a view from a sweltering red-stone koppie and 1 013 hectares of virgin land. Berekisanang, a Setswana phrase meaning fittingly 'We all work together', was founded as a trust, the workers bringing with them the 500 hectares in water rights from the Department of Water Affairs. Water is shifted by five big electric pumps from the northern canal to a plastic-lined dam on the farm, the largest in the Northern Cape.

The first vines were planted in August 2013. The first harvest, from 50 hectares, was made at the end of 2014, delivering 80 000 cartons of grapes each of 4.5 kilograms to European markets. The attraction of the area from a producer perspective is not just the heat (for sweetness) and plentiful water, but the ability to harvest and market just before Christmas when the prices for table grapes are at their peak.

The view from the koppie is now transformed. Where there was once virgin land, there is now 315 hectares – equivalent to 300 football fields – most in 5-hectare blocks of table grapes under cultivation nestling beneath white shade cloth, and surrounded by blocks of 118 000 grapefruit and other citrus trees, which are planted nearly 600 to a hectare. It is, the joint CEO Chris Conradie reminds us, 'the single biggest irrigated farm in South Africa built in one go'.

In full production, Berekisanang will provide employment for 600 workers plus an additional 1 300 seasonal jobs. A farm workers' trust owns a 17 per cent share, the Industrial Development Corporation 23 per cent and its risk-capital fund RCF a further 21 per cent, and Galactic Deals, majority owned by the Afrifresh Group, 39 per cent. The construction of 400 farmhouses by 2017 is being funded by a R42-million grant from the Department of Human Settlements. By then, it is planned, 200 hectares each of citrus (lemons, easy-peeler and grapefruits) and grapes will be in production.

Afrifresh was formed in 1992 by Conradie and Anton Viljoen, turning over R460 000. In 1998, it merged with Roy Fine's Sunpride to become one of the country's top five fruit exporters, controlling around 5 per cent of national citrus production. By 2008, it turned over R477 million, and by 2014 R2.6 billion, employing 4 000 people, enjoying diverse interests from wine to the global marketing rights for a number of iconic South African products including Ina Paarman's products, BOS ice tea and Mrs Ball's Chutney.

'The idea behind Afrifresh,' says Conradie, 'was to change the model of farming from a cash-flow dependent one to best practice. Instead of the farmer relying on intuition, we wanted to put farming onto a more empirical, data-driven system. But,' he admits, 'we have learnt a few things along the way. For one, there is a need to distinguish between the capital asset you are working, the land itself, which can have spectacular returns, and the operational side, where the returns are likely in the 10 per cent or so margins. This means that agriculture requires, as a business rather than as a speculative investment, patient capital, with a 10- to 15-year horizon.' The investment required for Berekisanang amounts, per hectare, to R5 000 for the land, R100 000 for water rights, and as much as R600 000 for investment. The shade cloth alone is R120 000 per hectare.

'Farming offers one of the easiest job-creation schemes available to South Africa,' says Fine. 'Unlike a call centre, these jobs are sustainable and permanent, over a generation.' He is also clear about the requirements from government to spur agriculture sector growth.

'The government can do a lot to provide cheaper finance and insurance, no doubt, but you cannot do this without skills and entrepreneurial know-how.' And there are several other 'rules' for success in farming, he says: 'You can't farm today on a small scale; you need to select your crop carefully against the climate and geography, and water; and infrastructure is important, as is raw material supply.' He is not fixated with the importance of export markets since it is 'not necessary for all products', or, indeed, of the need for value chains, save 'the need to establish a relationship with the clients – everything is all about relationships' and to ensure competition and transparency of pricing. And certainly 'there is no shortage of land. There are hundreds of thousands of hectares uncultivated.'

Processing failure

Among the priorities of government has been to fund projects that promote downstream processing. However, even with government aid, the manufacturing gains that are associated with farming can only be achieved if the enabling environment is present. For instance, in 2011, a R200-million tomato production and processing plant, Cape Concentrate, was opened at the Coega Industrial Development Zone in the Eastern Cape. With ownership originally split 58:42 between the Jonah Capital Group founded by Ghanaian mining magnate Sam Jonah and Makuba Amatshe Eastern Cape, the government provided funding through the Development Bank of Southern Africa, which covered the construction of a new plant and working capital for operations.

The aim at the outset was to produce tomato paste for the local market to rival Chinese, Italian and Turkish imports. At full capacity, the Coega plant could process 350 000 tonnes of fresh tomatoes annually, producing 48 000 tonnes of tomato paste, and creating 160 factory jobs and 2 000 positions across 30 farms in the Kouga region, most of which were to be leased to Cape Concentrate.[26] 'These were people who had not had work for 20 years,' reflected Leon Wait, who has been involved with the project since its inception in 2009.[27]

By 2014, however, Cape Concentrate was placed in business rescue, requiring a change of management and shareholding. The reason for its troubles was simple: there were not enough tomatoes, the plant processing just 10 000 tonnes in 2013, enough for just 1 000 tonnes of paste. 'The idea originally,' says Wait, 'was to put in irrigation and other systems into the farms, which would be transferred to the ownership of the farmers after five years. But the funding promised from the Land Bank never materialised. Furthermore, there have been big problems with logistics in getting delivery from the farmers, given we require 14 35-ton trucks every day at full production.' As a result, a new CEO and five-year turnaround business strategy was put in place at the start of 2015, including use of a resized crate system, enabling smaller-scale packing and improved pricing to farmers.[28]

Land is not enough to make a successful farming venture. Skills, knowledge and logistics are also necessary. The plight of the pineapple industry in the Eastern Cape illustrates another aspect to success and failure in farming: policy.

Prickly problems

It has proven increasingly tough-going across the Eastern Cape, the region with the highest unemployment rate in South Africa in 2012 at over 64 per cent.[29]

The first pineapples reputedly arrived in South Africa in the 1860s with sailors from the Dutch East Indies, modern Indonesia, who gave them to two girls they were courting in Grahamstown, one of the earliest settler towns in the Eastern Cape. They left the crown of the fruit out, and a farmer used it to plant more pineapples. Today the Bathurst region has 31 million pineapples under cultivation, though the number of farms has fallen from 56 to 16 as 'costs have risen and returns have remained, at best, constant', says local farmer Nick Bradfield.

Corder Tilney's family has farmed pineapples in the Kidd's Beach area near East London for more than five decades. He says, 'The costs have risen faster than the returns, which is why most guys are struggling.' He has *recently produced some comparative data on costs and returns between* 1974 and 2014. 'One tonne of pineapples in 1974 would earn enough for 250 litres of diesel. Today one tonne won't buy you 50 litres. One tonne paid for one man for 25 days; now it buys you 7.8 days at the minimum wage. The same sort of picture is true for other critical costs such as chemicals.'

Without economies of scale, with competition rising from Thailand, Brazil, Costa Rica, the Philippines and also Côte d'Ivoire and even Kenya,[30] he says, the margins are just too small. South Africa now produces 1.5 per cent of the world pineapple market.

'Let me give you an example,' says Tilney. 'The cost of land is around R25 000 per hectare in the area where I farm. The cost of planting pineapples, which you have to wait two to two-and-a-half years to harvest, is R23 000 per hectare, inclusive of ploughing, weed killer and labour, but without fertiliser. You have to carry your capital costs for this period, and then you will earn, at current rates, a return of R80 per hectare. It's hardly worth the effort.' Even black-empowerment endeavours, such as Pineco in

Peddie, set up with government funding, Tilney advises, 'are struggling' as a result. 'Without government support they would just go under.'

Tilney once employed 600 people on his farm, producing 12 000 tonnes annually. Now he does 3 000 tonnes with just 45 workers, the result of using less land and increasing mechanisation. As a result, 'production of Eastern Cape pineapples has fallen from 210 000 tonnes in 1994 to 63 000 tonnes 20 years later. This depressing situation is worsened further by the spectre of land reform and the high costs of production. 'The guys are saying why should I invest against the threat of losing half of what I am investing in?'

Today 90 per cent of pineapples are transformed into concentrate at a local canning facility, 95 per cent of which is for export. But where there were once seven canners, there is just one on the banks of East London's Buffalo River. 'Mittal put up the costs of tinplate to such an extent,' Tilney says, 'that we could not compete with Thailand and others in the canning business, hence the focus on juicing.' Around half of the cost of the can was in the tin. Now concentrate is shipped from canners Summer Pride in aseptic drums, having been through an elaborate process of vacuum heating and pressing.

Bruce Yendall, a Bathurst pineapple farmer, and past chairperson of the local producer body, agrees that 'agriculture is not the happiest place to be. There is too much red tape from government and too little support. At times we need extra staff, but we are too terrified to hire them, as you cannot get rid of them again when the demand reduces.'[31] Or as one of his colleagues put it, 'Farming is a difficult business. We don't need government to make it more difficult.'

A growing industry?

This chapter describes how some farmers have managed to grow significant agricultural enterprises and generate employment despite all the obvious constraints. Thus, while the absolute potential of agriculture is limited, and probably far less than the NDP suggests, addressing the challenges that agriculture faces will be one important part of a countrywide effort to generate more jobs.

Farmers are used to dealing with a difficult environment, and to finding the means themselves to resolve their problems. However, policy developments add new uncertainties. The reopening of the land restitution process for a further period of five years could see as many as 400 000 new claims with an estimated cost, according to AgriSA, of between R129 and R179 billion. Given that the Department of Rural Development and Land Reform's budget was just R3 billion in 2014, whatever the political aspects of the bill – as correct, restorative or unfair – it seems to be unaffordable. The farms under claim would also lose collateral value and therefore the ability to mortgage land to raise finance. In the 20 years since 1994, already R70 billion has been spent on land reform. Land ownership per se may also be less important than many believe, although it will always have a symbolic resonance in South Africa. And there are differences of size. While large, well-capitalised agricultural firms can operate in a leasehold environment, individual, smaller farmers tend to require security of tenure to borrow.

It is important for government to view land through the lens of twenty-first-century agricultural realities, including scale and technology, rather than that of the early twentieth century when much land dispossession took place. Indeed, agriculture is moving towards larger farms to achieve the economies of scale required to remain competitive. Smallholder and even medium-sized farmers struggle in this environment, which requires greater yields and capital costs. As Max du Preez has reflected, 'In the 21st century agriculture is not so much about owning land as it is pure business and entrepreneurship.'[32] Government must be supportive of increasing productivity by helping to provide the necessary infrastructure, notably water, capital and, critically, making sure that necessary policies are not too onerous for farmers to enforce. Getting from confrontation to competitiveness will require government investment in productivity through supporting research and extension schemes. Clearer land title, among 'white' farmers and those in the former homeland or communal areas, will also improve values and leverage for credit. Like any other sectors, those who survive and prosper will be the better farmer, marketer and entrepreneur, improving yields and technology, and inserting themselves into local and global values chains.

Higher wages and government regulations, which make it difficult to manage the size of the workforce and that are incentivising farmers to move towards greater mechanisation, should be confronted directly. The issue of disincentives for employment on the farm is especially important given that there are few other opportunities in the rural areas for economic advancement. The government must focus on a wage policy and labour regulation that can generate the most jobs, rather than simply the highest wage it believes that farmers can afford for their current workforce.

Finally, to achieve higher productivity, a more constructive dialogue with government is necessary. One Eastern Cape farmer put it, 'The mentality of a farmer is to control the things you can (ordering diesel, applying fertiliser, etc.) and try not worry about the things you can't (hail, flood, drought). Until now, government's intervention in the agricultural sector has formed part of the latter ... There has not been a platform for farmers to air their concerns/issues currently facing them/us.'[33] Nor, with some exceptions, has white agriculture been clear on how it must transform in order to be part of the new South Africa. As the debates described at the beginning of the chapter make clear, government and farmers are to an extent talking past each other and focusing on issues that are not the most critical to agriculture's future. All parties in the farming sector must develop the necessary structures so that they can work together in a sector that is changing very quickly.

4

Selling Forever?

The Services Sector

> Tourism is without any question of doubt the best export in the
> world. You can continue to sell tourism forever, for as long as it does
> not destroy itself.
>
> — Arthur Gillis, Marriott Group: Africa

An hour's drive north of Cape Town up the Atlantic West Coast is
the town of Saldanha Bay, the site of the Western Cape's Industrial
Development Zone (IDZ) and the focus of the local government's
efforts to become a leader in the oil and gas services sector by servicing
and repairing oil rigs.

Known once for its naval base and fishing industry, Saldanha is covered in a fine red dust, a remnant of its history as an iron-ore export terminal since the 1970s. The twenty-first-century plan for Saldanha is to
convert its existing IDZ into a Special Economic Zone (SEZ), providing
a facility to attract 20 per cent of the rigs that are either operational in
sub-Saharan Africa or passing South African shores. There are projected
to be 40 rigs per annum, or an estimated R7.2 billion worth of business. In
2014, however, Saldanha worked on just three rigs, with two others turned
away due to a lack of capacity. SEZs are eligible for up to 50 per cent rebate
in corporate tax rates, a youth wage subsidy and more rapid depreciation
of capital assets, in government's words, 'to promote national economic
growth and export by using support measures in order to attract targeted
foreign and domestic investments and technology'.[1]

Saldanha's upscaling will require landside services and infrastructure. However, it will also demand skills, which South Africans currently lack. For example, the IDZ could fill only 14 of 30 places on an Armscor artisan training course in 2014, despite interviewing more than 100 candidates. Or as Alan Winde, the Western Cape's Member of the Executive Council for Economic Opportunities notes, 'For the oil and gas services sector, we need 18 500 jobs; we currently have 4 500 in training.'[2] This will be necessary if, in Cape Town Mayor Patricia de Lille's words, 'we are to be good for more than tourism.'[3]

■ ı ■

Government and private services constitute an increasing percentage of the South African economy. There is a great deal of upside potential. Some of this, as will be seen, depends, as ever, on what government does (or does not do) about the labour regime and on fiscal incentives. But many of the factors that encourage investors are in the hands of local government: lifestyle, red tape, electricity costs (if not reliability of supply), rates, land availability, local transport and even the diplomacy that can attract specific companies.

This chapter offers a snapshot of key services by identifying crucial challenges and strategies for growth and job creation within a changing global context.

The changing role of services

Historically, agriculture is a developing economy's most important sector. As countries develop and their people get richer, services have become dominant in developed countries and an important sector, in part due to tourism, in almost every country in the world. As Figure 4.1 demonstrates,[4] services everywhere are making an important contribution to growth.

As income rises, consumer demands become less material and require greater and higher quality supplies of health care, education and entertainment, among other sectors. The comparatively high labour intensity of services ensures that jobs in this sector continue to increase as employment in agriculture and industry falls, given technological progress and increasing capital investment.

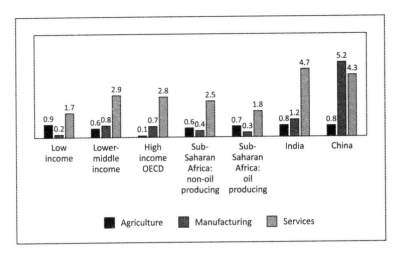

Figure 4.1: The contribution of services to growth, 1990–2012.

By the mid-1990s services accounted for almost two-thirds of world GDP, from about half in the 1980s. Even in countries still industrialising, the service sector is growing relative to the rest of the economy.[5] This phenomenon is true for South Africa, as is illustrated in Figure 4.2.[6] And South

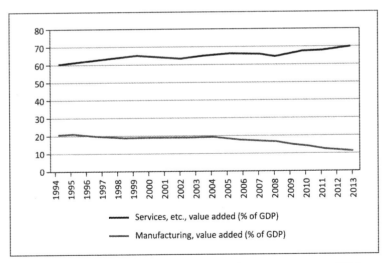

Figure 4.2: Services and manufacturing in South Africa as a percentage of GDP.

Africa still may be missing out on even more opportunities to promote services. However, the good news is that things can be done to change this; a jobless future is not pre-ordained.

South Africa's National Development Plan (NDP) recognises that a broad range of services is important to the economy, including finance, retail, tourism and transport. Services are viewed as a high-growth employment area under the Plan, with jobs in the sector increasing from four million in 2010 to between seven to nine million, depending on the scenario. The dynamics of whether the various industries within the service sector are actually poised to experience anything like the job growth the NDP suggests is analysed below.

Tempting tourists

The NDP foresees that the tourism sector could create a significant number of additional jobs by expanding the number of visitors to South Africa and increasing the amount of money they spend. Anti-apartheid activist Derek Hanekom, an Afrikaner who was jailed and exiled for his political beliefs and who has served on the ANC's National Executive Committee since 1994, was appointed as South Africa's Minister of Tourism in May 2014 and leads the effort to make South Africa a more attractive destination. Before this time, he served as Minister of Science and Technology from 2012 and, earlier still, Minister of Agriculture and Land Affairs during Nelson Mandela's government. He is bullish about South African tourism, 'which has been on a positive trend', he says, 'and for a very long time.[7] It is growing and resilient; with a steady rise in international arrivals', as highlighted by Figure 4.3.

The minister acknowledges that 'a significant chunk' of the arrivals are Zimbabweans on shopping trips, 'since the definition of a tourist is those who spend just one night in the country'. Still, 'there has also been a shift in some of our markets', notes Hanekom. 'China was our eighth largest market in 2010, but our fourth largest last year [in 2013]. India has also grown significantly.[8]

These positive changes are reflected in two other key indicators. 'It is an employment intensive sector', he says, 'with 610 000 formal jobs, or one

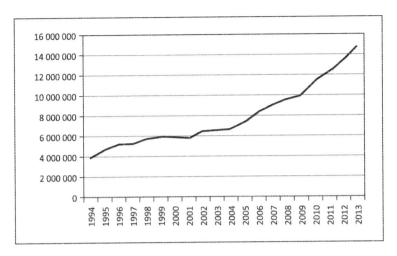

Figure 4.3: Total annual visitor arrivals in South Africa.

in every 10 jobs in the economy if you take indirect jobs too.' And the share of tourism to GDP has increased from 1.4 per cent in 1994 to 3.5 per cent 20 years later. He believes that tourism's contribution can continue to rise 'with more creative and targeted marketing and product improvement, otherwise known as "destination enhancement"'.

'Crime and perceptions thereof' also need to be worked on, he admits, as do the cost of flights, the perceptions of disease outbreaks 'such as Ebola', and visas. 'We have overstaying problems, which is well known, with people from Pakistan, Somalia, China and Bangladesh, so I can understand the security imperative behind the visa regime. At the same time, we should not model ourselves on those countries that demand visas, and we should avoid the sort of visa requirement that requires you physically have to be both fingerprinted and collect your visa in person. If we introduce such inconvenience, it will affect those wanting to travel without access to our diplomatic missions. We need,' he stresses, 'to move to something that is more efficient.' Twenty airlines have declared the newly proposed visa system 'a tourism, PR, economic and political disaster' and a leaked consultancy report for the Tourism Business Council of South Africa estimates that the policy could cost 100 000 jobs.[9] Whether the visa policy is actually ever adopted, the fact that it is being considered shows that the government's primary focus cannot be jobs.[10]

Hanekom is positive about the impact of global sporting competitions, specifically the World Cup. 'Sometimes the modelling calculation is incomplete. We need to ask whether the money comes back in other ways? Also if we deduct the money we would have spent anyway on infrastructure, but only fast-tracked the expenditure because of the World Cup, then the event was a catalyst.' He says that the event offered 'a permanent boost to South African tourism numbers, and lifted the graph permanently. One of our comparative advantages is our ability,' says the minister, 'to host big events. It brings people here who otherwise might not have come.'

The statistics, however, do not seem to back this up. The next section reviews the returns of the World Cup and what the Olympics might do for South Africa, both as a contribution to possible solutions to the employment problem and as an exploration of government thinking about public sector mega projects.

The World Cup effect

The 2010 World Cup in South Africa was undoubtedly a great logistical success. It also advertised the country in a positive way to a billion television viewers. But the event itself did not make money, at least not directly.[11] Out of 450 000 total visitors, just 309 554 people arrived in the country to watch the World Cup. They spent $513 million, under the estimated revenues of $900 million.[12] Indeed, the tourism numbers did not 'bump' significantly when viewed over the trends of previous years, as Figure 4.4 illustrates.

It is misleading to calculate how much money is spent in a city during such a sporting contest. A more accurate comparison requires an estimate of how much would have been spent without the events. For example, the 2010 World Cup did not increase airplane landings, though prices did rise, and hotel occupancy rates increased only modestly and were far from full.

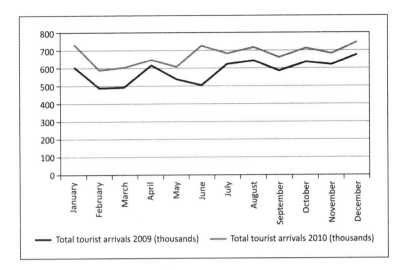

Figure 4.4: Tourist arrivals in South Africa, 2009 and 2010.

South Africa received 220 000 extra non-Southern African Development Community arrivals during the World Cup event and a total of 300 000 extra arrivals throughout the year, lower than predicted numbers.[13] The 'feel-good factor' and increased awareness of South Africa was a clear benefit (measured using a number of Google hits as a proxy), but it is unclear yet whether this will result in increased future tourism, trade and investment – it has not to date.[14]

While 17 000 construction jobs were added during the building phase of the World Cup in South Africa, this number was consistent with the general expansion of the economy and jobs added in other sectors, and construction employment actually fell faster than the rest of the economy after the completion of the stadiums.[15]

Overall, John Saker, chief operating officer of KPMG Africa, said: 'The big boost didn't happen. Businesses that directly served the World Cup did relatively well, but those without direct involvement struggled.'[16] There was also a diversionary effect on tourism numbers, as those who might otherwise have visited the country stayed away.

It certainly made money for FIFA, as much as $2.5 billion from television receipts and corporate sponsorship. Since 1998, overall World Cup revenue for FIFA has increased elevenfold.[17]

And the costs do not end with the last fan leaving. Even if the 2010 World Cup may have done wonders for South Africa's reputation, it has not done much for its finances, returning little more than 10 per cent of the country's total investment in the event. For example, according to De Lille, R80 million is required for the Cape Town Stadium at Green Point, built for the 2010 World Cup, to meet annual maintenance costs alone. Until now the city has not broken even with the operational, let alone the sunk capital, costs, receiving at best R12 million in annual income.[18]

In December 2014, it was reported that the Western Province Rugby Union would not move to the Cape Town Stadium from its traditional Newlands home.[19] The Union cited significantly 'higher' operating costs among other factors deterring the move.

It would take a touch of hubris – and arrogance – to claim that big sporting competitions can make money directly or indirectly for the host country, even though the 1984 Los Angeles and 1992 Barcelona Olympics are often cited as cases where these proved a boost to the city and its infrastructure. As the *New York Times Magazine* notes, '[T]here is strikingly little evidence that such events increase tourism or draw new investment. Spending lavishly on a short-lived event is, economically speaking, a dubious long-term strategy. Stadiums, which cost a lot and produce minimal economic benefits, are a particularly lousy line of business. (This is why they are usually built by taxpayers rather than by corporations.)'[20] While 'the Olympics have always been a debutante's ball for emerging economies, from Japan in 1964 and Germany in 1972 to China in 2008 and Russia in February [2014]', and there is some evidence that trade increases for the hosts, this is also true of countries that make losing bids. 'The benefit, in other words, came from the signal that a country was open for business, not from the spending itself.'[21] The same could apply to the World Cup, though such events are increasingly, if Qatar and Sochi are anything to go by, the province of authoritarian, if highly ambitious, regimes.

More important than mega sporting attractions is ensuring cheap, reliable, consistent access to South Africa for tourists. It seems particularly unlikely that South Africa's attempt to lure the Olympics, given the World Cup experience, will generate a significant number of sustainable jobs. The opportunity costs, in terms of what could otherwise have been done with the money, will in contrast be significant.

Getting people here and there

Arthur Gillis started in the hospitality business when he was just 15 and wanted a motorbike. 'My father told me to go out and work.'[22] So he did, initially as a guide at an ostrich farm in his native Oudtshoorn. After national service in the police force, he worked as a storeman at a hotel on Heerengracht Street in Cape Town. It was a humble start to a meteoric career. After a management buyout, he was a hotel manager at 23 and CEO of Protea Hotels at 31. In April 2014, he sold Protea, which had grown into Africa's largest chain, to Marriott.

Tourism, he argues, 'is not a difficult business to be in no matter what people tell you. And it is a great way of giving unskilled people a job. I can take anyone with a matric and teach them to be a receptionist, grill chef, cleaner or anything else.' It is also a great multiplier. 'I estimate that for every direct job,' he says, 'there are 10 in ancillary services, the majority of them in small and medium businesses. You ask a petrol station attendant at Mossel Bay when they sell more and they will tell you "During the holidays". It's the same for bakeries, for laundries, or other services.'

Tourism's growth is being driven, he argues, by technology and by changing life patterns. 'There is a blurring between tourism and leisure, with people adding on days to business trips more than ever before, partly because electronics have changed the proximity to the office.'

To realise South Africa's potential, 'we need to do two things', says Gillis. 'First, to recognise the advantage of international tourism in bringing new money into the economy, seeing tourism thereby as an export. Second, related to this, we then need to make it as easy and as seamless to get here as possible. We need an open skies policy. That is the most important aspect. This is why,' he says, 'the debate recently about whether to offer Emirates a fourth flight or not is stupid. Whether Emirates is a Pty Ltd [a private company] masking a country and operating on a non-commercial basis is no concern of ours. Rather we should be finding the means to treat our best customer well.' He adds: 'For every new [Boeing] 777 starting up a route to South Africa, I can justify open-ing a 300-room hotel.'

Related to the aspect of access, says Gillis, is South Africa's visa policy, which should be made as simple as possible. Concerning the proposed tightening up on visa restrictions that make it more difficult for some nationalities, especially the growing Chinese market, to visit, he says: 'I don't think for one second that anyone has thought this through properly. If you are planning your holiday, you are going to take the path of least resistance to get there, not one that involves travelling somewhere else for biometric tests and all sorts of hassle.'

National aviation: Champion or hindrance?

Good airlinks are obviously critical to the promotion of tourism given that many high-value visitors will come from outside the region. South African Airways (SAA) celebrated its 80th anniversary on 1 February 2014. It boasts a number of impressive aviation records. In 1953, for exam-ple, it became the first airline outside the United Kingdom to put the world's first jetliner, the De Havilland Comet, into regular service. It broke a variety of records in the 1950s with its Douglas DC-7 service between Johannesburg and London. At the beginning of the 1960s, SAA had 28 aircraft and 2 750 employees.[23] But following the imposition of an embargo on flights over Africa from 22 August 1963, SAA became a loss leader to keep international doors open for the regime, including having one of the cheapest first-class fares.[24]

The losses have continued in the post-apartheid period. In the 20 years since 1992, SAA has received a total of R16.8 billion in govern-ment bailout packages. In 2012, alone, this included a R1.3-billion loan; a R5-billion 'guarantee' for two years; and a R550-million bank facility for fuel and short-term commitments.[25] Two years later, the airline was in another restructuring phase, 'technically bankrupt', and surviving off state-guaranteed loans according to the Minister of Public Enterprises, Lynne Brown. In December 2014, it presented a 90-day rescue strategy to the gov-ernment that included a proposed R1.3 billion in annual savings and a review of some long-haul routes. This plan was to enable the full implementation of the airline's already approved Long-Term Turnaround Strategy.[26]

On 21 January 2015, South Africa's Department of Finance announced that a further financial guarantee for SAA had been approved. The new guarantee was for R6.488 billion, bringing the total guarantees up to R14.4 billion.[27]

As a result, every time an SAA flight takes off, a taxpayer pays. Regionally, African routes performed positively with a 17 per cent profit increase from R648 million to R761 million between 2013/14 and 2014/15.[28] However, SAA's long-haul intercontinental operations recorded an increased loss from R1.3 billion in the previous financial year (2012/13) to R1.6 billion reported for the 2013/14 financial year. The Beijing route, for example, had a R350-million annual subsidy, regardless of whether the flight was full, due mainly to the wrong aircraft choice (the fuel inefficient and costly four-engine Airbus A340-600).[29] In February 2015, notice was given to cut the loss-making Beijing and Mumbai routes, though these would be retained through a code-share arrangement with Etihad and Jet Airways.[30]

There are several reasons for this poor performance, which relate to the structure and the relationship between the airline and government as a state-owned enterprise (SOE).

First, there is no state-wide co-ordination policy for aviation, but rather a different set of impulses from the departments of transport, tourism, public enterprises and the Treasury – the latter, from November 2014, the government department responsible for the airline. Critically, South Africa must decide if it wants a policy that maximises the number of tourists who enter the country or if it wants to protect its national carrier. Given that the potential for jobs from tourism is far greater than will ever be generated by even a well-functioning national airline (which SAA is not), the choice seems obvious. However, the South African government is currently not in a position to even be able to evaluate that trade-off.

Second, SAA has 'never been properly capitalised', in the words of one local industry expert,[31] through an initial public offering or by government. The sale of 20 per cent of SAA to Swissair in 1999 collapsed after the Swiss carrier's 2002 bankruptcy. The government has been unwilling to cede ownership to enable recapitalisation, or to recapitalise the airline itself.

Third, in any airline, flight operations are the heart of the airline, but they remain 'distant' from the discussions. This reflects a problem across

South African SOEs. 'The easiest section to transform is human resources. The last is the section requiring the greatest technical skills. Inevitably,' reflects one pilot, 'the powerbase becomes HR, which moves from being a support function to one leading the company, rather than having the operational side in this role, which ends up being further and further away from the decision-making process.'

In sum, SAA first has to be recapitalised, either through an initial public offering or sale of a portion, or as an SOE. Second, it needs a mandate to make and execute technical decisions. Most importantly, the government needs to decide whether SAA is to be a loss leader for tourism and business promotion or (preferably) to liberalise the markets and stop subsidising SAA's inefficiencies at the expense of the taxpayers. Of course, this is not going to be without upheaval. The defence of state subsidy is on the grounds of employment and the competition its presence provides, bringing down prices. But this presumes that a liberalised SAA would not make it commercially – that implicitly government fails to back its own people's capabilities. And continuation of the subsidy to SAA ignores how many jobs could have been created if other airlines had been allowed to bring in more visitors.

There is some good news internationally. Across Europe and Asia, there is much life after subsidised yet high-fare national carriers, even though this is a tough business with very tight margins and constantly changing variables, especially with regard to fuel price. The question is whether to take the political plunge and commercialise the carrier and, if that happens, whether to concessionalise or privatise.

Either way, success ultimately depends on opening the skies to spur competition. The future of air travel, in South Africa as elsewhere, is unlikely to lie in protected, expensive national air carriers, especially for countries that do not have the easy access to cash that oil provides. Instead, the future lies in innovation, encouraging not suppressing the market, and cost competitiveness. South Africa should choose an aviation policy that maximises the tourism industry as a whole rather than simply continuing to support the losses of the national carrier.

■ ■ ■

Tourism is one measure of the health of the services sector. Retail is a guide, too, both of the health of the domestic economy and the challenges of logistics and local supply.

The cost of good intentions

From a macro perspective, the last 20 years have been good for the retail industry in South Africa, says Gareth Ackerman, chairperson of Pick n Pay Stores Ltd. The supermarket chain was purchased by his father, Raymond, in 1967 with five small stores, 130 employees, a capital investment totalling R500 000 and an annual turnover of R5 million. By 1969, he had added another five stores and listed on the Johannesburg Stock Exchange. In 1980, the group's 56 stores turned over R750 million, with 11 000 employees. Today the chain has 1 200 stores across eight countries, turning over around R70 billion.[32]

But it is not all easy. With 60 000 employees, there is a need for flexible hiring, which has been made more difficult by government attempts to eradicate labour brokers. Previously, most of the workforce comprised full-time staff because the trading hours were limited. As South Africa has moved with the global times, with a seven-day, 18-hour operation, it is 'impossible', he says, 'to have an inflexible staff complement'.

Pick n Pay is not alone in facing up to these changes. The first Woolworths store was opened in Cape Town in the old Royal Hotel in October 1931. The United Kingdom-based Marks & Spencer bought 20 per cent of the chain in 1947, setting the stage for close ties, which still remain. Today it has 600 stores in South Africa, employs more than 40 000 people between its African and Australian operations, and turns over more than R50 billion.

Simon Susman is the third generation of his family in the business. 'My grandfather, who had made his money trading in Zambia, lived next door to the Woolworth's founder, the United Party member of Parliament Max Sonnenberg. He went up to the Transvaal to run the stores, and we have been in the business ever since.'[33] Simon's father, David, was managing director before him, and a director of Marks & Spencer for nearly 20 years.

Susman says the key lesson from retail is that 'success begins in the shops. All good shopkeepers spend their time on the floor, managing the detail of their business. Head office,' he observes, is by comparison 'a place full of lies and defensive behaviour. The same is true for government. It does not get out there, and talk to industrialists and small businesses, the people behind the economy.'

He further maintains that there are two major issues facing business in South Africa, 'the fear of employers to employ' and 'the failure to manage and incentivise the workforce'. From his vantage 'the labour issue is an easily solvable issue. Currently it keeps millions out of work and ensures a culture of zero performance management.'

The result is 'that small businesses will do everything not to employ people, while big business has another strategy, which is to invest offshore and hedge the risk of exposure to South Africa's uncertainties. Yet this does not address our greatest sin, the millions of unemployed, which is also our greatest resource.' As a result we have 'multi-generational worklessness, which is very hard to change'. At the heart of this 'is labour legislation. If we can't untangle the unions from these questions, then at least we should delink the rural areas from the same requirements as the cities.'

At a practical level, Susman welcomes 'the occasional strike – it keeps us honest'. With such an attitude it is perhaps unsurprising that he helped to 'considerably' reduce the level of unionised Woolworths' workers through three actions: 'First, there is a formalised regular communications process in place directly between management and staff, with no third party involvement. Second, there is a progressive career path open to everyone, which is particularly appealing to younger staff. Third, every member of staff is part of a store performance-based incentive scheme. This drives a great deal of excitement.'[34]

Similar views are echoed by Mark Lamberti, the CEO of South Africa's Imperial Holdings, a giant logistics group, and formerly head of Massmart and Transaction Capital. He started his professional life as a musician. 'Since there was not a lot of work for a trombonist, I played some keyboards,' he laughs, but soon moved into retail before taking over six Makro shops in May 1988. By the time he left the [Massmart] chain just under 20 years later, the firm had grown from 1 500 staff to 24 436 across 238 stores – 'all sustainable jobs created with no subsidy from the government. The year before I left, I calculated that, together, the company tax, duties, VAT and PAYE amounted to 1 per cent of the income of the South African government. One decent growing enterprise has this impact, though the obstacles to the young entrepreneurs are now huge. Wave after wave of regulations are applied with seemingly no sense of cumulative impact on small businesses.'[35] He suggests: 'When unions are unhappy, they strike. When governments are unhappy, they make laws. When businesses are unhappy, they don't invest.'

■ ı ■

The most successful response to market needs in South Africa over the past generation has been the minibus taxi industry, which has supplied an integrated transport network for the majority of South Africans where one did not exist previously. However, government's current regulatory role is not seen as helpful to the industry.

Taxi driver

'Who is voting for this president, anyway?' exclaimed Vusi,[36] getting increasingly agitated. 'If you are coming from the government,' he said pointing, 'you must just go. The main problem is this government,' he said to murmurs of approval from the eight drivers cloistered in his taxi.

'They say anything to get elected, and they don't do anything. They go with the BRT [Bus Rapid Transport] when they say they won't, and they don't give us the permits we need, or the parking.' By now the group outside the Wanderers rank in downtown Johannesburg was excited – and getting angry. 'You look at him,' he said of the president. 'He spends R260 million,' referring to the Nkandla residence furore, 'and I live in my shack with my wife and two children. When he wants to get up to something, he goes to another room with one of his wives. What must I do?' he laughs.

Vusi, Steven, Boyz and their fellow drivers earn, they say, R700 a week. On a good day they will take five loads of 15 passengers. They do not own their taxis because they say they cannot get a permit to do so. 'We

89

apply, they take your money, and we never see anything,' they claim. 'They ask for R15 000 for a permit when it cost R200 in the olden days.' They believe they are preyed upon by the authorities and the ironically orange, blue and white Metro Police vehicle. 'They ask for "Tshotsho" [Sotho for a bribe] all the time. If they stop us and impound our taxis it costs R2 500 to get them released. That increases at R100 each day.' Amidst the head-shaking, mutters and increasing volume among the drivers, the same refrain is repeated: 'It was better under the last government.' As Frans, put it, 'They told us they were taking the apartheid permits, but they [the government] do not do anything for us. They are even worse. They are making money for themselves, and not thinking of others.' Or as Wilson said, remarkably: 'It was better under Botha.' This is an exaggeration, but is evidence of the level of frustration.

Before 1987, the taxi industry was highly regulated and controlled, with black taxi operators being refused permits. Then, the industry was rapidly deregulated, leading to a swift growth in the number of minibus taxi operators given the high demand. Employing directly and indirectly an estimated 400 000 people, the sector is 95 per cent black-dominated. The majority of vehicles are not owner driven (the average owner possessing 2.5 vehicles). Demonstrating the dynamism of the sector, there are nearly 1 200 new minibuses sold each month.

'It's a great entrepreneurial story,' says Dr Johan van Zyl, head of Toyota SA, which has more than 87 per cent of the taxi market with their Quantum Ses'fikile (We have arrived) model. 'There was a problem with sufficient buses and trains to and from where they transported people. The private sector solved the problem with a highly flexible system.'[37]

The industry is now worth an estimated R16 billion annually, with 250 000 taxis carrying two-thirds of South Africa's 23 million commuters, according to the South African National Taxi Council.[38] Buses (21 per cent) and trains (14 per cent) account for the remainder.

While it looks chaotic on the surface, it is hyper competitive and efficiently run. Rides work out, in 2015, at R11 per passenger per 'local' journey and increase depending on distance: R40 to Pretoria from Johannesburg, R25 Pretoria to Hammanskraal and R200 to Bloemfontein from Johannesburg, for example. It delivers a service that was previously not there.

That is why it has been successful against the odds. The early model of the Toyota Hi-Ace taxis were known as 'Zolas', in deference to the speedy 1980s' South African middle-distance runner, Zola Budd. Like the Olympian, taxi owners have had to possess resilience. 'They had to struggle to establish an industry by themselves,' said Van Zyl. 'They financed themselves, they created their own industry and their own rules and regulations, and they developed by themselves.'

Because the industry was largely unregulated and the official administrative bodies so corrupt, it was quickly consumed with turf battles over routes. These conflicts were worsened by political connections of various taxi associations and operators. Taxi-related violence claimed around 2 000 lives in the 1990s. While things settled down in the 2000s, the death toll was still over 140 by 2011. Most drivers carry guns.

Violence aside, the industry is also known for general lawlessness – vehicles that often seem to be death traps, and drivers with, at best, scarce cognisance of safety or of other vehicles. In a country with nearly 15 000 road deaths a year – one of the highest rates in the world, costing an estimated R300 billion annually[39] – minibus taxis are the worst offenders. According to a South African Institute of Race Relations report released in 2012, the minibus taxi death rate was 27 deaths per 10 000 vehicles, three times higher than the deaths for motor cars.[40]

The drivers themselves also face tremendous challenges. They can up their basic take-home pay by working longer hours once they have met their expected quota of passengers and income. Still, it is scant financial reward and considerable risk for drivers who are up at 5 a.m. and seldom home again by 8 p.m. South Africa's minibus taxi industry is evidence of both the good and bad of the country's political economy, of entrepreneurship in full flight and elements of lawlessness and *mafioso* activity. Whatever their lawless instincts and alleged links with crime and politics, if one had to devise a fully integrated, efficient door-to-door transport system free from state subsidy, it would be hard to beat the taxi industry.

Instead of providing the regulatory support they crave, or simply getting out of their way, the taxi industry sees government as attacking them. The evidence of dislike of government is obvious from every driver we spoke to. This explains why the only demand of the drivers of policy is 'for permits'. Given the violence and the lack of safety, the need for effective regulation is obvious.

However, government has not hit upon a strategy that could support the entrepreneurship of black taxi drivers while promoting safety. This is the kind of conundrum that has to be solved if South Africa is to move forward. In such a visible sector, government success would be highlighted. The taxis represent the kind of problem that successful countries solve. A successful solution would not be the end of what has to be done in South Africa, but this case, multiplied by other instances in other sectors, would be part of the solution to unemployment.

Services: Part of the employment solution

The shift to services is a key aspect of development, offering a massive upside in employment in retail and, especially, tourism. For example, the Western Cape region employs 216 000 in tourism, but just 79 000 in agro-processing and 129 000 (and falling) in agriculture. Services offer a lucrative alternative to the sweaty, finicky business of manufacturing. The sector also serves to diversify the South African economy so it is less dependent on the other industries.

But services will not flourish automatically. The government needs to provide the necessary regulation in a way that does not inhibit commercial development. For instance, South Africa must seek the least restrictive visa policy possible rather than, as at present, different departments seeming to war over the immigration stance that they favour due to their own particular optic. It must also focus, especially in the case of SAA, on the decisions that would promote the most jobs for the country. It would be best if SAA were configured so that it brought in the most tourists possible even if that led to a diminishment of its role as the national carrier. It is a continual focus on what policies will generate the most jobs on a day-to-day basis, while being able to make difficult decisions (like reconfiguring SAA) that will serve South Africa best. In contrast, mega projects – such as the FIFA World Cup or the prospect of the Olympics – may appear as a silver bullet to address many economic problems. But the record shows that they inevitably disappoint. The experiences of Singapore and Malaysia illustrate that critical decisions to build the economy were taken first and that it was only much later, if ever, that these or other Asian governments began to engage in international mega projects.

Government must also find more creative ways, as countries in Southeast Asia did, to confront problems that have been addressed in unhelpful, bureaucratic ways to date. As is clear from our study of retail, South Africa already has dynamic entrepreneurs who have a history of expanding their enterprises. However, their dynamism stands in stark contrast to the labour laws that do not give them the flexibility to hire the workers that they want to employ, as well as the Delphic bureaucratic behaviour they routinely experience. Similarly, the deregulation of the taxi industry was a tremendous boon to drivers and the customers they serve. However, these mobile entrepreneurs report that the post-apartheid governments have not been as helpful as they could have been in supporting an industry that provides a vital service. It is critical that government not only supports taxi drivers but finds a way to regulate them so that they become safer and, therefore, an even more attractive form of transportation. The need for focus and market space applies equally to manufacturing, to which our analysis now turns.

5

The Manufacturing Basics

Manufacturing is about jobs, growth, tax revenue, and beneficiation
– about everything that we as a country want to do.

— Iraj Abedian, Chief Executive Officer, Pan-African Capital Holdings

O n the N11 national route between Newcastle and Ladysmith
in KwaZulu-Natal province sits the Ngagane power station.
Commissioned in 1963 to meet manufacturing aspirations and to
fuel the mining boom underway, the 500-megawatt plant was one of 11 units
mothballed in the late 1980s and early 1990s. The original plan was to put
it back into service in 1996, when it would have a life of another 20 years.[1]

This was not to be. By 1994, Ngagane was deemed no longer necessary or viable for Eskom's Integrated Electricity Plan. Although the
plant was offered for sale in the mid-1990s, the sale did not materialise.
Recommissioning attempts with foreign investors in the late 2000s similarly came to naught. Today its four cooling towers, two smoke stacks and
the cavernous turbine buildings lie intact, if abandoned, in the veld, save
a friendly gate guard – testament to a failure of planning foresight in the
light of South Africa's current chronic energy shortages.

On paper, Eskom is an impressive story: ranked in the top 10 utilities
in the world in terms of generation and sales, with 27 operational power
stations generating more than 95 per cent of electricity in South Africa
and 40 per cent of all electrical power consumed in Africa.[2] But there are
considerable and chronic operational and strategic challenges. The common power outages experienced in recent years are economically disruptive and symbolic of greater structural failings.

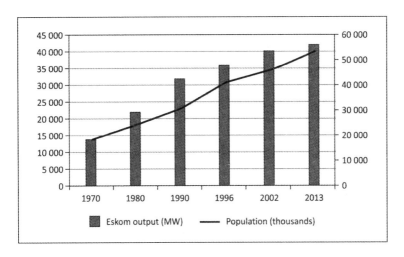

Figure 5.1: Eskom output and South Africa's population.

South Africa was once more than adequately supplied with electricity. In 1970, the country had an installed capacity of 14 000 megawatts for a demand of 12 000 megawatts. Thereafter, Eskom added generation to the grid at a rate of almost 1 000 megawatts annually. During the 1970s, it was calculated that generating capacity had to double every 10 years to keep ahead of demand. With new construction financed by hikes to electricity tariffs – in 1976 (twice), 1977 and in 1981 – by the early 1980s construction at five giant coal-fired power stations[3] along with the Koeberg nuclear plant at Koeberg was underway or committed to.[4] At the end of 1983, Eskom had 22 260 megawatts of generating capacity on order.[5]

By 1994, South Africa's total installed electricity was 35 963 megawatts, Mexico's was 35 374 megawatts and South Korea's was 29 222 megawatts. Then, in the mid-1990s, Eskom rid itself of 3 850 megawatts of power by closing power stations, including Ngagane, and committed to supply a fresh 1 000 megawatts each for the Hillside and Mozal aluminium smelters, the latter in theory supplied by power from Mozambique via Eskom. Along with Ngagane, others closed, included the small hydro station on the Fish River tunnel (5 megawatts); Camden (1 600 megawatts) near Ermelo; Grootvlei (1 200 megawatts) near Balfour; and Komati (1 000 megawatts) outside Middelburg. These were shut not because they were making a loss, but because 'they supplied energy at a greater cost than the newer "six-pack" stations installed in the 1980s'.[6] Eskom's marketing department, which had reportedly taken executive control from the previous doyen among the engineers and accountants, had become self-appointed experts in 'streamlining power generation'.[7]

Through these actions Eskom had effectively removed over 5 000 megawatts from the system. This situation was exacerbated by the provision of cheap power to industrial steam consumers, including South African Breweries and the paper mills, to persuade them to shut down their coal boilers and install electrode boilers.[8]

Today commerce uses more than 80 per cent of electricity in South Africa; households around just 18 per cent.[9]

By 2014, South Africa's installed capacity had risen to 44 149 megawatts. By comparison, Mexico's capacity had nearly doubled to 61 512 megawatts and South Korea's was at 84 874 megawatts.[10] Though it had fallen behind, South Africa did not commit to new power generation entities. This decision was effectively a bet against the rise in South African economic growth and consequent electricity demand.

Coupled with a rise in domestic demand, by 2014 the energy shortfall was 2 000 megawatts. Electricity outages had, by then, cost the South African economy an estimated R300 billion since 2008. Load shedding might reduce GDP growth by an entire percentage point in 2015, a stunning loss, and lock the country into low growth (2–2.5 per cent) perhaps even to 2019,[11] despite demand being suppressed by a trebling of prices (in nominal terms) since 2007. According to energy specialist Anton Eberhard, whereas South Africa's 'energy availability on average used to be above 90 per cent', over the last few years 'it has fallen precipitously to probably below 75 per cent'. Throw in maintenance scheduling and unforeseen technical dramas, especially when the grid is operating under strain, and there is a crisis of supply. These challenges are unlikely to be resolved any time soon given the delays to the giant Medupi and Kusile power stations, 4 800 megawatts apiece, whose commissioning date slipped well beyond the original 2014.[12]

The proximate causes of the electricity crisis seem to involve the state of Eskom's management over a sustained period. At some level this may have to do with politics, whether in the alleged form of direct interference (including allegations of orders for a no-loadshed policy at the cost of essential maintenance that led to a large backlog in repairs), or poor choice of managers at several levels, or poor board governance, or all of the above.

Corrupt supply arrangements have also been alleged.[13] At the time of writing, much of this amounts to subjective assessments of observers rather than (so far) proven fact. What Eskom's travails ultimately provide, however, is compelling evidence that the South African state does not have the capability to manage its current responsibilities. The likely success of it taking on more duties, perhaps to realise the ambitions of those who want a muscular developmental state, seem poor. It would seem reasonable for state authorities to first fix what is definitely their responsibility before looking to add to their portfolio. Indeed, at precisely the moment when South Africa needs to greatly enhance manufacturing to create jobs, it is underpowered. This is only one constraint facing manufacturers, albeit an important one.

The challenges to South African manufacturing

Manufacturing has been vital in alleviating poverty and inequality in South Africa over the past 100 years. Historically, manufacturing has gone hand in hand with urbanisation in addressing poverty. The *Oxford History of South Africa* notes, for example, that in 1924/5, 115 000 people were employed in manufacturing. That labour force grew to 141 000 'within a few years'. As a result, the 'poor-white' problem (the Carnegie Commission had calculated that of a white population of just over 1.8 million in 1931, more than 300 000 could be classed as 'very poor') had virtually ceased to exist.[14]

Manufacturing contributed 13.4 per cent of South Africa's GDP in the third quarter of 2014, making it the fourth-largest component of economic activity, behind finance, real estate and business services (20.3 per cent); general government services (17 per cent); and wholesale, retail and motor trade, and catering and accommodation (14.4 per cent).

However, manufacturing's contribution to real annual GDP growth has declined steadily, from 0.7 per cent in 2010 to 0.1 per cent in 2013. Moreover, the sector has shed more than 200 000 jobs since the 2008–9 recession, with 38 000 jobs lost in the third quarter of 2014 alone.[15]

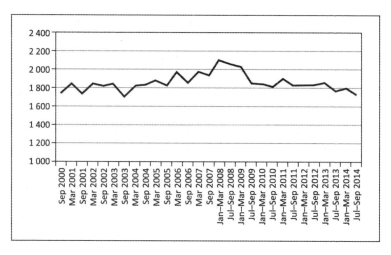

Figure 5.2: Total employed in manufacturing (thousands).

There has been, in the words of Gauteng Premier David Makhura, a 'significant decline in South Africa's industrial heartland' over the past quarter-century.[16] Makhura was a trade unionist, serving, among other posts, as deputy general secretary of the National Health and Allied Workers Unions, and he was also a member of the National Executive Council of the ANC Youth League. The province he governs accounts for around 36 per cent of South Africa's GDP, though it has the smallest land area of any province at 1.4 per cent of the total. Based on manufacturing, which followed the development of Johannesburg's mining sector, its economy is more than twice that of KwaZulu-Natal or the Western Cape. If Gauteng's manufacturing base is in trouble, the prospects for the sector overall in South Africa seem limited.

The decline of manufacturing has important implications. The Harvard group, which advised the South African government in the mid-2000s, believed that the country's chronic current account deficit was a major 'speed limit' to the economy. 'Economic growth increases demand for imports,' says Harvard Professor Matt Andrews, 'yet South Africa has no means to pay for them from its exports. Growth sustainability demands that the country produces goods it can export to the rest of the world. This was the same challenge South Korea faced in the 1960s, and their response was to develop industry.'[17]

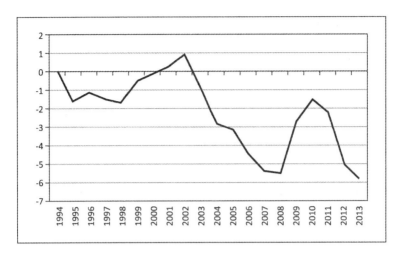

Figure 5.3: Current account balance in South Africa as a percentage of GDP.

There are other reasons why manufacturing is important, aside from the foreign exchange it can provide. As Toyota's CEO Johan van Zyl reminds us, 'The development of people, innovation, skills, and technology – all of this comes with engineering.'[18]

Paradoxically, South African manufacturers see the availability, productivity and quality of skilled labour, specifically researchers, scientists and engineers, as the most critical factor threatening production and competitiveness.[19] This challenge is a consequence of the misalignment between an educational system that produces poorly educated students, particularly in science, technology, engineering and mathematics-related subjects, and the skill requirements of the sector.

Government hopes that manufacturing will generate a significant number of new jobs. In the most hopeful scenario in the National Development Plan, the sector is projected to add as many as 700 000 new positions by 2030. The goal will be especially challenging to meet as the NDP projects that many of the jobs in manufacturing and other sectors will be created by small- and medium-sized firms, perhaps as many as 90 per cent of the 11 million positions needed by 2030. This is a challenge as South Africa currently ranks 43rd overall in the World Bank's ease of doing business index; it is 62nd in starting a business; 97th in registering a property; and

158th in getting electricity.[20] The Minister of Small Business, Lindiwe Zulu, says that the government's strategy to encourage small- and medium-sized firms in the sector will rest on 'addressing market failures and enhancing support measures geared for their growth and development'. This effort includes the Small Enterprises Development Agency, which had a total budget of R630 million in 2014/15. Another means was through, in her words, 'private and public sector procurement' and improving access to debt and equity finance.

Recognising that the 'cost of doing business in South Africa for small businesses is very high', Zulu says that her government is committed to try to reduce compliance costs for the sector by 'using technology, including cell phone technology' and 'jacking up government infrastructure, especially at the provincial and local level'. The government is also looking at other means of support, including mentorships and the creation of venture capital funds.[21]

Finally, improving prospects in manufacturing will be difficult because of the industrial unrest that has spread in recent years. South Africa now loses more days to strikes than during the era of anti-government 'rolling mass action' in the early 1990s.[22]

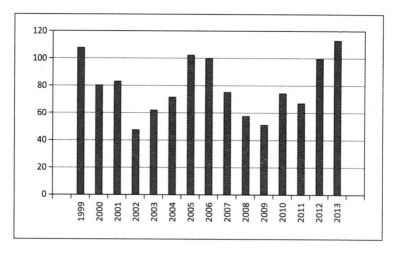

Figure 5.4: Number of South African strikes.

As Figure 5.4 indicates, the number of strikes increased from 2009 to 2013. Working days lost through industrial disputes in 2009 amounted to 1.5 million, a record 20.67 million in 2010, 2.8 million in 2011, 3.3 million in 2012 and 1.8 million in 2013. The first five months of 2014 were overshadowed by a platinum strike costing 7.5 million lost working days alone and a R23-billion revenue loss for Anglo American Platinum, Lonmin and Impala Platinum.[23]

The number of strikes has grown since 2008. In the view of ANC members, this has occurred because of ideological dissension within COSATU, notably between 'workerist' elements (such as the National Union of Metalworkers) and more traditional union elements, including the National Union of Mineworkers. The search for political power also has a business motive, because higher salaries equal greater levies. In this environment, violence has become a tool of negotiation. As a result, South Africa is 'one of the world's most violent, strike-prone countries.'[24] Denmark (159.4 days lost due to strikes per 1 000 employees), France (132) and Belgium (78.9) are among those that registered the highest rate of work stoppages between 2005 and 2009. The global yearly average for the same period was 30.6 days for every 1 000 working. Astonishingly, South Africa lost about 507 working days a year due to strikes over the same period.[25]

The costs to this chronic labour instability are high. According to Department of Labour data, R6.7 billion was foregone in wages due to striking workers in 2013, though the indirect costs are likely much greater, perhaps as much as R600 million per day.[26] Workers lost an estimated 47 per cent, or R10 billion, of their annual wages in the five-month 2014 platinum strike, with devastating consequences for social conditions and other businesses in the Rustenburg platinum-belt area. But other indirect costs are equally high. Dennis George, general secretary of the Federation of Unions of South Africa, observes that a 'culture' of striking, 'creates lots of problems with investor confidence when the workers and employers are at each other's throats.'[27]

While the right to strike is an important aspect of business competitiveness and a means to protect workers' rights, 'there is a need to find a way,' as one official put it, 'to limit disruptive strikes'. Or as a mining executive put it more strongly: 'No one will come to a country [to invest] where people go on strike for five months.'[28] From the perspective of business, and some in government, the absence of a secret strike ballot encourages widespread, frequent and damaging industrial action.

Put differently, the Tripartite Alliance has not delivered the peace dividend in the workplace.

The following case studies will examine the challenges to manufacturing in South Africa. It will place a special emphasis on the problems faced by small-, medium- and micro-sized enterprises (SMMEs), precisely the type of firms that the government hopes will contribute most to the reduction in unemployment. We find that while the national issues affecting employers everywhere are also present, there are additional challenges that must be confronted and that are specific to the sector if manufacturing in South Africa is going to be revived.

Coal to Newcastle

Originally a post halt between Durban and Johannesburg, Newcastle in South Africa was founded in 1864 as the fourth settlement in the colony of Natal, named after the British Colonial Secretary, the Duke of Newcastle.

Parallels with Newcastle's English counterpart city do not end with the name alone. The idiom 'coal to Newcastle', describing a pointless action, stems from the economy of Newcastle on Tyne being heavily dependent on the sale of coal, making any attempt to sell coal into the area foolhardy. Likewise South Africa's Newcastle is a major coal producer, feeding the steel industry and local power stations. And just as north-eastern England has suffered from the decline of British manufacturing, KwaZulu-Natal's version, today a city of nearly 400 000, the province's third-largest behind Durban and Pietermaritzburg, is in the throes of adjusting to new realities. Dealing with them is, however, not the government's task or in its power alone, though its actions – or inactions – can make a substantial difference.

In 1969, Ngagane apart, Newcastle was described as a one-horse town. Then came the announcement of the creation of the Iscor steel mill, envisaged as a three-phase development that would employ 25 000 by 2000. Investment followed in the town's infrastructure, including housing. By the time the cancellation of the second and third phases was announced in 1983, the plant employed 13 000 people. Privatisation in 1989 brought this down to 9 000, leaving 750 empty houses in the town.

Cancellation of the planned phases led to the pursuit of an aggressive industrial policy by the municipality. In 1983, the first foreign investment occurred with a Hong Kong-based company ramping quickly up to opening one factory per month, the newcomers attracted by generous decentralisation incentives. At its peak, the Riverside and Madadeni industrial zones housed 65 textile and apparel factories. The shift in South Africa's diplomatic relations from Taiwan to China in 1997 caused some factories from the former leave and the latter arrive. Today the textile and clothing sector employs 6 500 workers or one-third of the industrial workforce of the town, down from its peak of 35 000.

But it is pretty tough-going, reflecting the changing fortunes of an industry that has seen a decline from 250 000 jobs in the 1980s to little more than one-fifth of this number by 2014. The ending of incentives, fluctuations in the value of the rand, competition from cheap imports from Bangladesh, India and China in particular, and the establishment of the US' African Growth and Opportunity Act (AGOA) all undermined the competitiveness of South African-manufactured yarns and clothing. Under AGOA, South Africa was classified as a developed country and thus not eligible to convert cheaper third-country textiles into clothes for the US market, unlike Lesotho and Swaziland. A number of the larger companies – among them Nova, which manufactured denim (1 600 employees), Welcome and Nantex Textiles (2 200) and the Richfin knitwear plant (1 200) – left in the mid-2000s. Then, in 2011, the National Bargaining Council attempted to shut down several Chinese-owned factories to enforce compliance with the council's minimum wage. When they did so, the workers marched on the Bargaining Council and threatened to burn down its premises.

Now the industry is divided between so-called compliant and non-compliant firms, those that do or do not adhere to the minimum wage of R550 per week. This reflects, too, the size of the firms involved, highlighting the challenges the government has in promoting the SMME sector. According to the local municipality, the 'Council is dominated by the big players in the Western Cape, and the CMT [Cut, Make and Trim] guys in

KwaZulu-Natal do not feel they are part of this agreement between the employers and unions.'

In 2011 the non-compliant factories, actively engaged through the local Chinese Chamber of Commerce and Industry, took the Minister of Labour, the National Bargaining Council and the South African Clothing and Textile Workers' Union (SACTWU) to court, as the United Clothing and Textile Association (UCTA), in a challenge to the wage agreement and the Bargaining Council system. In March 2013, the court ruled in favour of the employers' UCTA, but only for 2010 – a hollow victory.[29]

It is a more complicated issue than simply the payment of a minimum wage. As the chair of Newcastle's Chinese Chamber of Commerce and Industry, Alex Liu, explains, 'While price is a big issue in the garment issue, the problem with the Bargaining Council's wage is about the way in which our business runs. While the Council says you cannot reward productivity, but rather years of service, this takes away the power of the factory owner to manage our factories and to reward those who are more productive. You simply cannot pay everyone the same as you will kill off the morale of the factory, and it would become unmanageable. It is not so much a question of affordability', he adds, 'as business logic.'[30]

Despite changing and tougher economic times, Chinese firms have hung on and adapted for two key reasons: many own their sites, 'which means they won't just pack up their businesses into a container and leave'. Also the municipality has attempted, by the businesses' own admission, to 'look after them as best as possible', troubleshooting with central government in terms of work permits, labour relations, environmental management and other issues, 'a mother and father' to this group. Part of the frustration felt by factory owners and the local municipality alike, however, 'is that Pretoria is not listening. We have no direct channels to government departments', they say, 'or even government in the province.'

The municipality has attempted to replicate Asia's business success by 'looking after our investors' with 'short turnaround times and preferences', though the incentives it can offer are limited to land, rates and electricity tariffs. 'What is a five-day process in Asia,' municipal officers reflect, 'can be a year-long frustration in South Africa.' They also realise the need to create factory facilities close to where workers live, such as in Madadeni.

Rather than attack them on wages, owners ask for greater government assistance in keeping the industry alive. As a start, they say, their factories should be allowed to purchase duty-free imported fabrics. 'The system of imports does not work because of corruption,' says Denis, a second-generation Taiwanese entrepreneur who, like others, preferred not to be identified. 'Those that are supposed to pay duty for clothing imports, don't, while we do, even though we are adding value through jobs. Even with all of our mills working, already 95 per cent of fabric is imported. The local mills simply cannot supply the entire industry. We should be allowed to use imported fabrics based on the value we add locally.'

As a result, other Chinese want out. 'I will tell anyone,' says Robert from China, who started by working in a factory in Lesotho before opening his own at Madadeni, 'don't open a factory in South Africa. There are too many problems with labour. The Department of Trade and Industry,' he maintains, 'should help with funding the non-compliant factories. Instead they give R1 billion to the so-called compliance businesses, where less than 20 000 work.' Members of the Chinese Chamber are, expectedly, universal in their criticism of the trade unions. 'The role of the trade unions needs to be specified. In South Africa, their role is unique. SACTWU wants to have the benefits of capitalism, given its investments in businesses, yet remains a standard bearer of socialism,' says Liu. 'They want to be in charge of everything, while they intimidate our workers and hassle our businesses,' he says, while waving a summons against him. 'They can't be in politics while making a profit.'

There is another challenge that is implicit in the presence of these factories, 40 years after their arrival in South Africa, as a mainstay of Newcastle's economy. Current production, by the owners' admission, reflects 'a very basic industry'. Why then have they not ascended the value chain? 'It's about education, skills and a mindset change,' says Aaron, who runs a jersey knitwear plant. 'Ninety per cent of the children of the first generation of Taiwanese factory owners in South Africa are now working around the world – they are products of a good education. But it is also very difficult to start a business in South Africa. There is too much red tape, and government will not assist but rather makes life difficult for you.'

And then there is the question of vertical integration – there is no supply chain and market for higher-tech goods.

One solution for small businesses is to opt out of the compliance requirements. However, that is most likely when there is no requirement for BEE eligibility for state contracts. What should be clear is that when compliance costs are increased, there are consequences for unions and government alike.

Besieged in Ladysmith

The difference between success and failure among businesses in Ladysmith, just over 100 kilometres from Newcastle, is not in the presence of such vertical linkages. Rather, it is a similar set of issues around compliance, the ability to manage union militancy, and the extent to which they have adapted to changed South African realities, and globalised their markets.

Once the centrepiece of a 118-day South African War siege, Ladysmith was described at that time by Dr James Alexander Kay, a local resident, as 'an awful hole, celebrated for heat, dust, storms, wind and insects'.[31] Even today, it is a hard sell for businesses. Ladysmith is on the route between Durban and Johannesburg, and there is plenty of (unskilled) labour around. Ithala, the parastatal that administers the bulk of the properties at the main industrial area at Ezakheni, offers a rent-free period and cheap rentals at less than a third of the rate in the major cities, cheap and reliable electricity and water supplies, and a one-stop shop for newcomers.

But that is where it ends. The incentives that led to the creation of three industrial areas in the 1980s, at Ezakheni, Nambiti and Danskraal around the town, no longer apply. Labour is restive and the local municipality seen as corrupt and useless. Although Ladysmith has an interesting history, its size (with a population of just 65 000) makes it difficult to attract skilled engineers and technicians from the bigger cities.

Defy is South Africa's biggest appliance maker, supplying half of the local market with 1.5 million freezers, fridges and washing machines made annually at three plants. Now owned by the giant Turkish Koç group, its labour force has been beset with wildcat strikes, 11 in 2013 alone, and productivity problems that were compounded by a seven-week national strike in 2014. Its challenges are aggravated by the relative absence of engineering services in the region, and the need to outsource tool making, a critical element of the appliance manufacturing process, to Durban and elsewhere.

But it is not labour's responsibility alone, say Defy executives, to repair the relationship with management. Progress demands better training and understanding, and the importance of promoting workers from within by creating opportunities.

Defy was, by 2014, busy upgrading its manufacturing processes and range with input from its Turkish owners, with one eye on an increasingly lucrative southern African market. A similar revamp was underway at the nearby Dunlop tyre plant, since 2013 owned by the Japanese Sumitomo concern. The investment is a play on South and sub-Saharan Africa's burgeoning car market, despite the increase in international competition, and South Africa's special advantages of a developed infrastructure and established vehicle manufacturers.

There are four tyre manufacturers in South Africa – Dunlop, Bridgestone, Goodyear and Continental. About 40 per cent of the South African tyre market is imported, some of it a target for accusations of 'under-invoicing' and 'dumping'. Dunlop produces 9 000 tyres a day for a 70 000 daily national market.

Sumitomo is busy investing R1 billion in new manufacturing facilities, which will increase daily production to more than 15 000 by 2020 through four shifts working seven-day weeks.

Yet, like Defy, Dunlop's recent labour experience has been turbulent, despite very high wages. The cheapest cost-to-company worker earns R2 800 per week, 'about six times the wages of a similar worker in India', says the local Dunlop CEO, and 'higher than Eastern Europe'. More than half the plant earns more than R17 000 per month, while, by comparison, a graduate engineer will be on just R45 000, on a par with others in his profession countrywide.

In January 2014 Dunlop suffered a two-week strike, and a further three weeks in July. As a result the company has created a special agreement – Project Ubunbane (Unity) – cancelling all previous labour accords and starting afresh, though there are some doubts about whether this can stick 'given the battles to enforce the law'. During the strikes, the company took a decision not to dismiss the workers because it was fearful of the violence at the Marikana platinum strike in August 2012. 'The police service was not in a position to manage a process like that. Management even had to leave the premises under armed guard,' remembered Dunlop's executive. But it spurred Dunlop to get a grip on its labour relations. 'While labour is problematic,' says one manager at the Ladysmith plant, 'we have to find a way to improve relations with our shop stewards and workers.'

Overall, a similar story

The message of the need to change old ways of doing business is clear, too, from another Ladysmith business at the other end of the technology spectrum, Durban Overall, a leading manufacturer of work uniforms.

Started by diesel mechanic Steve Tandy in 1990 with just 12 workers, by 2014 the business employed 1 400 across four sites, 1 200 of these in Ladysmith. By his admission, he operates at the 'bottom end' of the industrial chain, though the average weekly wage of the workforce is at R700, well above the minimum.

His frustrations arise in part from the failure of local fabric suppliers, with just two of the 'big six' still operating. 'It's impossible to compete against the Chinese and others in terms of costs despite 22 per cent duty,' he states, 'though smaller manufacturers often benefited from the flexibility of having a local supplier. If we had a decent modern mill in the Southern African Development Community region that could take advantage of the local production of cotton, it could make a big difference.'

But Tandy is a believer in local labour. 'We can make cars with local labour, so why not a basic overall? We need a mindset change. We have enjoyed a 250 per cent increase in worker output, measured in terms of garment per worker, just over the last three years, by improving training at the factory.' In 23 years he has never experienced a strike, he believes, because nearly all his workers are women 'who carry the nation, and are the best of all workers when treated well and fairly. Anyone,' he adds, 'who wants to pay R250 per week, is not interested in providing a job, but simply hiring slave labour.'

He is scornful of local procurement initiatives, which 'have not been implemented fast enough and are subject to so much corruption. We attempted to set up a co-operative, buying in and supplying the fabric at cost to the workers to enable them to benefit from local tenders. But these are corrupt schemes, benefiting middle men importing goods and trading on their connections.'

As a rule, local factory owners berate BEE provisions, which add significantly to the compliance burden. There are eight levels of compliance with a scorecard judged on the issues of Ownership, Management Control, Employment Equity, Skills Development, Preferential Procurement, Enterprise Development, and Socio-Economic and Sector Specific Contribution.[32] Worse than that, factory owners complain that BEE entrepreneurs use their racial status and connections in government to procure items abroad and sell them locally, adding no value to local labour in the process.

Still, it is possible to make money. The ability of Ladysmith's factories to do so seems to depend on a combination of a willingness to adapt and manage the regulatory disorder and weight of compliance, and the relationship with the unions.

But for other bottom-end businesses, compliance, corruption and labour present a crippling combination.

Rearranging the furniture

According to the Department of Trade and Industry, South Africa's furniture sector is the third-largest, labour-intensive manufacturing industry behind the construction and clothing and textile sectors, peaking at R15.6 billion in output in 2008.[33] It is a sector, too, where obvious growth possibilities exist. Between 1995 and 2000, for example, worldwide trade in furniture increased by 36 per cent and it was by 2000 the largest low-tech sector, with global production valued at $350 billion, of which South Africa enjoyed just a 0.4 per cent slice. According to the Furniture Bargaining Council, 31 375 people were employed by the sector in 2015. The sector ranges in size from the smaller 'backyard' traders, with two or three people, to larger entities with over 2 000. Around 76 per cent of the companies are located in Gauteng.[34]

Despite possessing key aspects of the value chain, notably the raw material in wood, and apparently being well positioned for growth, the recent story of this sector is a sorry one. While the global furniture industry grew by an annual average of 13 per cent between 2004 and 2009, South Africa achieved a growth rate of just 3 per cent over the same period. In the three years from January 2008, 883 companies closed in the furniture sector across South Africa, resulting in nearly 10 000 job losses. This trend has continued to accelerate.

There are a number of reasons behind this decline, but the key ones include cheaper imports (mainly from China and Vietnam, but also from Europe) and the high costs of South African labour. The 'cost to company' of an entry-level worker is R3 200 per month, far more than his or her Southeast Asian counterpart. Usually, however, the suffocating cost of compliance is the number-one complaint of local furniture manufacturers.

Take 'Colin' who has run a factory in Johannesburg for 20 years, employing 480 people in 2014. It was a business he got into by mistake, when one of the suppliers to his retail business ran into financial trouble and he took over a small duco factory making spray-painted furniture. For him and 'Bert',[35] who also runs a smaller business on Rosettenville Road with about 150 employees making sofas, the biggest challenges for their businesses are, first, the costs of regulatory compliance and, second, the volatility of the rand.

'Rather than spending time, as a small, creative business entrepreneur should, on his product, marketing and sales, we are overloaded with government paperwork, which requires a full-time person to keep up with it,' says Colin. Not only do the small percentages deducted for various levies add up in terms of costs, 'which we can seldom afford the time to recoup', but also compliance with BEE stipulations adds a further demand on time. However, without lucrative government contracts, further growth would not be possible. Even Statistics SA forms 'take several hours a month, if only to inform everyone how many jobs we are losing in manufacturing'. A further negative compliance aspect is in the increasing challenges of firing, which discourages taking people on.

Job losses are, from an employer perspective, an entirely predictable result of labour practices and union activism.

'But don't get this wrong,' emphasises Bert. 'No one employs someone with the aim of eventually firing them. It costs a lot of money to train them and so on. But it can cost even more to get someone who is damaging your business out. Not having this flexibility is not conducive to employing people. And the problem is more deep-seated than just skills, however.' From his vantage, 'It goes to the heart of issues around work ethic, which is far more difficult to create and entrench.'

Many of the businesses are dependent on imported fabric for their items, which are liable for import duties. About half of the input costs of a sofa, for example, is the fabric. While rand strength may reduce their scope for exports, it should help with the cost of imports and vice versa. Yet, many producers are small, making it impossible for them to import in bulk directly, thus incurring additional middle-man charges. These expenses put them at a further disadvantage to Asian competitors who are sourcing cheaper inputs. South African manufacturers have asked, so far unsuccessfully, for an exemption of tariffs based on the levels of labour-intensive beneficiation added to their products. Avoidance of duties by furniture importers – *corruption* in a word – is widely speculated on, as is the role of Chinese government incentives in improving their export competitiveness.

Ironically, given that furniture is an industry heavily reliant on credit purchase schemes (so-called hire purchase in South African parlance), the greatest day-to-day challenge for the proprietor is in managing a workforce '95 per cent of whom are in such shit because of opening accounts and heavy borrowing', whether this be from stores, credit cards or micro-lenders. This in turn leads inevitably to garnishee orders, which force the employer to deduct loans at source from the individuals' pay packet, a source of continuous friction in the workplace. The level of indebtedness also, anecdotally at least, worsens insider-theft.

Another challenge for manufacturers is the concentration of the retail sector, dominated historically by four big companies: Ellerines, Lewis, JD and Shoprite. But the sector melted down in 2014. Accumulated losses of R3 billion, partly a result of its relationship with the African Bank, drove the biggest retailer, Ellerines, with over 1 000 stores, into business rescue in August 2014. In part, some of these tribulations are about right-sizing an industry that has expanded with the bubble of credit and expectations in post-apartheid South Africa.[36] The total number of furniture stores (2 600) rival the 2 800 Shoprite, Spar and Pick n Pay supermarkets across South Africa, though the latter have a combined sales more than five times that of the furniture retail sector.

For all of the above challenges, in the right conditions, the furniture sector could flourish. Colin's firm makes 1 200 recliner chairs a month, while 8 000 more are imported from China. Bert is on a monthly production of 4 000 upholstered chairs and couches, a fraction of the Chinese import orders. He and Bert realise that the only way to grow is to improve competitiveness. That, in turn, demands improving productivity, tightening up against illegal imports and the corruption that enables them, giving space back to the innovator and entrepreneur.

■ ■ ■

The Eastern Cape is at the epicentre of South Africa's industrial decline. The phasing out of apartheid-era decentralisation incentives in what were then known as the border areas, combined with increasing trade liberalisation, has resulted in an exodus of factories. Again, however, the costs of labour and compliance, along with an unhelpful Bargaining Council regime, are barriers to competitiveness and growth, and are frequently cited by local entrepreneurs to explain why the region's deindustrialisation continues 20 years later.[37]

No Bargaining Councils, please

Frame Park is a metaphor for what has happened to industry in East London. Once the site of blanket maker Waverley, which employed over 5 000 workers in its pomp, today the vast factory site has been converted into an office park, dominated by government offices. For jobs that paid taxes, substitute jobs that spend taxes.

The loss of industrial sector jobs is commonplace in the city, at least 7 300 since 2010. Over the last 10 years, says the chair of the Border Industries Employers Association, 'we have lost the equivalent of the workforce of more than three Mercedes-Benz factories', in reference to the doyen of the city's industries.

A drive through the Wilsonia industrial area confirms the extent of the deindustrialisation. Unlike nearby Dimbaza, where factory buildings have all but disappeared, in East London factories have been replaced by depots, conduits for goods made elsewhere and traded locally.

A view of East London's main Oxford Street confirms the downturn. Tatty retail outlets hawking cheap goods abound. Today the Buffalo City municipality is the biggest proprietor, with 5 100 employees, though the industrialists roundly dismiss the usefulness of the local government. 'We have nice industrial policy', says one official, 'but it never hits the ground in the province. It happens by luck if something gets implemented.'

Speaking at a roundtable of industrialists held at the old Marley tile factory in East London, where employment is around one-third of its 380 peak, the official gauges 'the extent of municipal dysfunctionality by big firms like Johnson & Johnson and Nestlé having to pay for their own garbage removal'. The municipality is characterised by lots of political infighting, and a lack of political oversight. Given that business is seen as 'largely white', he says, 'government routinely asks of itself: "Why should we support it?".'

This situation is amplified by a high turnover of government personnel. It takes years to build up relationships and get to grips with the issues. However, the turnover of officials is quick and newcomers have to start from scratch. Moreover, the officials are often too politicised, too fraught by 'power-plays', claims business.

Local industrialists admit that these changes are a result both of global and local forces, of globalisation and the impact of cheaper competition from China.[38] Labour inflexibility and costs, productivity, red tape, a lack of responsive government, costly electricity inputs and transport expenses to the nearest container port of Port Elizabeth are also variously cited as reasons for the downturn. The journey to Coega, 300 kilometres south, costs over R9 000 per container.

They all agree on one thing: they have survived despite a government that can and should do better.

US-based firm Venture Otter is one of those companies that invested in South Africa, buoyed by the opportunity of the post-apartheid environment. Twenty years later it is disinvesting, tired of South Africa's 'fixation on transformation'.[39] Where once 1 600 employees worked making automotive components, today there are just 17.

Government missteps have even more exacting consequences.

South Africans purchase 1.8 million new televisions each year. The country was very late in getting television. Prime Minister Hendrik Verwoerd compared it to atomic bombs and poison gas, claiming that TV sets 'are modern things, but that does not mean they are desirable. The government has to watch for any dangers to the people, both spiritual and physical.' Dr Albert Hertzog, then Minister for Posts and Telegraphs, went a little further, saying that TV would come to South Africa 'over [his] dead body', denouncing it as 'a miniature bioscope [cinema] over which parents would have no control'. It was regarded as the 'devil's own box, for disseminating communism and immorality'.[40]

Remarkably, the country survived the introduction of television in 1976. East London was in at the start, with the assembly of Telefunken sets at Tek Electronics' Wilsonia site, based on technology from the French Thomson concern. Activities diversified into the manufacture of M-Net decoders by the mid-1990s, by which time Tek had been taken over by Plessey.

In October 1998 Plessey was bought out by Dimension Data, which, in turn, hived off the manufacturing wing to Tellumat, which continued to make TVs, decoders, circuit breakers and prepaid electrical meters until it was bought out by management in 2002. Renamed Vektronix, the firm continued with the decoder business, taking the analogue production over the two million mark, and inaugurating the new Pace PVR decoder in June 2013, building 300 000 units in the first 18 months.

But the firm's big breakthrough came in May 2005 when the company manufacturing Samsung televisions in South Africa went into liquidation. With a foreign exchange guarantee from the Industrial Development Corporation, Vektronix commenced plasma screen production under the Samsung brand. By the start of 2014, it had built more than one million cathode ray and plasma sets, with a capacity of 2 000 televisions and 1 800 decoder sets a day from its 300-strong workforce, 80 per cent of whom were women.

The term 'assembly plant' does not do the operation justice. The plant is dominated by multimillion-dollar circuit-board lines capable of assembling and soldering 220 000 components per hour, the processors and chips fed into the process through cassette reels. The boards, populated with as many as 1 200 components, are photographed and X-rayed after assembly. Plasma TVs, prepaid control and battery boxes for solar power and decoders move swiftly along the production line.

Then, in November 2013, Samsung dropped a bombshell: it was going to open its own plant at Dube Trade Port Special Economic Zone (SEZ) in Durban. The government was offering a special SEZ corporate tax rate of 15 per cent (over the usual 28 per cent) and, reportedly, exemptions on foreign work permits. Vektronix (and the other two South African assemblers of Samsung televisions) would be losing out to a government subsidy, encouraging the plant to move elsewhere, putting one-third of its workforce at risk.[41]

East London's industrialists have a raft of positive suggestions for government, though they suspect no one is listening. Mostly, they look for greater subsidisation: 'Make scheduled labour and electricity a double tax deduction,' suggests one. 'Expand the SEZ scheme, with lower corporate tax rates and exemptions from Bargaining Council prescriptions, to encompass previous industrial estates, for example those around East London, Butterworth, Dimbaza and Queenstown,' proposes another, along with the need to boost local industry by giving 'local procurement an empowerment rating'.

Instead of believing that government is out to assist in recognising, as one business person put it, 'that employment is a form of empowerment', the feeling among the group, which represented firms with 1 400 employees, was 'nobody cares or wants to help you, and nobody sticks to the rules'. Or as another asked: 'Should we be surprised? There is a lack of experience by policy-makers in industry, shop stewards apart. Instead of taking up the cause of the unemployed, they have given that voice to the employed.' There seems, at the moment, to be extremely limited dialogue between these industrialists and government. They appear to be talking past one another.

How is government responding to these challenges?

How government wants to help

Government's proposals to build industry centre around an unusual combination of grand infrastructure schemes, incentives for SMMEs, and an Industrial Policy Action Plan that links with SEZs and the Manufacturing Competitiveness Enhancement Programme.

For the Department of Trade and Industry's chief economist, Stephen Hanival, there is a 'relatively simple' economic issue that 'we are dealing with: manufacturing margins have come down, and come down massively. The reasons for this are quite reasonable and rational. Trade liberalisation was perhaps too fast and too deep. We also can't have electricity prices rising by 110 per cent in three years and expect to remain competitive. Getting even access for business to municipal services, such as water and electricity, is sometimes hard work. In sum, there is a margin squeeze – companies are not making enough profits to employ people.'[42]

Hanival speaks for many in government when he says that 'we do not want to follow the race to the bottom' in industrialisation, not least since lower (or higher) domestic salaries will 'have an impact on domestic demand'. Moreover, highly unequal societies 'are unsustainable in the long run'. So the government would prefer to get out of those sectors, ultimately, where the margins are slight, and invest instead in those where there are more gains to be made. Despite the temptations, he says, the Department of Trade and Industry is not into 'picking winners'. The department 'talks state intervention but we don't really do it. Our problems are about margins – about competitiveness. While the government has spent heavily on social infrastructure – water, housing, solar-heated hot water – we are not spending nearly the same on establishing industrial areas.'

At the other end of the government scale are the large infrastructure ambitions. 'Reindustrialisation will create quality jobs,' says Gauteng Premier David Makhura, 'but a reindustrialisation strategy without initiatives will not work.'[43] His province is home to 13 million South Africans, with (at least) 2.3 million unemployed.

To turn business around in Gauteng, his administration has a number of proposals: an Aerotopolis SEZ Hub around O.R. Tambo airport linking into the East Rand's Ekurhuleni industrial area; a new inland port between

Nigel and Heidelberg, which will overlay with a bus factory at Dunnottar; a River City on the Vaal; another logistics hub around Lanseria to the north-west; an Agripolis agro-industrial zone to the south; a Smart City or Technohub for manufacturing technology products; a Pharmaceutical Hub linking up with the province's three universities; a New Centurion with United Nations offices, the African Union and the biggest convention centre in the continent south of Pretoria; and an Innovation Hub overlapping with the Tshwane metro. His aim is to create two million jobs in five years.

It is a long shopping list, but necessary, he says, to turn the country's most important economy around. There are two driving forces: first, acknowledgment of the extent of deindustrialisation and the shrinkage of the mining sector; and second, the costs of apartheid spatial planning, which had people living far from where they worked. The answer to these problems is, Makhura says, to promote the 'Township Economy' by providing a supportive environment for SMMEs in an economy currently 'dominated by monopolies'. To change this, 'we need to incentivise small business, creating better infrastructure in the cities, bringing government's industrial policy to support as well'.

How government can help

The manufacturing sector in South Africa has gone through a pronounced decline over the past two decades. In part this is due to the 'double-transition' of the early 1990s: from apartheid to democracy and from an isolated import-substitution economy subject to sanctions to one integrated with the world economy. The decline of manufacturing is not that different, too, from experiences in many other countries, given the shift of manufacturing resources to Asia.

Yet, it reflects South Africa's uneasy position between different worlds. With an effective 36 per cent unemployment and a largely unskilled workforce, it is suited to 'sweat labour', though it has the immediate aspirations of a first world economy in terms of salaries and labour conditions. It is, therefore, uncompetitive against many mainly Asian exports. Government-enforced high wages add to the competitiveness problem. And employers avoid recruiting staff or adding to their labour force because of the difficulties in releasing workers. Manufacturing is also stifled by issues of regulatory compliance, the cost and reliability of inputs, especially electricity, the reliability and predictability of policy, corruption, competitiveness and the premium placed by BEE demands, and the role of institutions such as the Bargaining Councils in setting sector-wide wages.

In the absence of the 'labour tool' to improve competitiveness, those acting on behalf of manufacturing industries have advocated trade remedies (that standards are maintained and no illegal goods slip through), increasing the size of the local market (through local procurement and branding such as Proudly South African) and for measures that might lessen the costs of compliance and reliability of service inputs.[44] One acute problem, however, is that the dialogue between business and government on these (and other issues) appears 'trapped in banalities, such as "business and government need to lead" and "business and government need to get together".[45] Changing the role and influence of the Bargaining Councils is central to understanding how competitiveness in SMMEs, in particular, can be improved.

The present system seems rigged against the unemployed. A handful of large engineering firms, for example, collude with big labour and big government under the current labour regime in agreements that suit their agendas. In the case of big business, they compensate for excessive wage increases without productivity gains by inter alia shedding labour at the expense of the large majority (some 9 000) of small and medium firms that have little or no such flexibility. The outcome is inevitably business closure, non-compliance or 'informalisation', as was seen in the case of Newcastle's apparel firms. This is ultimately bad for business, government and labour.

There are ways out of this bind, but they demand unwinding the cosy relationship between big business and labour, and putting the interests of small businesses and the unemployed first. One goal for South Africa is to radically improve its position in the ease of doing business index and other metrics, especially in the ability to open a business and other aspects of compliance. These indicators have been a focus of Asian countries for many years and are increasingly an area of concentration for others, including in Africa. Government regulations and actions should at all times be evaluated in terms of the burden imposed, especially on small business and job creation. Rather than only focus on incentives, the government should encourage innovative financing tools, including the conditions that will expand the aforementioned 'start-up' venture capital market and mindset, one of 'initiative, risk-taking and agility', which has proven key to taking business ideas and concepts to reality in other dynamic economic environments.[46]

Finally, we do not believe that large-scale plans to promote manufacturing, in Gauteng or elsewhere, will work as long as the incentives facing employers go against hiring. Much as with our analysis of the World Cup and the Olympics, mega projects to promote a goal cannot substitute for economic systems that align employer and labour interests with the national goal of employing more people. South Africa does need more industrial infrastructure, and there is nothing wrong with big dreams, but they will inevitably fail unless the basic, seemingly more mundane, issues are settled.

6

Mining
A Trail of Crumbs and Riches

> Having a job is more than just about income, but about defining a
> person, and giving purpose. It's about who you are.
>
> — Ayanda Khumalo, Chairperson, Free Market Foundation

'Underground,' said the Afrikaans mining captain, 'it's like a complete society.'

He was speaking to legendary South African artist Johnny
Clegg about the operation at AngloGold Ashanti's TauTona mine near
Carletonville west of Johannesburg, the world's deepest, during the musician's filming of *A Country Imagined* in 2009.

Opened in 1962, TauTona – otherwise known as Western Deep Number
3 shaft – runs to a depth of 3.9 kilometres. 'The four of us, my producer,
the cameraman and soundman and myself went first,' recalls Clegg, 'for a
20-minute induction, in which all the various aspects of mining and safety
were explained. We were shown what looked like an ant farm – a cutaway
of the mine and its tunnels.'

Capable of carrying 70 miners, the cage drops at 16 metres per second,
or nearly 60 kilometres per hour. 'We plunged down a kilometre, as Dirk,
the mine captain, explained to me that the mine runs on air and water continuously being pumped in and out. There were lots of broken air pipes,
which you passed at speed with a loud hiss, giving me quite a startle, causing a chuckle among the toughened miners.

'We then crossed to a sub-vertical shaft and entered another cage,
down another kilometre, and again, until we had reached 3.9 kilometres

underground. As I stepped out, I saw a big, white spray-painted sign on a red background, saying "It's OK". I asked Dirk what this meant. He said "No, ja, it's OK, Johnny." I asked again. He said, "You know, it's like a big underground society. The deeper you go," he said, "it becomes like a big creature. In this environment, you can occasionally have a mental speed wobble. Then you look around and see the sign and it's," he smiled, "OK". It was a bit of mine psychology.

'I was overwhelmed by the sheer scale of the operation. When you see what is going on down there, it's a breathtaking economic activity. The thing that sticks in my mind is that, in a way, humans are imbued with a mad courage, the same courage that sends people to the Moon or to Mars, into alien environments.

'Everybody down there was part of a group of wild frontiersmen, part of this inhospitable landscape, creating a frontier that does not exist, a group of real explorers. When I got to the top, I realised that underneath my feet was an urban planet being mined by very brave humans.

'Dirk wanted us to film the gold in the rock. It was a dull, greenie-yellow, between 9 and 10 centimetres thick. In the stope where it was mined was only space for two miners with drills. I had a very distinct evocation of Hansel and Gretel following bread crumbs through the forest. It was like a fairy tale, following the seam, not knowing quite where it was going to land up.'[1]

The heart of the matter

Johannesburg was, of course, founded on the basis of what lay beneath its soil, even though Sotho-Tswana mines and iron-smelting furnaces had been at work for centuries. The main Witwatersrand gold reef was discovered in June 1884 on the farm Vogelstruisfontein, triggering the gold rush and the start of Johannesburg in 1886. The first settlement at Ferreira's Camp was established as a tented camp, reaching a population of 3 000 by 1887. In November 1886, a portion of the farm Randjeslaagte was laid out as a village and named Johannesburg. Within 10 years, Johannesburg had over 100 000 inhabitants. Nearly 130 years later, the population of the Gauteng province was 13 million, or one-quarter of South Africa's population.[2]

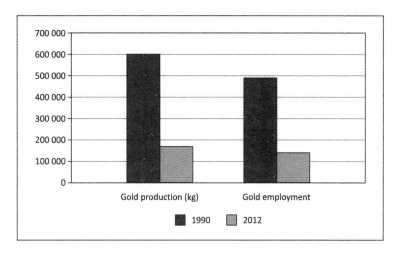

Figure 6.1: South Africa's gold production and employment.

Henry Barnard, 48, is the mining manager on Sibanye Gold's Hlanganani shaft at its Driefontein operations, near Carletonville. Once known as Number 5 shaft, Hlanganani (meaning, 'come together') reflects Sibanye's own translation as 'We are one'.[3]

Sibanye was created in 2013 from an unbundling of Gold Fields Limited. Sibanye's initial three mines were considered deep, high-risk, labour-intensive operations with a limited future.

Today that future looks brighter, thanks to trimming costs and getting labour and the local communities more on board. There is much still to be done.

Barnard wanted to be a doctor like his famous heart-surgeon uncle, Christiaan. But with his father a miner in Barkly East and, later, Kimberley, and not many opportunities for expensive education among him and his 14 siblings, the die was cast. 'It was before TV,' he jokes of the size of the Barnard bunch. He has spent 31 years on the mines, all bar the last three of them full-time underground.

Barnard has worked at only two mines: first at Anglovaal's Hartbeesfontein and then, from 2005, Driefontein. Such longevity is today unusual in an industry blighted by closures. Where Anglo American, for example, once ran 45 gold mines, today it runs just five. The rapid decay of Welkom, once the epicentre of the Free State Goldfields, confirms what happens when mines close: the heart is ripped out of the local economy.

Some 52 000 tonnes of gold, 30 per cent of global output, has been mined over 126 years from South African mines, with a peak of 1 000 tonnes in 1970, or that year 70 per cent of world production. Now, production has fallen to 167 tonnes. Though gold is still (after platinum) South Africa's second-largest mineral export and mining employer, with 130 000 workers, this is down on the figure of 540 000 in the mid-1980s.

In part, the difficulties experienced since then relate to the changing role of the unions and salary structures in a business where, today, electricity and staffing costs comprise 75 per cent of Sibanye's costs.

Despite the pruning of numbers and attempts, now, to build solar energy alternatives to its 550-megawatt needs, the cost structures are fundamentally difficult to change. Underground it is much the same drilling, blasting, digging and scraping operation as it was 100 years ago. The operations are somewhat more efficient and much safer, despite the depths and the increasing logistical complexity of getting people down and ore out from the working stopes to the gulleys, into trains down the ore pass and up to the surface in skips where it is crushed and refined. Getting the ore out is much easier said (or written) than done.

There are 2 800 miners down and up Number 5 shaft every day. They send up 3 500 tonnes of ore daily. From each tonne between 6 and 7 grams of gold is extracted.

Due to trimming management above ground, Driefontein has managed to improve productivity (measured in square metres mined per 19-person crew per month) by 40 per cent. This has caused the cost per tonne mined to drop from R2 600 to R1 600, increasing the mineable reserves from 13.5 million to 20 million ounces in the process. 'As the "pay limit" [the break-even point] falls,' notes Shadwick Bessit, Sibanye's senior vice president and technical head, 'our life of mine gets longer. Unless we keep reducing our overheads, especially personnel, eventually we will have to close even though the resource will probably not be depleted.'

William Osae is Driefontein's head of operations. A Ghanaian by birth, he has decades of mining experience across southern Africa and mineral types. He says that 'the unions spend a lot of time talking about wage increases, but hardly ever talk about productivity increases. There needs to be better balance', he exclaims, to ensure long-term prosperity of the industry.

Across the gold sector, the general trend is that labour and other costs have risen exponentially while productivity and returns have fallen. Yet, the outside view of the industry, in gold and other minerals, remains largely stuck in the 1970s, as one of exploitation and poor living and unsafe work conditions.

Without political support in their attempts to keep costs down, it is difficult to imagine a long-term future for a sector where it costs R15 billion to sink a 1.5-kilometre shaft, which will take 10 to 15 years to pay back. Absent business confidence to invest for the long term in ultra-deep mines, the reserves will remain down there. And the costs of not achieving Osae's 'better balance' will be seen in further unemployment in Carletonville, an area already hard hit by mine closures. The extent of illegal mining, with an average of more than one arrest every day on Sibanye's operations, is one indicator of the scale of the unemployment crisis.

South Africa still has the biggest gold reserves worldwide. With better policy, including government using the Tripartite Alliance to deliver a peace dividend into the workplace, these could be a long-term resource for jobs and the fiscus. Henry Barnard's eldest son is training to be a chartered accountant. 'But the other one,' he smiles, 'wants to be an engineer on the mines.' Government's challenge is to make it possible for him to be so.

The mining challenge

Concern about South Africa's political direction and its policies has meant the country has been badly positioned to gain fully from what lies under its soil.

A 2010 Citigroup survey put South Africa as the world's richest mining country in terms of its reserves, worth an estimated US$2.5 trillion, easily more than Russia and Australia with around $1.6 trillion apiece.[4] However, South Africa's mining sector has been declining at an average of 1 per cent per annum during the 2000s, while the global top 20 mining producers have been growing annually at 5 per cent. In 2011, South Africa's global share of greenfield mining projects was just 5 per cent; Australia's was 38 per cent. At the time of the Citibank report, experts maintained that with the right regulatory environment, South Africa could at least double coal, platinum, iron and manganese outputs within five years. It was estimated that this could add a further 100 000 each to direct and indirect jobs.[5]

During the previous commodity boom, between 1973 and 1981, about 1.8 million private sector (non-farm) jobs were created in South Africa, or 200 000 per year. By comparison, only 100 000 new jobs were created in the eight years between 2003 and 2010, equivalent to half a year in the 1970s, despite sanctions and a high rate of inflation.[6] The last decade was thus 'one of the big missed opportunities', says Joel Netshitenzhe, President Thabo Mbeki's strategy adviser. 'South Africa,' he notes, 'could have performed much, much better in taking advantage of the minerals' super-cycle.'[7]

In the National Development Plan, mining is hardly seen as a high growth area. In the best scenario, jobs go from 297 000 in 2010 to 437 000 in 2030. However, these gains will not be realised in an environment where business confidence has been severely dented by mining legislation, by demands for state-controlled beneficiation as part of a government mining strategy and by frequent talk of nationalisation. Such long-term policy issues are especially important where investments require immense amounts of capital and where projects must continue for many years in order to yield a profit. In a 2011 survey conducted by the Fraser Institute, for example, South Africa's attractiveness as a mining investment destination slipped as a result of 'obscuring government involvement in the sector'. The report ranked South Africa just 67 out of 79 for attractiveness for exploration investment among countries such as Zimbabwe, Venezuela and the Democratic Republic of the Congo.[8]

Mining legislation

Not surprisingly given mining's role in the economy, discussions on the Mineral and Petroleum Resources Development Act (MPRDA) started in 1992 in order to move South Africa from a private to a state-based custodial system of mineral rights. The Act, which came into effect on 1 May 2004,[9] provides a mechanism for conversion of old-order rights and applications for new rights. Fundamental to this process is adherence to the Mining Charter on Black Economic Empowerment, which was put into effect in October 2004. Under the Charter, mining companies have to ensure 26 per cent black participation, failing which there would be no success in either the (old-order or new) rights applied for. The Charter also prescribed a number of additional requirements, including procurement of services by black-owned companies, employment equity targets and improved labour and social plans.

The Act is generally seen as a positive step. In the words of industry lawyer Peter Leon, 'Let's give credit where it is due. It's created a junior mining sector that didn't exist before 2004; it has stopped mining companies sterilising reserves, which is positive, and there's much greater black ownership of the mining industry and in employment equity.'[10]

However, there have been several unintended negative consequences.

First, the deals had to be funded and securitised, which contractually locked black participants into transactions. During the boom times up to the end of the last decade, therefore, they were prevented from selling, and their dividends were recycled into payments. When commodity prices fell, they went 'underwater'. Thus, while bankers may have profited from the transactions, the new stakeholders received far less.

Second, and most importantly, essentially, in the words of one mining legal expert, it was 'the same old cake bitten by different people'. Very few deals injected new finance and created new mines. It was 'a false economy of frenetic activity'. While some entrepreneurs may have gained fresh access to prospecting rights, these 'were usually quickly flipped to white miners'.[11]

In March 2014, a proposed amendment to the Act was published, which, in particular, gave the minister discretionary powers involving beneficiation, in directing the holder of a mining right to address specific concerns of certain groups around mining areas, and also the power to restrict exports. The original version of the amendment, published in December 2012, gave the minister the power to determine a 'strategic' mineral, and thus the percentage to be sold domestically, the aim being to force producers of precious metals to sell at reduced prices to encourage local beneficiation.

With subsequent concessions made by government on the determination of pricing and the designation of minerals as strategic (or not), the amendment was supported by the Chamber of Mines.[12] 'A little like turkeys voting for an early Christmas,' as one seasoned industry entrepreneur put it.[13] Such relative policy timidity may prove to be a tactical manoeuvre in a strategic, long-term industry. For, at the start of 2015, the ameliorated proposed amendment was sent back to Parliament by President Jacob Zuma. The government's overall attitude towards mining appears to have been driven by various impulses: the industry's historical links to processes of exclusion and dispossession, and more recently, by the opportunities for greater inclusion and empowerment. Ideology has also played a part, which explains the existence of the ANC's commission on state intervention in the mining sector, leading a form of creeping nationalisation, the objective being to create a state-mining company at the centre of activity.[14]

There is widespread public sentiment in South Africa, often just scarcely below the surface, that big firms are hurting the consumer and the public by imposing unacceptable costs and preventing the development and diversification of business. Capitalism, they would argue, has to be brought under control or managed to play a more responsible role. 'In industry after industry,' writes Felicity Duncan, 'there are only one, two, or a handful of competitors dividing up the market. This means that prices in South Africa are much higher than they should be, that the quality of products and services is lower than it should be, and that South African companies are less innovative and efficient than their peers in more competitive environments.'[15]

In the same vein, South Africa is seen to be losing out on the beneficiation of local products, and that pricing has a role to play in this regard. For example, South Africa produces 80 per cent of the world's platinum, yet it manufacturers just 15 per cent of global catalytic converters. And this share of converters is falling. The relative cost of manufacturing in South Africa is responsible for this decline, of course, but for some it is odd that South Africa should be a price taker on London-based markets, especially where most of the input costs of platinum are South African.

A variation on this argument is that the price of South African commodities should be cheaper in South Africa because of their origins, from polymers to steel. South Africa should thus have a natural comparative advantage to beneficiate these products because they are dug or pumped out of the ground locally.

Robin Renwick, former British Ambassador to South Africa, has noted that the issue of 'developmental pricing' as contained within the MPRDA would simply 'switch off investment in South African mining'. As a result, of the 7 000 people attending the annual Mining Indaba in Cape Town in February 2015, said Renwick, 'not a lot of them are looking to invest in South Africa. Most of them are looking for investments in other African jurisdictions that are less complicated.'[16]

More accurately, as we describe below, mining houses are investing, but not in labour because of how difficult industrial relations have become above and below ground.

Marikana

On 16 August 2012, a contingent of the South African Police Service opened fire on a group of striking miners at Marikana, a town in the Rustenburg local municipality. Thirty-four people were killed in the incident, and at least 78 were wounded. It was the single most lethal use of force by South African security forces against civilians since the Sharpeville massacre of 1960.

This was the apogee of the Marikana miners' wildcat strike from 10 August to 20 September, at a mine owned by Lonmin, which ultimately cost 44 lives. The strike occurred in pursuit of a monthly pay raise to R12 500, a significant increase in the miners' monthly salaries. But the event also occurred against a backdrop of inter-union tension between the COSATU-affiliated National Union of Mineworkers (NUM) and the surgent Association of Mineworkers and Construction Union (AMCU). NUM lost its organisational stranglehold at the mine after its membership dropped from two-thirds of the workers to below half, and its leadership began to be seen as 'too close' to management.[17] The strike ended on 18 September 2012 with the acceptance of a 22 per cent pay rise and a one-off payment of R2 000.

By 2014, AMCU was making inroads into NUM's membership on the gold mines, firmly on the ascendancy in the platinum belt.

Mncekelegi Ndabeni is the AMCU shop steward at Siphumelele Number 2 mine in Rustenburg. Under his white overalls is a green T-shirt with the date 16 August proclaiming 'never again'. From Dutywa in the Eastern Cape, his older brother was a miner, too, with Impala Platinum, and encouraged him to get a job as a winch operator. Known as 'Rasta' on account of his dreadlocks, Ndabeni explains that just 13 of the 400 people on the mine 'are NUM, and 200 are AMCU. What we want are for the workers, not for politics,' he says in reference to AMCU's rival union.

Still, AMCU's rise is a raw expression of the desperation of workers, the gulf between their situation and the perceptions of politicians, and the naivety of management focused on technical and logistical challenges. The causes of the strike were less to do with AMCU, however, than the underlying 'material conditions' in which the miners found themselves.[18] A great many experienced financial hardship, partly a result of having 'second families' (in addition to those in their home region). The migrant workers had moved out of the hostels by using a 'living-out' allowance to relocate into informal settlements with their families. As a result, the miners faced considerable expense and many were served with garnishee orders. Many found themselves in a vicious cycle of taking on more debt to service existing obligations. As the official report into the Marikana episode revealed, 'for both garnishee orders and maintenance orders … the average amount per order has increased steadily between 2008 and 2013 to amount to over R1 600 of their monthly income'.[19]

Add the failure of traditional workers' structures, including NUM, and local tribal leaders to assist, inexperienced and militaristic policing, and throw in the chronic corruption in squandering the 'D accounts' (a developmental municipal fund set up by the government to help mine workers), and the perfect storm of Marikana erupted. Moreover, the Lonmin board proved politically out of touch. It was all about a political, governance, policing, economic, corporate and union failure.

Nor did the violence end with Marikana. On 23 January 2014, workers at South Africa's three largest platinum producers – Anglo American Platinum, Impala Platinum and Lonmin – went on strike, demanding a doubling of wages. After five months of the longest and most expensive strike in South African history, they settled for a more modest pay increase spread over three years.

From the perspective of the mining companies, the strike was related to pay, but also to politics and wider issues of delivery. 'It's like,' reflected one platinum miner, 'you are trying to dance with your union partner, but someone is continuously pulling the rug from under you due to unmet expectations and lack of delivery of socio-economic goods.' Uncertainty with labour makes more difficult – and costly – the revenue-technology-profit calculation that drives investment. These calculations are likely to be complicated by a new labour militancy, as the movements seek to outcompete each other for members.

A simple equation

The Bushveld geological complex, in which platinum is found in South Africa's north, was created millions of years ago with the injection of magna under high pressure and temperature into the earth's crust. This took the form of a variety of parallel layers, shaped like a soup bowl: chromite deepest, then the UG2 reef comprising platinum and chromite, the Merensky reef (so named after Hans Merensky who surveyed it in the 1920s) consisting of platinum group metals (platinum, palladium, rhodium, ruthenium, iridium, osmium), some gold and silver and base metals (nickel, copper, cobalt) and chromite. Various subsequent tectonic shifts disturbed the neat bowl, leading to three major deposits around Rustenburg, Burgersfort and in Mokopane, the so-called Western, Eastern and Northern limbs respectively. The reef itself is a strip running between 900 millimetres and 1 500 millimetres thick through the rock, over thousands of square kilometres, and at recorded depths greater than 3 kilometres. The deepest mine – Zondereinde – operates at 1 200 metres.

The depth of the reef complicates its extraction, since the nature of the base rock means that the temperatures are twice that of corresponding gold mines. Whereas a gold mine will require a cooling plant – usually a 30–40-megawatt unit – at 1 500 metres, this is necessary at 750 metres for platinum. Platinum working costs therefore increased at a faster rate.

Anglo American Platinum Limited (Angloplats) accounts for 40 per cent of global production across eight mines in South Africa, and one in Zimbabwe, plus another eight South African joint ventures. By 2014, with the majority of miners being AMCU members, all of its 50 000-strong work-force were on a 'guaranteed' minimum pay (including a 13th cheque, housing and health benefits) of R12 500 per month, as part of a three-year agreement with the union that included a first-year 10 per cent annual increase.

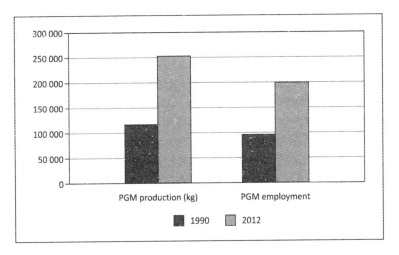

Figure 6.2: South African platinum group metals production and employment.

South Africa possesses around 80 per cent of known global reserves of platinum, a resource essential to the manufacture of catalytic converters in cars. As such, the government would like the country to be a price set-ter not a price taker based on this resource capture and to intensify local beneficiation. But the reality is more nuanced and the future likely increas-ingly mechanised.[20]

The kudus on his necktie give away Gordon Smith as a Wits University graduate. With more than 30 years of experience in gold, diamonds, base metal, coal and platinum, he is a mining engineer and industry enthusiast to his fingertips. He explains a compelling formula for assessing the viabil-ity of a resource and mine: 'You are granted a right to mine for 30 years with a 30-year option for an extension of an asset with certain charac-teristics: depth and thickness, different grades and spatial and geographic aspects. This determines the mix of technology and labour that can be used, whether labour-intensive, conventional hand-held pneumatic drill breast stoping methods or more mechanised "room and pillar" techniques (on reef dips of less than 10 degrees), using remote-controlled, low-profile equipment to both cut and move the ore around.'[21]

Price is also not entirely in the miners' power either, since it is a function of demand and alternatives. The platinum price has declined from its peak of $2 000 an ounce in 2008 to $1 200 by 2014, reflecting less demand for European vehicles and over-supply. Moreover, the second-largest 'producer' today is from recycling.

The more uncertain or punitive the regulatory regime is around mining, the less likely it is that investors will put capital in projects. Even if South Africa might be one of the few places to mine platinum, costs will dictate whether it is mined.

Possible changes in government policy or to the empowerment charter, as threatened, for example, by the promulgation of the aforementioned amendment to the MPRDA, inject fresh uncertainties. One solution to simplifying this equation is to introduce further technology. The development of tracked, remotely controlled mining equipment has moved quickly from off-the-shelf Low Profile (1 800 to 2 200 millimetre profile) equipment through Extra Low Profile (1 300 to 1 700 millimetre) to lithium battery or fuel cell powered Ultra Low Profile (900 to 1 200 millimetre) prototypes, avoiding unnecessary cutting of non-ore-bearing rock and enabling work in tight confines.

In 2013, Angloplats turned over R52 billion, producing 2.3 million ounces of refined platinum, with a profit of just under R2 billion. This represented a turnaround from 2012, where a strike resulted in a R6.33 billion loss. An amount of R15.6 billion of turnover went to salaries and benefits for its 50 000-strong labour force. Its peak production was in 2006 at 2.6 million ounces with 64 000 people, when one-third of its output was from highly mechanised mines.

Over the next decade, as technology develops, Angloplats likely will reduce its workforce to below 20 000, while slightly increasing its output. 'This is not what government wants,' says one executive, 'but you can't continue to give significant wage increases above inflation. Something has to give.'

Anglo is not alone, far from it.

Northam Platinum's operations at the country's newest platinum mine,

Booysendal, on the border between Limpopo and Mpumalanga, about 35 kilometres from Mashishing (the former Lydenburg), offer a glimpse into this future.[22]

When at full production, Booysendal will produce 160 000 ounces a year. There, strata control observers, not gumbooted, sweating miners muscling and shaking about drills, use fibre-optic cameras to probe the seams and stability of overhead rock formations by employing the room and pillar method of mining rather than the more narrow stopes. Multi-drill booms, mechanical shovels, automated roof bolters and large utility vehicles are the technological order of the day. When Booysendal hits full production, it will employ 1 200 people to produce 160 000 ounces of platinum group metals. In contrast, Northam's other mine at Zondereinde (on the northern extremity of the western limb of the Bushveld Complex in Limpopo province, near Thabazimbi) produces 300 000 ounces and employs 9 000 people.

Northam, the country's fourth-largest mining company, is headed by Paul Dunne. He says that mechanised mining is 'a significant differentiator', both with lower overall costs and improved safety.[23] 'This is not a debate', from his perspective, about the 'cheapness of labour', but rather about 'skills and competitiveness'. Of course, mechanisation will not be possible – or at least cost-effective – on all reefs, he admits. 'Mechanisation versus conventional mining', explains Dunne, 'is driven by the ore body and thus the opportunity.'

The same technology-revenue-labour imperative exists in other sectors. Take Venetia, currently De Beers' most profitable South African diamond mine.

Romancing the stone

'I care for myself and others' reads the slogan on the back of the broad-shouldered mine manager's orange-and-blue, high-visibility safety shirt. He was explaining in guttural tones and general terms the expansion of the giant open-pit diamond mine at Venetia mine in South Africa's northernmost Limpopo province. More than a kilometre wide, the pit's contoured terraces weave their way as deep as 450 metres across its four Kimberlite ore bodies.[24]

Inside giant Caterpillar 789 185-tonne and 793 221-tonne dump trucks scurry around, while six giant shovels scrape its sides; on the lip, a steady hum of diesel engines provide the backdrop to the manager's briefing. It is an earthmoving business or, as one miner put it, 'it's not even about ore; it's about moving waste'. Either way, it is a long way from the glitz of the diamond markets of New York's West 47th Street or London's Hatton Garden, the expensive jewellers. Venetia is a long way from Versace and Vuitton. Still, it is at the heart of a global industry. Responsible for as much as 5 million carats annually, over two decades Venetia has moved 600 million tonnes in search of 60 million tonnes of ore and some 60 million carats of diamonds. It is the jewel in De Beers' South African crown, responsible for half the country's production.

Opened in 1992, 20 years later a decision was taken to extend Venetia's commercial life to 2043. Two 1 000-metre underground shafts would be sunk in a R20-billion expansion programme in search of another 90 million carats. As President Zuma noted at the groundbreaking ceremony in October 2013, this investment signals that 'our mining sector is poised for growth, and that it has a bright future'.[25]

Rather than scooping out the diamonds from the top, in layman's terms, the shafts enable the undermining of the Kimberlite pipe by excavating from the bottom, where the pipe's contents fall down before they are brought to the surface. Much of this process is robotic: drilling, blasting and then the movement of ore into a load haul dumper truck, which tips into a silo and onto 40-tonne trucks. They run driverless, gyro-guided on a loop to a crusher, after which the ore is reloaded into skips and hoisted to the surface.

This future requires 'about 30 per cent' less labour compared to a conventional underground mine. While labour costs are likely to remain the same, with higher salaries for better-qualified workers, 'the maintenance costs', reflects a 30-year De Beers veteran, 'will come sharply down. There's no testosterone, so no sudden braking or accelerating, or crashing into the side. And there are no lunch breaks and absenteeism. The vehicles run smoothly between regular maintenance cycles.'

Sinking of the shafts is increasingly mechanised. Safety considerations have slowed the rate of descent. Gold mine shafts have been dug at a record 400 metres a month. But that involved extreme risks, losing sometimes a worker per 10 metres. The Venetia shafts, 7 metres in diameter, will achieve just a quarter of this sink rate, but there is absolutely no appetite for risk to life and limb. As a result, De Beers loses more people to private car accidents than accidents in its mines. The sign at the entrance reads, 'Welcome to Venetia mine. Zero Harm to People, Planet and Profits.'

Still, South African society demands an expansive view of the company's responsibilities. Despite its location on the crossroads of trade with Zimbabwe, the town of Musina, an hour away and home to many of the mine workers, is sagging. The local high school, built for 800 pupils, houses more than 2 000, with 80 to a class, sometimes four sharing a single desk. Roads are falling apart, critical electricity infrastructure tottering too. De Beers has built 12 schools over the past decade, with the Limpopo Development Trust supporting establishment of local poultry, brickmaking, agriculture, vehicle repair and garden services, and has assisted with improving electricity poles and substations. De Beers' stated aim is 'to build a community that is not solely dependent on the mines'.

Regardless, given the poor education provided, meeting this ambition is some way off. While long gone are the previous days of building a mine inside a fence, cut off from the local community and first world safety standards, Venetia has become something of a supplement to the weak local government.

The modern business' role might differ from the usual mining model; however, some things stay the same. 'We are not going to be in this business,' reminds De Beers' Chief Operating Officer Martin Preece, 'if we're not making returns.'

Venetia could have kept mining profitably without major new investment until the early 2020s, then to be sold or closed. De Beers' decision to do otherwise reflects the shortage of gem diamonds in a global market boosted by Chinese and Indian demand. Yet, the mine's relatively positive future will not result in significant employment gains.

Coal and energy

Coal is today the largest revenue earner of the mineral sector in South Africa, above gold, iron ore and the platinum group of metals. But its importance goes beyond money to powering the economy.

'While it is true to say that the success of South Africa's modern economy was underpinned by the growth of the gold- and diamond-mining sectors,' notes writer Jade Davenport, 'the industrialisation of the economy could not have been achieved without coal and iron ore.' The exploitation of the country's vast iron-ore resources in the North West and Northern Cape provinces and the establishment of a parastatal iron and steel industry in the 1920s stimulated South Africa's industrialisation. But it was coal, 'first discovered in the 1850s but developed on a significantly large scale as the needs of the mining industry began to expand from the 1890s onwards, that provided the entire power base of the country'.[26]

South Africa is the seventh-largest producer after China, the US, India, Australia, Indonesia and Russia. A quarter is exported, two-thirds are used for electricity generation, and much of the rest consumed by Sasol, the world's largest coal-to-chemicals and synthetic fuel processor.[27]

Employing around 50 000 workers, the sector earned R101.3 billion in 2013. A 2014 review of the country's coal endowment by the Council for Geoscience revealed that the country's run-of-mine coal reserves have increased from 55.3 billion tonnes in 1987 to 66.7 billion tonnes, despite 7.5 billion tonnes of coal having been extracted in the past 24 years.[28] The increase is due to higher resource estimates for the Waterberg, Tuli and Soutpansberg coalfields – all in Limpopo – following extensive exploration. It is estimated that coal mines in South Africa are capable of sustaining current usage patterns for another 200 years. [29]

Coal should have a bullish future. However, its fortunes depend on the performance of Eskom, policy choices on energy and the global demand and price.

South Africa's energy demands are such that new mines are needed urgently. Fossil fuels accounted for 45 per cent of the world's total energy demand growth in the past 10 years. In the next 30 years Eskom will require an additional 4.5 billion tonnes of coal, of which 2.5 billion tonnes

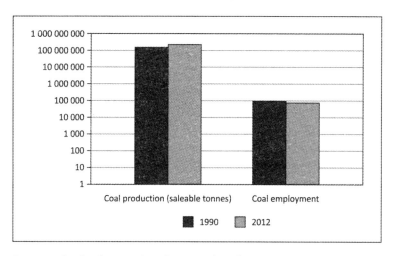

Figure 6.3: South African coal production and employment.

are still unsecured. Indeed, it is estimated that the electricity utility will face a 'supply cliff' of as much as 60 million tonnes a year as early as 2018.[30]

The National Development Plan also sees coal continuing to be the dominant fuel in South Africa for the next 20 years. In particular, development of the Waterberg has been designated a priority by the NDP, given that Eskom would like to source coal from that area to keep power stations in Mpumalanga running after they have exhausted their local sources of supply.[31] The government decision to go ahead with the purchase of eight nuclear power stations, which could cost eventually as much as $100 billion, is inexplicable on the grounds of the cost and the country's enormous coal endowment.

However, there are significant barriers to coal realising its full potential. Eskom has stipulated that a substantial portion of its coal is to be procured from companies that are black-controlled. Yet, these companies lack access to finance. A typical new coal mine supplying a power station with 10 million tonnes of coal a year will require an investment of R10–15 billion. (The production of a 1 600-megawatt power station uses around four million tonnes annually.) Eskom's projected deficit of 60 million tonnes a year by 2018 would, therefore, require an investment of R60–90 billion. Even assuming that investment funds are available, securing mining rights, water-use licences and environmental permits in a reasonable time frame is challenging, while all the time the costs of a weakened transport and energy infrastructure, labour and fuel mount.[32]

There is also regulatory uncertainty. Under the MPRDA Amendment Bill there is a threat that government could declare coal a 'strategic' mineral, resulting in price or export restrictions.

After a start in the mining business at Anglo American, Sipho Nkosi founded Eyesizwe Coal in 2001. Six years later he became the CEO of Exxaro Coal, formed from the unbundling of Kumba Resources and the merging of Eyesizwe with Namakwa Sands. The former president, also, of the Chamber of Mines of South Africa, he believes that the future of coal rests in finding synergy between exports and local sales to Eskom, ensuring the former requires investing in mines, but also infrastructure. For example, the cost of shipping a tonne of coal from South Africa to Gujarat in India is between $11 and $12, while from Indonesia it is just $7 to $8. The future of coal depends, he points out, on continued investment in coal-fired power stations, if not by Eskom, then 'by allowing Independent Power Producers to build and operate their own facilities and to employ national transmission infrastructure'.[33]

Coal, like the rest of the mineral sector, faces real challenges in expanding and increasing employment. Yet, other debates occurring in South Africa also may impose further burdens on the industry.

The beneficiation bogey

For every tonne of reef and earth mined and moved up from 4 kilometres underground on the best mines of the West Rand, just 6 grams of gold are recovered. Ten tonnes have to be dug out for every carat (0.2 gram) of diamond found at Venetia.

Platinum mining has equally challenging ratios of effort to reward, which make calls for greater beneficiation absurd for the miners. The extent of the jargon is a hint at the complexity: 'jackpots', which position hold 'elongate supports' bundled with wire into groups of three to keep the overhanging rock at bay, blast 'barricades' manufactured from recycled plastic hanging like bamboo curtains, 'hydro-bolts', 'buntons', the 'dip' of the reef, 'camlock' jacks, Anfex explosives in their orange dustbins, 'kib-bles', 'creep stops' to keep the hundreds of kilometres of 640-millimetre gauge train tracks on course, 'hoppers', 'box fronts', 'super elevation' of train lines around bends, and regular 'trimming' of headgear cabling as a maintenance measure.[34]

The technical complexity is further defined by the process to extract minerals. The relentless regime of 'drill-blast-clean-support' extracts the ore, which is scraped by means of winches and shovels from the mining face to a centre gulley. From there it is scraped, again, to the stope box where it is emptied into trains that proceed from a cross-cut to a station tip. Thereafter, it is tipped down an ore pass and hoisted to the surface in 7-tonne skips every two minutes, where it is sent to the crusher. From there the ore is moved to a concentrator. The concentrate is smelted, which removes silica, and the resultant smelter matte is processed further in a convertor to remove iron and sulphur, the latter then made into sulphu-ric acid for sale. The slow-cooled convertor matte is crushed and fed to a magnetic concentrator plant, which splits up the magnetics (the platinum group of metals) for the precious metal refinery. The platinum, palladium, rhodium, iridium, ruthenium, gold and silver are then extracted, while the 'non-magnetics' are sent to the base metal refinery to garner copper, nickel and cobalt. The platinum is moved by helicopter to a secure facility thereafter.

Things change all the time, throwing up unexpected challenges. Not only does the global price for the resource fluctuate, so do demands of workers (though only in one direction). Copper cable theft has also become a plague, requiring that overhead electric cables be gunnited together with concrete. Otherwise its plunder for desperadoes, who dig their way underground into the maze of tunnels and gulleys and sometimes over weeks unpack the wire for resale. 'It's a manifestation of unmet expectations and economics,' says one miner, while surveying the gunnite. 'Unemployment and the price of copper [wire] have created a major issue for our security teams.'

And it is extremely tough. Working the narrow stope is immensely claustrophobic, hot and humid, dirty and very noisy as the compressed air-driven drills 'drrrrklaatsdrrrrklaatsdrrrr' their way into the rockface panels. There gumbooted miners, dressed in their white overalls, blue battery light-packs hanging off their belts, sweat rising under their white plastic helmets, crouch down on their orange knee pads in an area seldom much bigger than 1.5 metres high. It is a place for tough men and, increasingly, tough women.[35]

And at the end of it all, in order to acquire 4 grams of platinum, one tonne of ore has to be drilled, blasted, shifted, treated, heated and refined before it is ready to be able to be made into something else. Little wonder, then, when politicians speak about beneficiation, it leaves the miners a little perplexed.

While mining companies devote enormous efforts in turning the ore into platinum, seemingly the ultimate form of beneficiation, they cannot affect the price. The price of platinum is set by the global market because that is where the principal demand is. Equally, the price of South African-produced goods is set globally.

The focus on local beneficiation is driven, it would seem, by the belief that companies should strive to acquire a little more domestically than a cost-plus price for their raw commodities. Yet, South Africa pays the international price not only for reasons of demand (in the case of platinum), but because the cost of capital is determined by international markets and expectations. The return on investment depends on the weighted average cost of capital, a rate determined by the source of its funding – whether this be from shares, debt, options, subsidies, bonds and so on. This rate is not dictated by management, but rather by investors.

Of course, one can appreciate the conundrum facing government: it wants cheaper inputs for industry to grow and jobs to be created. But competitiveness is not just a function of the price of commodities, even if this could be determined locally, but also of skills, logistics efficiencies and costs, electricity inputs and productivity.

Embrace mining

Mining is clearly not one thing. At one end of the difficulty spectrum is gold, with exceptionally deep ore bodies and volatile seismic shifts; at the other is coal, with highly mechanised procedures. However, both these commodities, and all other minerals are affected by price changes, and the costs and reliability of inputs, notably electricity, transport and labour. Government policy provides the framework, but too often is seen less as a constant than a constantly changing target. Policy predictability is especially critical in mining given the length of the investment horizons, requiring up to 15 years of operations before they begin to turn a real profit and not just repay the capital investment. The periodic spotlight shone on the issue of beneficiation is not helpful because, at the most basic level, the prices of the minerals that South Africa produces are determined at a national level. South African miners have shown no hesitation to add value up to the point that it makes commercial sense.

Mining houses have, in their own words, kept their heads 'below the parapet' in government interactions, in the main because mines are difficult to move if policy and the political going gets tough. Given the challenge of labour relations and regimes, 'the response has been, wherever possible, to mechanise'.[36] The effect of the crippling five-month 2014 platinum strike is likely only to further that tendency at a time when South Africa requires as many jobs and as much global trade as possible.

Just at the time when mining has declined in importance in the face of restive labour and ramping costs, the government has advocated investments in the oil and gas sector. However, these initiatives likely will not be taken seriously by investors in the face of regulatory uncertainty and the Tripartite Alliance's hostility towards the existing extractive businesses.

'Agriculture and mining should be the biggest drivers of employment among the unskilled,' says Northam's Paul Dunne, 'a building block for our economy. Instead we have growing divides of income and increasing inequality, noticeably between the cities and the small towns, which are being overwhelmed by people and unemployment. The answer,' he says, 'is simply for the government to embrace mining.' As former Mbeki adviser Joel Netshitenzhe has noted about the aims of economic policy more generally, sustainable job creation and growth goes hand in hand with investment, and that requires, in turn, winning the confidence and trust of the private sector.[37] For mining, in particular, given the capital investment, this requires policy predictability over a generation. The greater the stability in the labour market, itself a function of responsible government policy, the ruling party's relationship with its union ally, and (as will be seen in Chapter 8) business actions, the better the prospects for increasing employment.

7

The Social Wage and Education
From 'All-Pay' to a Paid Job?

> There are literally two economies in South Africa. The entry of any-
> one into the First World economy is education. But if you are selling
> sweat capital – unskilled and uneducated labour – there is no way
> in.

— Laurie Dippenaar, Chairperson, FirstRand Group

Signs for SASSA – South African Social Security Agency – are particularly prominent in rural towns, from Keimoes to Clanwilliam.
Once a month, workers take the day off to collect what they term
'all-pay', something that 'everyone' is deemed to receive in the form of
child support payments and other forms of welfare.

As noted in the Introduction, there have been huge improvements in
the social wage, with 44 per cent of South African households receiving
one form or another of social welfare grant, dramatically reducing poverty levels. Since 1996, the number of social welfare recipients has grown
from 2.4 million to 16.1 million and the nominal value of welfare payments
has grown from R11 billion to R113 billion.[1] Concurrently, according to
Statistics SA, by 2015, about 21.5 million people, or little over 41 per cent of
the population, lived in poverty. This figure had decreased from 27.8 million, or 56.8 per cent, just five years before.[2]

At the same time, South Africa has made a massive investment in
education. It currently spends more money on education as a percentage
of GDP than Canada, the United Kingdom, South Korea, Brazil and the
US; more as a percentage of GDP than any other African country.[3] These

expenditures are crucial because, as will become clear, social grants by themselves cannot lift people out of poverty. The grants are, thus, at most, a bridge with the hope that the employment of a well-educated workforce will be the ultimate game changer for South Africa.

This chapter examines whether social grants have worked, and compares the South African experience to evolution of government grants in Brazil and Mexico. If grants are a short-term solution to poverty, education is the generational fix. But is the current education system adequately preparing young South Africans for the job market?

The origins of South African welfare

The origin of the social grant system is murky. Certainly, the Freedom Charter envisioned a system where all had the right to work: 'The state shall recognise the right and duty of all to work, and to draw full unemployment benefits,'[4] but nothing was really said about direct government payouts. By the time 'Ready to Govern' was developed in 1992, the ANC had recognised the need for a social welfare system. However, it was very much positioned in the form of a social safety net for those who could not work: 'Social Welfare includes the basic rights to shelter, food, health, employment, education and all those aspects that promote the physical, social and emotional well-being of all in our society. In addition, provision will be made through a social safety net for those who are unable to care for themselves because of certain problems (i.e., the disabled, women, children, youth, families in need of care, the aged and those in chronic emotional distress). The task of rehabilitating and integrating juvenile and adult offenders will also be addressed.'[5]

However, it also was clear at that point that the ANC still considered employment to be the major means to reduce poverty. In a line that many in the ANC probably would deride later as close to 'neoliberal', the liberation movement continued to note in 'Ready to Govern', 'We do not encourage the handout approach to social welfare provision because it does not address the root causes of social problems.'[6]

The origins of the current system can be traced to the Reconstruction and Development Programme. The RDP envisioned, 'A comprehensive, non-racial, unitary and democratic welfare system, including a negoti-ated national social security programme, must be introduced to aid the distribution of goods and services within the framework of public respon-sibility.[7] Even in the populist RDP, there seems to have been the assump-tion that the welfare programme would be relatively narrowly targeted. The 'social safety net' was to be limited: 'Social assistance in the form of cash or in-kind benefits should be given to those most at risk (such social assistance could take the form of work opportunities in public works programmes; the provision of food, clothing and health care to those in need; cash in the form of disability grants, foster care grants, maintenance grants, or grants for veterans according to predetermined criteria).'[8]

The ANC was then still clear that it viewed employment as the pri-mary means for poverty alleviation and was obviously suspicious of a large social welfare system. Indeed, the words in the RDP seem almost impolitic given the demands of a large number of South Africans in the run-up to the elections: 'Although a much stronger welfare system is needed to sup-port all the vulnerable, the old, the disabled and the sick who currently live in poverty, a system of "hand-outs" for the unemployed should be avoided. All South Africans should have the opportunity to participate in the eco-nomic life of the country.'[9]

The 1996 Growth, Employment and Redistribution (GEAR) pro-gramme endorsed a limited social welfare system. It noted: 'By far the greater part of welfare spending is devoted to social grants, which assist some three million elderly or disabled persons or needy children.'[10] The authors of GEAR clearly were worried about the trajectory of public sector expenditures, though they stressed that 'strengthening of the redistribu-tive thrust of these [government] expenditures remains a fundamental objective of economic policy'.[11]

The current scope of the South African social welfare grant system seems to be a post-Mandela phenomenon, taking off under Mbeki, who seems to have elevated social grants to a central position in South Africa's poverty alleviation strategy. In some ways, the social grant could be seen as a redistributive measure that complemented the Mbeki-designed black empowerment programme: 'President Thabo Mbeki's unequivocal commitment sent a clear message to the bureaucracy that social grants provided the central pillar for the poverty eradication strategy. In the 2002 State of the Nation Address, he announced a government-led campaign to "register all who are eligible for the child grant", and in 2003 reinforced his support for the ongoing effort by publicly thanking all those "who had rolled up their sleeves to lend a hand in the national effort to build a better life for all South Africans", citing first "the campaign to register people for social grant".[12]

Zola Skweyiya, who joined the ANC at 16 in 1958 and spent many years in exile working to support, among other things, Umkhonto we Sizwe, was appointed as Minister of Public Service and Administration in the Mandela cabinet in 1994. Five years later, under Mbeki, he was moved to Minister of Social Development, where he served until 2009. The origins of the welfare scheme, he recalls, were a combination of 'a social democratic mindset of what had happened in some European countries like Britain, France and Sweden', but fundamentally of 'the need to encourage people to be better by placing their children in school to create a better living standard for all. On coming into power there were very high hopes, and we made promises which we found we could not deliver on, especially with jobs. You must remember,' he says, 'that in 1994 Africans were not getting social grants. So this scheme essentially extended what was there already.'[13]

Social grants in operation

A much tougher tax regime has enabled the ANC government to generate resources to ensure redistribution to the previously disadvantaged. By 2014, child support grants, the most extensive of the government's welfare payments, covered almost 12 million children up to age 18. The largest number of grant recipients was those who receive child support (71 per cent), followed by old age grants (18 per cent) and disability grants (7 per cent). Others types of support include the foster care grant and the care dependency grant.[14]

Table 7.1: The system of social grants in South Africa.

	2013/14 (rand/month)	2014/15 (rand/month)
State old age grant	1 265	1 350
State old age grant, over 75s	1 285	1 370
War veterans grant	1 285	1 370
Disability grant	1 265	1 350
Foster care grant	800	830
Care dependency grant	1 265	1 350
Child support grant	295	315

This system also follows international trends. Public welfare in developing countries has increased both in terms of coverage and scope in recent years. It is estimated that a fifth of all those living in developing countries now receive benefits, and that coverage is growing by 3.5 per cent each year. Grants are also expanding in Africa: 37 countries had cash handout schemes in 2013, up from 21 just three years earlier.

The social grant system is well designed. As Finance Minister, in 2007, Trevor Manuel noted: 'One of the clearest ways in which we are able to act against poverty is through our system of social grants.' He said, 'There is strong evidence that South Africa's social grants are well targeted and account for a substantial share of the income of poor households. Grants are associated with a greater share of household expenditure on food and hence improved nutrition, and the child support grant contributes measurably to the health status of young children. Statistics SA data show that the proportion of households where children often or always went hungry decreased from 6.7 per cent in 2002 to 4.7 per cent in 2005. This means that we can say,' he observed, 'to many more children, hunger is no longer knocking on the door.'[15]

Contrary to urban (and rural) legend, the evidence shows that the social welfare system does not support teenage pregnancies, or encourage laziness or alcoholism or absentee parenthood. A study by the Centre for Social Development in Africa shows that '[grant] monies are mainly used for food and some basic non-food items such as school fees and uniforms, health and transport', that the overwhelming majority (more than 92 per cent) of children live with their caregivers, and there is no evidence that grantees stop looking for work. Indeed, the report notes that 'grant recipients do not wish to be "dependent" on cash transfers and continue to place a high value on paid employment' and that they are 'extremely motivated to get work and want to exit the welfare system as soon as they can'.[16]

There is no doubting the social stability offered by the grants. It has been a revolution for those at the bottom of income distribution. Yet, while the system offers a safety net, despite the grant system, there is still widespread and very high inequality, driven by the difference between having a job or not.[17]

There are few who understand South Africa's current social situation as Senzo Mchunu. He was born in eNhlwathi in the area of KwaHlabisa, eMkhanyakude District in KwaZulu, taught at St Augustine's High School at Nquthu (a prominent rural school), and has served in many important posts, including as MEC for Education in KwaZulu-Natal. Since 2013, he has served as premier of KwaZulu-Natal and provincial chairperson of the ANC.[18] Surveying the vast province as part of a wide-ranging discussion of regional and economic trends he observed, 'We have more than three million people on grants in the province. There is still "poverty of the stomach".'[19]

It is the fiscal sustainability of the social grants that is most concerning, more so than any possible negative impact in creating a dependency mindset. Indeed, questions about the sustainability of the grant system have come from unusual quarters. President Zuma, perhaps reflecting the old ANC position, said in November 2011 that South Africa 'cannot sustain a situation where social grants are growing all the time and think it can be a permanent feature'. Taxpayers, he said, should develop the country 'rather than feed the poor'.[20]

Grants were expanded during the 2000s, an era of relatively high growth and fiscal expansion in South Africa. However, even as early as 2004, Trevor Manuel expressed disquiet over the sustainability of the programme, especially given that disability and foster care grants had climbed by 30 per cent during each of the previous two years.[21] Eight years later, there were further worrying signs in that welfare grants were catching up to the growth in government revenue.[22] While government revenues had grown by 491 per cent from 1996 to 2011, from R114 billion to R674 billion, welfare expenditure increased tenfold between 1996 and 2014. And there are, as we show below, related concerns about the tax burden.

Yet, the social grant programme continued to be supported and is widely popular beyond its immediate recipients. It is not particularly surprising that organised labour is in favour of the social grant system. Poverty alleviation is, of course, a critical objective of the Tripartite Alliance in which COSATU participates and the redistributive nature of the social grants is clearly attractive. Workers whom COSATU represents do not pay significant taxes. As a result, the fiscal burdens produced by the social grant are not immediately obvious to the unions. Finally, and critically, the social grants programme and its very real success in reducing poverty moderate the pressure on the South African government and on the unions to develop new, radical measures to create jobs that might have hurt organised labour.

Indeed, Mbeki, as part of the effort to expand the social welfare system, largely dropped the previous ANC opposition to a general social welfare system that would amount to large-scale handouts. During Mbeki's presidency, social welfare, to a significant extent, replaced job creation as the major thrust of poverty alleviation. This was a mighty gift, among other things, to the unions, which had seen with the GEAR report what a job-creation strategy might look like and how their own interests might be hurt. They were, therefore, motivated to support another way that poverty could seemingly be reduced.

A redistributive impulse?

The sustainability of the social grant system needs to be evaluated in terms of overall levels of government expenditure. Even though grants are pegged, currently, at what government considers a sustainable level, they are no substitute for private sector jobs, not least given the relatively unsustainable fiscal burden of public sector employees. Studies show that while social grants, as a proportion of total government revenue, rose from 12.6 per cent in 2008 to 14.2 per cent in 2012, during the same period, the total civil service remuneration bill increased from 31.7 per cent of revenue to 42.2 per cent. Between 2000 and 2012, the average per capita income of civil servants more than doubled to R211 788. As a result, between 2008 and 2012, total state employment rose by 13 per cent, but the remuneration bill went up 76 per cent.

If these spending trends continue, social grants and state jobs together would account for all government revenue by 2026, assuming average yearly revenue growth of between 9.7 per cent and 9.9 per cent between 2012 and 2030. Even if there were sharp increases in personal and company tax, VAT, the fuel levy and excise duties, 'the SA version of the fiscal cliff would merely be deferred for two or three years'. One reason for this pessimism is South Africa's relatively narrow tax base.[23]

However, government has made important efforts to make sure that the resources that it does devote to the social grant reduce poverty as efficiently as possible.

Technology to the rescue

Corruption in the social grant system has been widespread, by former minister Skweyiya's admission, though this has been reduced by a biometric system that stores fingerprint and voice records for authentication when cash is disbursed.[24]

Net1, a South African payment technology firm launched in 1989, has been distributing social grants in a number of provinces in South Africa since 1999. In 2011, it was awarded a national contract by the South African Social Security Agency to register all social welfare beneficiaries and to allocate all associated grants. Net1's Universal Electronic Payment System uses biometrically secure smart cards that operate in real time but offline, unlike traditional payment systems, which require immediate access through a communications network to a central computer. The offline capability means users can conduct transactions with other card holders even in the most remote areas as long as a smart card reader, which can be portable and battery powered, is available. In 2011, Net1 launched its latest development platform that allows the Universal Electronic Payment System to operate seamlessly with the National Payment System.

Net1's founder and CEO Serge Belamant was, in the 1980s, responsible for the design, development, implementation and operation of the

Saswitch network in South Africa, a world leader in ATM transaction switching.[25] He has patented many of the solutions the company uses, such as the Funds Transfer System, the emergency Finger, the variable PIN and Secondary Verification Methodology.

Net1 has registered 21.3 million people, 40 per cent of the South African population, for the welfare system, which distributes R120 billion annually, equivalent to about 12 per cent of the South African budget. More than half of welfare payments are effected through 10 000 Net1 pay points and participating merchants using biometric-enabled cards, the remainder through the usual PIN-enabled ATMs.

'We take a truck into a remote area once a month that is fitted with between two and four ATMs,' says Belamant. 'We park it in a designated place, put up a tent and dispense cash, either in species or in electronic form on the card, or both.' Previously the government used vouchers, which the beneficiaries collected at the Post Office. 'Merchants would exchange them for cash after a 20 or 25 per cent discount, and there was much fraud,' he says.

Belamant says that Net1's technology has saved the South African government more than R3 billion a year, with the removal of more than a million invalid applicants. The biometric readers are heat-sensitive to remove spoofing by the use of latex, for example, and also statistically monitor acceptable levels of read errors. If the reading is too perfect; sorry, please check another finger.

The fundamental change for beneficiaries is that the new system has integrated them as part of the National Payment System. They now have banking accounts and have access to a realm of financial services, such as money transfers, debit orders, loan finance, insurance products and the like. South Africans' financial inclusion has been achieved, at least technically.

The social grant experience demonstrates that when government is committed, it can find solutions to corruption and inefficiency, often by tapping the ingenuity of the private sector. If the social grant experience was duplicated in other areas, South Africa could see a significant improvement in governance. The key is to tap the best of both the government and the private sector.

Still, even a well-designed system can be improved by the experience of others. Skweyiya has said that South Africa wanted to emulate the positive aspects of what he terms 'the Brazilian Way' in using grants to improve access to health care, nutrition and education. How well does the South African experience match up? The same comparative question applies to the Mexican grant system.

Brazil's Bolsa Família

The Bolsa Família social welfare programme was introduced by the Brazilian government of President Luiz Inácio Lula da Silva in 2003 as part of the Fome Zero federal assistance scheme. Programa Bolsa Família (PBF) provides financial aid to poor Brazilian families conditional on participation in school and health programmes. While the Mexican programme Oportunidades was the first nationwide plan of this kind, with 12 million Brazilian families benefiting, covering more than one-quarter of the population, some 50 million people, the PBF is now the largest cash transfer scheme in the world.

The PBF pays out between R$14 to R$140 reals (US$4.30 to US$43) a month, depending on family earnings and the number of dependants. The money, which operates through a Citizen Card debit card system, is given preferentially to a female head of household, since empowerment of women is seen as key to the investment in children. Use of such debit cards has helped to reduce corruption, and to dissociate transfers from individual politicians or political parties.

On the plus side, the transfers have assisted in directly dealing with short-term poverty. Government statistics show that PBF has lifted 36 million Brazilians out of extreme poverty, defined as those who live on less than US$35 a month. Between 2002 and 2012, for example, the number of Brazilians living in extreme poverty decreased from 8.8 per cent to 3.6 per cent. The PBF was found to have been responsible for about 20 per cent of the drop in inequality in Brazil since 2001.[26]

The programme also has had a significant impact on the nutritional circumstances of the poorest families, with children in public schools receiving at least one free meal a day. Surveys conducted by the federal government among PBF's beneficiaries indicate that the money received by households is spent, in priority, on food, school supplies, clothing and shoes.[27] The Federal University of Pernambuco showed also that 87 per cent of the money is used by families living in rural areas to buy food.[28] According to the United Nations, hunger has consequently decreased from 22.8 million people in 1992 to 13.6 million in 2012.[29]

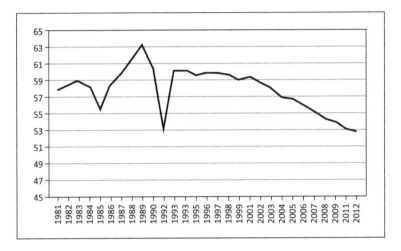

Figure 7.1: Brazil's Gini coefficient.

One of the most recurrent criticisms is that the Brazilian programme discourages the search for employment; that people supposedly give up trying to find a job, content instead to lounge around on the PBF. However, a World Bank study found that this was not the case. Instead, the study reported, working adults who claimed PBF grants were inclined to take greater risks and work even harder, in the knowledge that the subsidies gave them a safety net.[30]

Among the sharpest critics are left-wing academics, who have studied welfare policies for decades. They warn that the PBF is simply a new way of maintaining a profoundly unequal status quo.[31] This criticism has resonance in South Africa given that the grants may have quieted immediate pressures to reform the economy, but they are only really relevant if the grants are considered a permanent solution to poverty, rather than a temporary means to address hardship. The impact of the PBF on poverty during this century is also less important than the effect of large increases in the minimum wage and in pensions, demonstrating that employment is the ultimate tool to reduce poverty. Over the last 18 years, for example, the minimum real wage in Brazil rose more than 100 per cent, resulting in a 'huge increase in income distribution at the bottom', as the average real wage escalated over this time by around 10 per cent.[32] The most people will benefit if they will get better jobs by having more and better skills. According to the economist Fernando de Holanda Barbosa, ultimately educational improvements, already responsible for 30 per cent in the reduction in Brazil's Gini coefficient, are the most sustainable means to addressing income inequality.[33]

The Mexican illustration

Mexico's cash grant scheme, Oportunidades, was founded in 2002 to extend an earlier, rural-based scheme, Progresa, to urban areas. Like Bolsa Família, this social inclusion scheme offers payments to families in exchange for regular school attendance, health clinic visits and nutritional support. Payments are made directly from the government to families, reducing the likelihood of corruption. By 2011, Oportunidades helped support 5.8 million households and covered all 100 000 towns and municipalities across Mexico.[34]

Regular external evaluations were, at the outset, established as a key aspect of the programme, which changed its name to Prospera in 2014. Its aim has been to enable people to break out of an intergenerational trap, where the parents were poor and their children did not go to school but instead went to work. The children, therefore, were assured to remain poor, as without education, they could not get a good job. When they, too, became adults, their own children would perpetuate the cycle, from generation to generation.[35]

Like Bolsa Família, there are those who see Oportunidades as having remarkably positive impacts, such as increasing school attendance and facilitating access to health care for the poor. Others view it as institutionalising a culture of hopelessness and unemployment, while some argue that 'in order to be transformative, it needs to be responsive to particular vulnerabilities and it needs to address the underlying causes of poverty'.[36]

Overall, viewed from a South African vantage, 'Oportunidades faces the same problem we do', says South Africa's former ambassador to Mexico, Malcolm Ferguson. 'Ending poverty is dependent on creating an education system, which, in Marxian terminology, is the factor that can change everything, enabling people to find their way out of the poverty cycle. While the state can provide a measure of social justice in such grants,' he emphasises, 'and a necessary policy construct for business, more is required for success.'[37] But like the South African and Brazilian examples, while these programmes do not necessarily lead anywhere, they help make the status quo bearable for a great many of the underprivileged.

Graduation

Without necessary skills to acquire a decent job, graduation from welfare is unlikely. Yet the state of South Africa's education system is perhaps the greatest tragedy and missed opportunity since 1994. The successive failures relate to both historical legacy, no doubt, but in the successive 20 years, they are also due to the corrosive role of trade unions and absence of political will to improve the system. The International Monetary Fund noted in December 2014, 'South Africa's challenges stem partly from poor service delivery. For example, although spending on education is high compared to other developing markets ... outcomes are poor.'[38]

In fact, the bang for the buck is dismal. Just 28 per cent of South African government (National Senior Certificate) school matriculants qualified for tertiary studies in 2014, about 12 per cent (or 150 752) of those who started Grade 1 in 2003. Dropout rates increased sharply from the first year, so that only slightly more than half the cohort that began school together (1.25 million) wrote matric in 2014 (688 660), making the effective pass rate 41.7 per cent.

In the same 2014 exams, the Independent Examinations Board tested those 1.5 per cent of the candidates in private schools (10 451 in 191 schools). The pass rate in those schools was 98.38 per cent, and 85.45 per cent qualified for university entrance.[39]

Effectively this means South Africa has two education systems: a private system for a small number of students that performs well and a public system that serves the vast majority poorly.[40]

A 2014 report by the World Economic Forum ranked the quality of South Africa's maths and science education last out of 144 countries. It was placed 140th in the quality of its education system, 117th for Internet access in schools, and 133rd in the quality of primary education. The World Economic Forum's global information technology report put South Africa ahead of only Yemen and Libya in the overall quality of its education.[41]

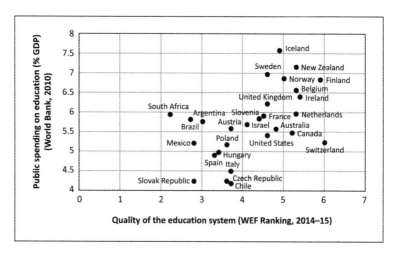

Figure 7.2: Education expenditure versus quality.

The reasons for poor educational performance are known. Better teachers produce better skills. In South Africa, however, teacher non-attendance levels are above 10 per cent. Furthermore, many teachers are not equipped to teach the classes they have been assigned, yet remain protected by their unions at the expense of their students. A 2014 study found that the content knowledge of 79 per cent of Grade 6 mathematics teachers was below the level required for learners to pass Grade 6. It also found that just 16 per cent of Grade 6 pupils were taught by maths teachers who had at least a Grade 8 or Grade 9 level of content knowledge. Nearly two-thirds of Grade 6 pupils were taught maths by teachers who only could manage Grade 5 work. Yet, the study was unable to find evidence of any sort of training and professional development intervention, which had helped to improve the knowledge of maths teachers. Another investigation found a sample of 253 KwaZulu-Natal teachers scored an average of just 57 per cent when given a matric maths past paper to write.[42]

This situation only can worsen already skewed income trends. Research shows that teachers with relatively high levels of maths content knowledge were concentrated in the wealthiest 20 per cent of schools (that is, those in quintile five). Yet less than 10 per cent of the teachers in quintile one (the bottom 20 per cent), two (20–40 per cent) and three (60–80 per cent) schools were able to handle questions at the Grade 8 and Grade 9 level.[43]

Just as poverty can ensure a vicious cycle of low skills and joblessness, poor teachers breed a cycle of educational dysfunctionality, where many children do not have first-hand experience of a proper school environment and therefore perpetuate poor performance. Astonishingly, South African children receive, on average, instruction for only about 40 per cent of their time in classrooms.[44] Holding teachers responsible by imposing sanctions may be a key, first step in breaking this low-performance cycle. Although COSATU acknowledges the crisis of education, it denies that this responsibility starts with the role of its affiliated South African Democratic Teachers' Union, representing 260 000 members, 70 per cent of the country's teaching staff.[45]

At the same time, the poorly functioning educational system is not training the skilled workers that the South African economy needs. The failure of existing systems, including the Sector Education Training Authorities, are part of this general dysfunction. ADCORP, the largest South African labour broker, has found that only one in a hundred applicants for call centre jobs are suitable for the posts; down from one in 70, five years earlier. Decline in the quality of applicants reflects, from the ADCORP perspective, 'a deterioration in overall educational standards.'[46] The dearth of skills does not apply only to the white-collar workforce. As the snapshot on Saldanha Bay's ambitions to create an oil and gas service centre in Chapter 4 illustrated, there is a shortage of artisans, reflecting a failure in the system that feeds this skills cohort.

Education standards have a direct correlation to unemployment. The level of unemployment among South African graduates is under 6 per cent, a rate that has remained more or less constant since 1994, even though the number of graduates has grown rapidly, from 463 000 in 1995, for example, to 1.1 million in 2012.[47] The chances of finding a job have historically been much greater also with a secondary matric qualification. Just 16 per cent of the unemployed (broadly defined) in 2009, for example, possessed a matric.[48]

As a result, the country continues to suffer from the seeming paradox of having many positions that require skills remaining vacant, even while a very high number of unskilled people seek work that does not exist for them. It is critical that the educational system be reformed so that students with the skills required by the national economy graduate in large numbers. Such a development would help business and also cause a significant decline in poverty and the demand for government grants.

Education is a necessary but sometimes, as Zimbabwe's collapse suggests, an insufficient condition for success.[49] Although that country enjoyed a first-class education system, absent the right political choices, it suffered economic instability before descending into state failure for the majority of its citizens. However, a well-functioning education system is certainly a *necessary* condition for success, especially for poor people to break out of the cycle of poverty. Educational success is associated with income. Those who are employed have the resources to send their children to good public or private schools. As a result, South Africa's inequality, fundamentally the result of the inequity between those with and those without jobs, will likely cross generations.

Squandering the dividend?

Public policy can assist the poor, although simply spending more is not enough. South Africa has devised a system of social grants that works to keep people from destitution. However, the very significant resources devoted to education have not resulted in bridges that will allow the children of the poor to participate in labour markets so that they can do better than their parents. The educational system also is not helping to alleviate the significant skills shortage in many sectors of the South African economy.

It is imperative that South Africa creates a generally accepted timeline where students can expect to graduate from welfare and move to jobs.

'Maybe,' says farmer Paul Cluver, 'we need to make peace with the fact that we pay people to do nothing. But this will work only if we can produce enough with the rest of the economy. You can't have both – a static economy and an increased number of dependants.' Indeed, as Cluver put it, 'The welfare system is not an unacceptable price to pay as a society towards those who are suffering. It is providing stability. But,' he asked, 'are we squandering the benefit of this stability in not using it to put another system in place?'[50]

8

A Bridge to the Future?

We must maintain our reputation for being a good place to live and work, because we lose that at our peril. If people think that we are not interested in attracting investments, that talent is not welcome, that we've turned inwards, I think that's the end of us.

— Lee Hsien Loong, Prime Minister, Singapore

Despite the challenges to South African business and to job creation described throughout this book, there is an enormous amount of entrepreneurial energy waiting to be unleashed. This chapter examines several case studies of visionary experiments that have succeeded or failed, and several policy directions where South Africa might like to go.

Clearly, to create world-class firms with good jobs, a supportive policy environment must exist. We examine first how the policy environment has affected the motor vehicle industry. This industry serves as a link between South Africa's past and its possible high-tech future in areas from aerospace to pharmaceuticals. However, creating world-class firms is not an easy path. Competitiveness is dependent on several factors under South Africa's own control, such as labour, technology and capital; and others that are less so, including the size of the local market and distance from rich international customers. It is to this future that the study now turns.

■ I ■

Ford is South Africa's oldest vehicle manufacturer. It opened its first factory in 1923 and, aside from a 10-year divestment interregnum, it has been in the country ever since.

The street names 'Motor', 'Bearing' and 'Propshaft' offer a clue about the location of Ford's Silverton assembly plant east of Pretoria. Originally established by the Sigma Motor Corporation in 1968 to assemble Chrysler products, today it only makes one model: the Ford Ranger pickup (South African 'bakkie'). With annual production around 90 000 vehicles, some 400 per day, one leaves the production line every 2.2 minutes. Two-thirds of these are destined for export markets, mainly to Germany and the United Kingdom.

Most of the 1 780 manufacturing staff is on the 'Trim, Cut and Finish' assembly line. The Bodyshop, where robotic arms place and weld the steel panels and the Paintshop are both highly automated. A 'Pick to Light' scanning system, borrowed from the Minnesota plant, enables the right parts to be delivered to the correct car. Assembly is dictated by a computerised 'Error Proofing Station' denoting the status of each task. All of this is essential given the different spec vehicles under production for different markets: 1 600 permutations from colour, engine type and size, left- or right-hand drive, single-, double- or rap-cab.

The machines help Ford cope with the skills shortages. Ford used to train 150 artisans a year on the job, about three times more than it required. This role was handed over to the government's Sector Education Training Authorities (SETAs),[1] set up in 2000 to address skills shortages and needs. These are seen to have failed in their mandate because of acute management problems. One government report on the SETAs, meant to be confidential, said, 'It is not clear per the strategic plans and annual performance plans whether the scarce skills needs, as identified in the sector skills plans, are being addressed.'[2]

Still, the company has 'the fastest production line in Africa', says its CEO Jeff Nemeth.[3] But there are many challenges for Ford and others making cars in South Africa. The future of mid-sized plants, such as Silverton, with a capacity of around 100 000 units a year, especially those far from export markets, is inevitably scrutinised in an industry where the economies of scale of manufacturing operations is more important than any other aspect, technology included. 'The focus,' says Nemeth, 'is always on maximising scale.' Although the South African Ranger plant takes just 28 hours to produce each vehicle compared to 38 hours in Thailand, freight costs for the South African-produced vehicle are eight times what they are in the Southeast Asian country. This differential provides an indication of the South African competitiveness challenge.

Until it temporarily disinvested due to pressure from anti-apartheid activists in 1988,[4] Ford had constantly been the 'number one or number two' seller in the South African market, according to Nemeth. By 2010, the South African Ford chapter was at a crossroads. Forty per cent of its 40 000 annual production was made up of the Ford Bantam bakkie, an 'orphan' vehicle, as South Africa was the only place it existed. The existing Ford Ranger was also reaching the end of its life, with between 1 300 and 1 400 units per month, and 'just a handful of Focus' cars being built. It was 'big decision time', recalls Nemeth. If Ford was 'to build a new platform, it needed all new types of automation and investment'. At the time, South African productivity compared unfavourably with many of Ford's 40 global assembly plants; each of the earlier-model Rangers took 20 hours to produce in Minnesota, but 75 hours in South Africa.

It was a 'turning point about what South Africa meant to Ford. The decision had been taken to close Australia, with double South Africa's market and just three car manufacturers, compared to South Africa's seven. To keep South Africa open and to invest, we needed enough scale at a competitive cost,' says Nemeth.

The target was 75 000 vehicles annually. 'The largest segment in the Middle East and sub-Saharan Africa,' reminds Nemeth, 'was the compact pickup, and particularly robust in South Africa. But we estimated that if we could export 25 000 and sell the same number to the domestic market, we were still 25 000 short. We then started to think about Europe, which was being supplied out of Thailand at the time. South Africa's Free Trade Area gave us some advantages in this regard, and then we had another 25 000 and we were at our target.

'But in the wake of the crisis of 2008/9, when the [Ford] board was cutting everything, these achievements still did not carry the day.' While Ford was laying off 10 000 workers it did not want to contemplate a $300-million investment in a new range in faraway South Africa. The loss of three months of production due to strikes at Ford in 2010 and four weeks the following year caused a high level of concern in Detroit. 'It came down to being a conversation,' says Nemeth, 'about Africa. While South Africa is a mature market with limited opportunities, Africa is the final economic frontier. We believed that we would have to open a plant in Africa at some point even if the South African plant was closed.' Africa 'carried the day'.

Even so it was a tight calculation, 'the sums showing that we could break even with the plant'. Policy support from government was critical. 'The decision would never have flown without the MIDP [Motor Industry Development Programme], and we had lots of discussions with the Department of Trade and Industry to determine a clear line of sight on future policy.' Without this support, the plant would have closed, or been sold, at the end of its platform life – which, with a 27-year-old Bantam as its mainstay, was imminent.

Hence the decision to invest in a new Ford Ranger line at Silverton. In so doing, Ford aims for a small slice of 65 million new cars sold annually across the world. South Africa accounts for under 1 per cent of this market, or 600 000 units. Africa comprises three times this figure, the bulk (850 000) destined for North Africa. By 2015, the Silverton plant had improved its competitiveness to rank second best among Ford's 40 plants worldwide. Still further advantages, Nemeth believes, lie in accessing the African market via preferential (free) trade agreements.

■ ▪ ■

Keeping the South African car industry alive has, however, been a controversial exercise in subsidies and protectionism. The alternative posed is to lose, as has occurred in Australia, the industry altogether, given the lack of economies of scale in the South African market, and with it 50 000 direct jobs and the contribution to the balance of payments.

But what is the opportunity cost of the government's policy? What does a process of graduation from protectionism look like? And what lessons are there from the motor vehicle industry and other higher-tech sectors for South Africa's employment growth prospects?

Scale, scale ... and export

Ford's story of increasing capital intensity and single-model production is replicated across South Africa's six other vehicle manufacturers
– Mercedes, BMW, General Motors, Toyota, Volkswagen and Nissan/
Renault. Whereas in 1995 they together produced 41 different models,
17 years later this was reduced to 13, even though the number of vehicles
manufactured has increased from 390 000 to 540 000 units.

In East London, Mercedes-Benz has invested in state-of-the-art technology to manufacture its C-Class model. It seems rosy from the outside.
More than 60 000 vehicles were manufactured in 2012, mostly for export.
The plant has been exporting sedans to right-hand-drive markets since
2000. But in the process, the business has returned to virtually what it
started out as in the form of Car Distributor's Assembly Pty Ltd 60 years
ago – an assembly plant. Today robots weld and spray the steel panels that
are imported from Germany, while workers screw together a kit of nearly
all foreign-supplied parts. Little wonder that the number of workers has
declined to 2 500 from 7 000 just a few years ago.[5]

Similarly, BMW produced 'between 15 000 to 16 000 3 Series in the
mid-1990s, along with 5 000 5 Series, 240 7 Series and a dozen or so 8
Series cars', says Nico Vermeulen, director of the National Association of
Automobile Manufacturers of South Africa. 'Now it only makes one model
– the 3 Series – for local and international markets, exporting 60 000 of its
80 000 annual production.'[6]

Certainly one of the reasons for the loss of jobs was continuing labour
volatility. On leaving South Africa at the end of 2014 to take over as head
of VW in Brazil, David Powels has said that labour disruptions were the
'hardest and darkest' days of his eight-year leadership tenure. Speaking
of the 'desperation as the plant stops', he stressed that everyone lost during such stand-offs, not least the damage done to the country's reputation.
'We have to change the attitude and mindset of both parties to find a less
destructive and disruptive way of settling disputes. It starts with reasonable demands,' he reflected, 'and maturity.'[7]

In addition, these changes may have been necessary in the transition of
this South African industry from a protected low-volume market to one

attempting greater international economies of scale.

'Before 1994,' reminds Vermeulen, 'South Africa's motor industry was protected by a combination of a 115 per cent tariff and a local content programme, first by weight, then by value. This was a path to nowhere for an industry that fluctuated between annual local sales of 200 000 and a 1981 peak of 301 000. These volumes were inadequate to retain seven major subsidiaries of multinational companies.' The result was the appointment of a Motor Industry Task Group charged with coming up with a 'blueprint for sustainable growth in an industry that had become fat, lazy and highly inefficient behind import duties. It needed a wake-up call.'

The Task Group gave birth to the MIDP, which quickly brought down tariffs, while at the same time encouraging exports to increase volumes and improve economies of scale. The MIDP allowed for export credits to be used to offset duties on imported parts.

As Johan van Zyl, the head of Toyota South Africa, observes: 'If you had to remove the duties from motor vehicles into South Africa, it would be much easier to import them than to produce them. We are far away from the big markets from a logistical point of view, so it does not make sense to do this. Without the MIDP we could not have survived, and the motor vehicle industry would be like the textile industry, it would be dead. South Africa had to quickly reinvent itself. The MIDP transformed the industry from an isolated, low-tech, low productivity one, to one that invested more in people, in productivity and technology. The imperative to find export growth, through the rebates, was shock treatment to become competitive.' He says that it is unlikely that the 'industry will be in a position in the foreseeable future when we can do without protective tariffs'.[8]

The result was that by 2012 the automotive sector accounted for 12.1 per cent of total South African exports, growing from R4.2 billion in 1995 to R86.9 billion in 2012. Exports of cars and trucks grew from 68 031 in 2000 to 276 819 units by 2012, and similar increases were reported among components. The main export market was the European Union (R34 billion, or 39 per cent) followed by the US at R20 billion and Africa at R17.8 billion. The motor industry's contribution to South Africa's GDP is estimated at 7 per cent.[9]

At the end of 2012, the MIDP was replaced by the Automotive Production Development Programme (APDP), which seeks 'to shift the emphasis away from an export focus to one that emphasises value addition and scale in the production of vehicles'.[10] Under the APDP, tariffs will remain at 2012 levels (25 per cent on vehicles, and 20 per cent on components) until 2020. There is a system of duty-free import credits based on production targets (rather than the MIDP's export-based scheme) and a system of cash grants of 20 per cent designed to further stimulate production. However, there remains concern within the industry about policy predictability. There are now discussions about changing the APDP, 'an agreement that was supposed to remain as is until 2020', just two years into its life, jeopardising the government's credibility with the local franchises and theirs, in turn, with their head offices. As Powels put it, major changes to the APDP could indicate to investors in the sector a reversal of the government's 20-year record of policy stability and predictability. Coupled with labour issues, political tensions and sovereign downgrades, any changes in the APDP would 'put further doubt into the minds of foreign investors'.[11]

The MIDP changed into the APDP because of the challenge of World Trade Organization prescriptions, and the importance, says Van Zyl, of finding a balance between local and export sales, 'a market neutral position'. And, rather like welfare, at some point there is a need for graduation. 'You cannot in the end be driven by protection alone,' says Elisabeth Bradley, daughter of the founder of Toyota South Africa, Dr Albert Wessels, 'but rather by making things at a lower cost. Somehow we seem to have missed that message.'

Despite Toyota's status as the number one best-selling vehicle manufacturer in South Africa for 35 years, from Van Zyl's perspective, there remain significant challenges. For one, local component suppliers are uncompetitive against the economies of scale of overseas competitors, and they are still dependent, too, on imported items and vulnerable to exchange rate fluctuations. 'Even though we might produce an average of 150 000 vehicles each year, with 600 000 shock absorbers, for example,' says Van Zyl, 'we have that across a range of different models. So we are making small numbers. And South Africa cannot obtain the same basic inputs, such as steel, at cost as our suppliers elsewhere, which seems strange for an iron and steel exporting country.' Moreover South Africa 'still suffers from the logistics challenges through its ports'.

While the government lauds the contribution that South Africa's car manufacturers make to the balance of payments, an evaluation of the programme has to consider both the widening automotive trade deficit (R49.2 billion in 2012), and the costs to the economy. In its 2011 Budget Review, for example, the Treasury calculated that the annual subsidy to the motor industry was R17.8 billion, comprising tax allowances, cash grants, preferential financing from the Industrial Development Corporation, and the costs to consumers from higher prices due to import tariffs. For the 36 000 workers then directly employed, this worked out to R585 000 per worker for a sector where workers earn on average R143 000 annually, or if the downstream 80 000 workers are included, R205 000.[12]

Is it really worth it?

The defence of such subsidies is that there is 'no country – Australia apart – with a vehicle manufacturing sector', responds Vermeulen, 'that does not offer protection'. Equally, the subsidies 'have to be weighed up against the contribution made by the upstream and downstream aspects of the entire industry' – from servicing to sales, and catering to media and advertising. Vermeulen estimates the overall value of the sector to the economy to be in the range of 'R200 to R250 billion plus'. Of course, even if South Africa thought that these costs were justified, they could not be repeated in other industries given the fiscal constraints.

A small player

The opportunity presented by the global automobile market is big. South Africa remains a small player, however, in the global car market. Much of the recent global growth has been driven by emerging markets, not least in East Asia.

Joe Studwell's engrossing *How Asia Works* describes how the Japanese copied the US, British and German industrialisation model of protectionism, built behind tariffs and using monopolies, and founded on close co-operation between business and government through, in the

Japanese case, the Ministry of International Trade and Industry. This government-business prototype was emulated, in turn, by the Taiwanese and (South) Koreans.[13]

Subsidies, tax breaks and even free land were part of what governments in the region provided. In return, business had to maintain a rigorous export focus. Where there has been success with this model, it has been a story of learning, foreign technology importation, discipline, continuous, ongoing expansion, and an export-oriented system, including a weak currency. In 1968 Chung Yu-jung's Hyundai company obtained permission to assemble Ford Cortinas. Inadvertently, Ford's US and United Kingdom headquarters in Detroit and Dagenham helped a real competitor on its way. Studwell points out that in 2010, Hyundai with Kia sold 5.7 million units worldwide, tying with Ford as the fourth-biggest global auto group. Technology has helped is global ascendancy. It took 41 000 workers to make one million Hyundais at its Ulsan plant in 1994; and 34 000 to make 1.6 million in 2013. In all, not bad from knocking together a few Ford Cortinas less than 50 years earlier.

Whether this sort of industrial model is possible partly hinges on government discipline: a willingness to efficiently administer the relationship with business, demanding a top-class interlocutor. Not many countries possess the capacity of a Ministry of International Trade and Industry or Taiwan's Industrial Development Board and South Korea's Economic Planning Board.

Success also demanded the discipline of getting out of those businesses that prove unable to graduate from protectionism or subsidies – less picking winners than, Studwell notes, 'weeding out losers'. While protectionism 'is an entry ticket to industrialisation', he points out, 'it is expensive and inefficient because it adds cost, punishes consumers and invites retaliation'. This transition is more difficult in less disciplined markets. The idea of getting out of failures, or allowing them to fail, applies equally, too, to government's role in parastatals.

Regardless, such lessons from others have not stopped the South African government from attempting to finance apparently forward-thinking schemes.

Too few Joules

On the face of it, the Joule was a good idea, a means of moving people with less pollution in the increasingly congested cities of Africa and elsewhere.

Coupled with fears about rising oil prices and declining reserves along with pollution, the stage was set for an increase in electric vehicle production. Global sales of electric vehicles were expected to number as high as 20 million by 2020. These projections were driven, in part, by the Chinese government's target of the half-million units of production capacity by 2015 (from just 6 000 in 2011) and, under the 12th five-year plan, ownership of five million battery-electric vehicles and plug-in hybrid-electric vehicles by 2020.[14]

Enter the Joule.

Founded in 2005, Optimal Energy was responsible for the Joule, South Africa's first electric car. Funded by the country's Technology Innovation Agency (with a US$5-million stake) and the Industrial Development Corporation (with 22 per cent of equity), the Joule was praised by motoring journalists for its performance and styling. According to Optimal's CEO, Kobus Meiring,[15] the company had, by 2010, signed an agreement with the German automotive developer EDAG to be their main industrialisation partner, with the aim of creating 'around 1 900 direct jobs, with a further 8 500 created in supporting industries'. Meiring expected the car to make its 'first profit in 2014. We are developing the plant for 50 000 units per year working on two shifts, expanding to 75 000 per year quite comfortably,' he said.[16]

Hubris is little substitute, however, for hard engineering facts. On paper, it looked perfect. It seemed to be well positioned to enter a market where demand outstripped supply. It appeared also to be the answer for South Africa having a high unemployment rate, but not wishing to enter the 'race to the bottom' on the basis simply of low wage rates. Instead, it would rely on technological innovation and top-class styling. Cape Town-bred Jaguar designer Keith Helfet, responsible for the iconic XJ220 and F-Type, was brought in to style the body, while a 120-strong team of local talent was assembled to produce the drivetrain and engine at the heart of the Joule. The new car supposedly attracted 'the best engineers in the country' with some reputedly 'even offering to work for free', according to the official project history.[17]

In the end, production of the Joule prototype was outsourced to Hi-Tech Auto in Port Elizabeth. Just five were eventually manufactured before their funders, erm, pulled the plug. Although the Joule benefited from engineering input by world-renowned firm Zagato, it died an expensive death. It was 'a cock-up', says Hi-Tech's Jimmy Price, with aerospace engineers involved who were 'not geared to producing cars' and dual operations in Cape Town and Port Elizabeth. 'It was a case of the wrong people aiming too high with an intention to produce 50 000 units a year, and they did not have the technology. I ask you,' says Price, 'which electric car is selling those volumes? It was just unrealistic from the start.'[18] A realistic market assessment was distorted by the need to target 50 000 units to qualify for the government's subsidy scheme.

The Department of Trade and Industry's Stephen Hanival has a contrarian view. 'Had the oil price not dropped as much as it did, perhaps it would have been a success, perhaps it would have been the winner to pick. We need to look at other factors, not least the cost of having an overvalued exchange rate, like Australia, and the impact on its motor manufacturing sector. We need also,' he says, 'to tie such initiatives in with our natural resources, such as with fuel cell research.'[19]

To its supporters, the Joule's failure is portrayed as one of funding and support rather than leadership, concept and engineering. 'In the end,' wrote Hannes Oosthuizen, former editor of the local *CAR* magazine, 'the fact that the Joule's designers were not given the opportunity to further refine the vehicle for production is disappointing enough. But when you realise that the Joule would have been a world-class product, the disappointment turns to heartbreak. I would be astonished if South Africa ever comes as close as this to having its own car (of any type or propulsion) ever again.'[20]

However, no matter the heartfelt sincerity, the Joule was a Potemkin effort, demonstrating that success is not a silver bullet or prototype away. At the heart of the engineering, the Joule relied on a General Motors' drivetrain and suspension. 'The project had very limited resources, people and money, just peanuts,' says one engineer involved in the battery system. 'Although we made it look like it was ready for production, we were nowhere near industrialising it.'[21]

The reason for the Joule's failure, says Toyota's Van Zyl, is 'really quite simple. Designing, developing, and manufacturing are all quite difficult stages. And together with marketing and selling, it is very difficult,' he emphasises. 'Selling needs backup, and a big network. You need to sell against brands. It was foolish to have thought that a small start-up could compete against the big manufacturers who can pump billions into the development of a car.' As one commentator notes, the projected budget to commercialise the vehicle was a moving target, changing 'over time from R500 million, to R1.5 billion, to R7 billion, to R9 billion. Amortised over expected production, that works out to a hefty R180 000 per vehicle in sunk costs. At a projected price tag of R250 000, they'd have to sell 36 000 of them just to break even, assuming zero operational costs.'[22]

'They also went for a small car at the bottom end of the market,' says Van Zyl. 'As they say in our industry: small car, small money. Perhaps Joule would have been better off going the route of the Tesla [luxury and sports cars], to the high end.' Tesla, a firm co-founded in Palo Alto by Pay-Pal originator, South African-born Elon Musk, gained fame with the launch of their Roadster sports car in 2008. But hitting the top end would not necessarily have made a bad idea into a good one. Joule did not play to any strengths, financial or technical, South Africa possessed.

As Vermeulen notes, 'Why did we think that we were going to have different results from other manufacturers – including BMW, Toyota and Nissan with their own hybrid vehicles? Why should a South African vehicle work where others have failed?' Indeed, such projects, like the motor vehicle industry per se, have very high upfront capital costs and technology requirements, which a country like South Africa, for all of its special skills, cannot afford. The path is littered with the failure of such attempts.'

The sky is the limit?

Sir Pierre van Ryneveld was the founding commander of the South African Air Force (SAAF). A First World War flying ace, he was knighted for his pioneering trip back to South Africa in a Vickers Vimy bomber with co-pilot Quintin Brand. He established the SAAF in February 1920, just 18 months after the Royal Air Force was created as the world's first independent such force, and directed it until 1933, when he was promoted to Chief of the General Staff, a post he held until 1949.

Appropriately, off the street named in Sir Pierre's honour close to the Swartkops Air Force base in Pretoria is Aerosud, South Africa's leading aeronautical engineering and manufacturing firm, producing 1.4 million parts annually for Airbus and Boeing. It now has an international reputation for its product reliability, innovation and problem-solving.

Formed in September 1990, Aerosud has its origins in the team that produced the Rooivalk attack helicopter. Aerosud's CEO, Paul Potgieter, started work originally at the Council for Scientific and Industrial Research in 1974. Five years later, together with Pierre Dippenaar, he moved to Atlas Aircraft Corporation, a division of Armscor, to start the Rooivalk project. However, already by the time of its first flight in January 1990, despite having cost R950 million (in 1980 rands), the project was under threat not only from the reduction of post-Cold War, post-Angolan-Namibian arms expenditure, but also as a target of those within the SAAF. 'Even though we managed to convince the Defence Force to continue to support Rooivalk, this experience made me realise,' says Potgieter, 'that we had to move outside of the traditional defence sector. So we started our own company.'[23]

Aerosud's first contract was ironically for the SAAF in re-engineering the Mirage F1 fighter with the MiG-29's engine, an engineering project made possible by the end of the Cold War and the thaw in relations between South Africa and the Soviet bloc. 'The Mirage F1 was still a very good aircraft, which required only updated avionics and a more powerful, more economical engine, which the Russian Klimov RD-33 offered.' Fitting the engine was technically challenging, the type of project with which Aerosud has become synonymous, and one which the Mirage's original manufacturer, Dassault, said could never could be done. 'The result,' recalls Potgieter, 'was an aircraft that outperformed the standard Mirage by a wide margin, which would have served South Africa well for many years to come.' The Mirage project came to an end with South Africa's decision to purchase the Gripen fighter as part of the strategic arms packages in the late 1990s.

As the MiG project wound down, Aerosud, then with 'around 60 employees, mainly ex-Rooivalk and Carver', branched off into producing galleys for Airbus while acquiring a contract to update Mi-24 helicopters for the Algerian military. Soon after 9/11, the company received its first contract from Boeing, as part of a commercial offset resulting from South African Airways' purchase of 737s.

Today its products for the commercial sector also include parts for the Airbus A320 and A350, and the wing tips, cargo liners, cockpit wall and liners, and gallery structures, among other parts, for the production run of the military A400M transport. Delays with the latter project, and the South African government's cancellation of its A400M order, however, 'nearly proved a catastrophe' for Aerosud, the founders having to find R150 million to keep the company going and staff employed.

With 850 employees, by 2014 Aerosud had an order book of R5 billion for the next five to seven years, with an anticipated turnover of R1 billion by 2017. Aerosud's success is, in part, down to its cost advantage over some of its rivals, not as a result of cheap labour, rather the efficiency and innovation of production processes. For example, in the manufacture of track cans, which house the arms for the wing flaps and slats, and which pass through fuel tanks in the wings, the firm has invested heavily in welding skills and processes. While commercial rivals have a 50 per cent scrap rate, Aerosud has a 98.3 per cent pass rate. By 2014, the firm manufactured more than 1 000 such units a month, enough for 38 passenger aircraft.

Equally, the investment in continuous fibre reinforced thermoform plastic manufacture of carbon parts has given Aerosud a cost advantage. While other processes require six to eight hours oven-time to manufacture parts, this high-pressure, heated press has a part cycle time of just six to eight minutes.

The importance of innovation in production is among the lessons that Potgieter has learnt over his 40 years in the sector. 'If we were to rely only on labour [costs] as our distinguishing factor,' he says, 'we could never make it. Our rates are not that high, but on average our education levels are behind our competitors.'

A second lesson is of the role of government, both as an investment partner and in helping to ensure a necessary skill base. Aerosud has enjoyed a productive relationship with the parastatal Industrial Development Corporation as a co-investor.

Skills have proven more problematic. 'Apartheid was wrong,' reflects Potgieter, 'but if it had not been for the investment by the state in military programmes, Aerosud would not exist today. The pioneering mentality of South Africans along with their can-do manner and ability to think out the box, coupled with such investment,' he says, created the mix necessary for such a high-tech business. 'The aviation business,' observes Potgieter, 'is not like the motor industry – a highly repetitive manufacturing business – but rather one that is more specialised, demanding much greater variability.'

But whereas there was a relative surplus of skills in the 1980s, a quarter-century later the contraction of South African Airways and Denel's apprentice training schemes has led to a chronic shortage, not least since the original trained cohort are mostly the wrong side of 50. Hence Aerosud's investment in its own training school (with 30 to 40 apprentices at any one time) and the establishment of an innovation centre for refreshing thinking and skills – a critical component of South Africa's manufacturing capabilities, as was highlighted also in the previous chapter.

Globally competitive, Made in South Africa

Stephen Saad does not dwell on risks. In Aspen he has built the fifth-largest generics pharmaceutical company in the world. Despite operating in one of South Africa's most economically depressed regions in the Eastern Cape, it has been possible to build a world-class pharmaceutical business, manufacturing 20 billion tablets a year for more than 150 countries across the globe.

In 1998, Aspen listed at R2.40. By the end of January 2015 it traded at more than R438.00, giving it a market capitalisation of around R200 billion and making it one of South Africa's top 40 companies, listed 14th on the Johannesburg Stock Exchange's top 40 index on 30 June 2014.[24]

By 2006, Aspen had become the biggest supplier of antiretroviral drugs in Africa, concluding distribution deals with Merck, Sharp & Dohme, Bristol-Myers Squibb, Roche, Tibotec and Gilead.

For Saad, Aspen's success illustrates what can be achieved in South Africa.

'As a globally competitive pharma company, Aspen has been able to rival many of the top pharmaceutical companies in Asia,' he says. 'Being an African company, no one ever credited Aspen's ability to compete in this high-technology industry. Looking at a country like Japan, however, logic would dictate that it could never compete with Africa as a small island with many inhabitants and limited natural resources. It needed a plan to survive without handouts and it did so. If you look at Africa with all of its resources and its size – 20 per cent of the world's land and 15 per cent of its population – the contest seems unfairly skewed in its favour. With a vision, supported by discipline, focus, courage, perseverance and passionate people, it is possible to triumph against all odds. If Japan did it, so can Aspen.'

A graduate of Durban High School and the then University of Natal, Saad trained as a chartered accountant. He entered the pharmaceutical business through Quick Med, a prescription drug distribution company that operated across black townships. Quick Med merged with Covance to form Zurich, which was sold for R75 million in 1993.

Saad served out his restraint-of-trade period by turning around the loss-making Varsity College, later sold for R100 million. Then he returned to pharmaceuticals with the launch in 1997 of a new company, Aspen Pharmacare, so named as he wanted to bring about a fresh, clean image.

His first move was to buy the moribund SA Druggists for R2.4 billion in 1999, a move he has described as 'the biggest risk we ever took'.

After acquiring SA Druggists, the real challenge was to make Aspen globally competitive while building a reputation for quality, a non-negotiable in the pharmaceutical industry. Although it was possible to produce more cost-competitively in South Africa than in Europe, the real threat came from the East.

Saad made regular trips to India, visiting Hyderabad, Mumbai and Bangalore. The numbers were intimidating. 'It's quite daunting at first when people say they make tablets at X dollars a thousand and I know I can't even turn my machines on for that.

'When we compared ourselves with Asia, we were more than twice as expensive. It was a real, real problem for us. We had to come up with a model. To manufacture a billion tablets from South Africa and compete was never going to be possible, our fixed costs in quality alone before even making a tablet, meant we were more expensive. The only solution for us lay in betting on ourselves to get the economies of scale.'

The answer lay in volume. 'We needed 10 billion tablets. At five billion or six billion, we absorbed our overheads and could compete with Asia. To do this, you had to mechanise, build for much more capacity and bet that we could significantly expand our sales volumes globally,' he said.

The end result was a highly mechanised and flexible facility that Aspen has been able to constantly expand. 'We are still investing significantly in our manufacturing capacity locally and abroad – both in terms of additional and enhanced facilities as well as world-class manufacturing equipment. Our greatest investment though is in the more than 10 000 people who work for Aspen around the world.'

Its competitive production costs offered multinational pharmaceutical companies, such as GlaxoSmithKline, an opportunity to extend the life of some of their products.

When the US decided to invest billions in rolling out Aids drugs under the President's Emergency Plan for Aids Relief – known as PEPFAR – Aspen was able to offer high-quality, affordable production, having built a facility approved by the US Food and Drug Administration.

'That was one of the milestones that changed the perception of the business and it really drove our business growth in South Africa. We could meet with specialists and they felt comfortable using our products. We became a one-stop shop,' says Saad.

Saad, who chairs the Sharks rugby franchise in his spare time, and played rugby overseas, counts leadership as Aspen's primary resource. 'And,' he added, 'there is a very big difference between management and leadership. Leadership means you have to roll up your sleeves and work. It calls for accountability, trust and execution to ensure delivery at all costs. While plans are needed, execution is what decides winners from losers.'

'I'm going to say something very controversial here. Corporate South Africa has often underwhelmed me. We are quick to point fingers at other sectors, but sometimes we need to appreciate that we ourselves may be overpaid. If you've run a restaurant successfully you make a million bucks a year, yet some of us are making R20 million a year – I'd like to see how many people could run 20 restaurants successfully before asking for a R20-million pay package. It goes to my point on the need to execute – it's so easy to churn out bland corporate excuses.'

He does not hide his contempt for bureaucracy. 'Bureaucracy signals an absence of leadership. Take our Port Elizabeth-based facilities that manufacture approximately 10 billion tablets. To compete with us, a multinational will have 10 factories with a billion tablets from each, split across all sorts of geographies. They will have regional managers, managers of the regional managers and a huge head office structure. At our manufacturing site, there is no boardroom. There is no executive dining room – bring your sarmies.'

Aspen has made use of the 121 Tax Allowance Programme on capital investment and the Manufacturing Competitiveness Enhancement Programme, along with a tax break for research and development.

With the Port Elizabeth state-of-the-art manufacturing site in place and undergoing ongoing investment, Saad's next battle is to get Aspen's most ambitious capital expenditure investments to date – a high-potency plant and a number of expensive sterile manufacturing units – up and running. The staff who run this hi-tech operation are locally recruited. To fill any education gaps, Aspen offers intensive on-the-job training as well as tertiary education opportunities.

South African workers often are described as unproductive, something that annoys Saad. 'I think there is more of a problem with South African management than with South African labour.' In his experience, workers, 'if treated properly and managed properly', can radically improve their productivity.

Saad has faced the same South African labour situation as everyone else. Yet, he has not suffered competitively on the global market.

When Aspen bought the old SA Druggists operation, Saad's first meeting was with the trade union representative. 'He said something to me which I will never, ever forget, because it was so foreign to me. He said: "How could I possibly ask the workers to be more productive? If they are twice as productive, you will need half as many jobs."'

Saad says he could not duck the reality, telling him: 'Yes, there will be job losses, but if we get it right, we will increase and grow our jobs.' If his plan worked, workers who were laid off would return to a more successful company. He also promised workers that they would become shareholders and made good on this promise.

The constant focus on productivity has led to a doubling of the number of employees. And, says Saad, they are well paid, somewhere between the high pay of Europe and the low pay of Asia. 'The problem I noted in India with dependence on low-cost labour is that ultimately it will make you inefficient, no matter where you are,' he says.

'Economic growth and bridging the education deficit in our country are key to addressing both our social challenges and ensuring a stable democracy going into the future,' he says. 'Creating an environment conducive to economic growth by attracting foreign and domestic investment by instilling investor confidence, improving our export performance and enhancing private-public collaboration in improving education outcomes are pivotal. To this end I would ask the president how he and cabinet best ensure policy cohesion and consistency in implementation of policy and how he would reduce red tape and administrative burdens that are hampering growth and turning investors to other investment destinations.'

Pitching a success

In 2014 Canvas and Tent won the award for the large exporter of the year in KwaZulu-Natal. The origins of the tent manufacturer, which employs 860 workers at its Ezakheni factory, are in South African Defence Force requirements and contracts. By 1996, with the decline in military demand and expenditure, the business had collapsed, being bought out of liquidation by a private Pretoria-based entrepreneur Eric Goldblum and Nedbank. Since then it has, in Goldblum's words, 'grown organically', securing large British Army contracts en route, and also moving into the top-end safari, deployable mining and United Nations camp business.[25]

'It was very difficult in the beginning,' says company CEO Louw Bekker. 'Our design process was done by hand, and our frames were outsourced. We went over to the United Kingdom three times a year looking for work, initially trying to supply canvas. Then we got a contract to repair 20-odd container loads of British Army tents, which arrived from Afghanistan, before we picked up an order for four 600-man British Army camps as a supplier could not deliver. This changed our lives. We improved our design as the orders flowed in, and upgraded our machinery and increased the number of jobs.'

By 2014, 60 per cent of revenue was from export orders. Although the military work has dried up with the ramping down of involvement in Afghanistan and Iraq, Bekker, who worked previously at the South African Bureau of Standards, says that '97 per cent' of employees are from Ladysmith, while '80 per cent' were 'employed at the gate'. Canvas and Tent runs a training school, with 20 graduates annually, though there are still shortages in skilled labour.

A R15-million grant from the Industrial Development Corporation was used to purchase overhead carrying lines from Sweden and the latest technology in cutting machines. 'This has,' says Bekker, 'put us into a different league with regard to automation.'

It has not all been easy. In 2008 the firm suffered a paralysing strike, one result of which is that it employed a change manager, and another the retention of a labour consultant. 'We slept in the workers' homes and took taxis to work,' recalls Bekker, 'and visited their places of worship. This helped us to build a team,' a process aided no doubt by having one of the higher wages on offer in the area.

Even in those sectors of the economy where labour relations have been historically fraught, a different management style can change things for the better.

High risk, very deep, complex, fraught ... but profitable

Neal Froneman is CEO of Sibanye Gold, the largest producer of gold in South Africa. Sibanye, meaning 'We are one', was formed, as Chapter 6 on mining noted, in 2013 from an unbundling of Gold Fields Limited, the company started by Cecil Rhodes and Charles Rudd in 1887. 'It was spun off because our mines are deep, high-risk, labour-intensive operations.[26]

'We were able to take the assets performing badly in Gold Fields' hands and turn them around in two years,' he says, 'into the best performing gold share internationally. We were able to do this because we have tabular ore bodies with good grades that are extensive, and because we were able to get our costs down. With 55 per cent of our costs in the form of people, we "displaced" 7 000, but saved 35 000 other jobs in the process.'

Froneman is equally clear about the challenges South Africa faces.

'It's difficult to operate here because of regulatory uncertainty and a very inefficient labour system, which reflects our history and the political role of organised labour.' But he does not accept that it has to be that way. 'More than anything,' he adds, 'the unbundling was driven by a vision of a company that I did not accept had to be high risk because of the deep ore bodies and inefficient because of our labour regime.'

This demanded a more proactive role with his workforce and the community.

Froneman moved Sibanye headquarters from the Gold Fields operation in corporate Sandton to Westonaria, right near their four mines. To win the hearts and minds of the mine workers, he has started regular and direct dialogue with them, and not only through the unions. 'We have taken back the right to communicate and engage directly with employees – stupidly in the past we had become almost a surrogate of the unions in this regard.'

The next stage was to assist with worker education, not least to help them budget and deal with their debt. 'Our miners are burdened with garnishee orders, and we have helped them with numeracy programmes and assisted in consolidating their debt.' Sibanye has evidence that 'union elements', says Froneman, were behind a number of the micro-loan schemes. It found 177 such orders to be illegal.

And Sibanye engaged directly with the communities in which they operate. 'Instead of building schools that we then handed over to the municipality to hand over to the community while crowing how little the mining companies do for them, we now deal directly with these communities. We need stable and supportive communities without which we don't have a viable business.'

Sibanye is also investigating profit-share arrangements, the aim behind all of these initiatives to 'get the employees to think much more who is helping them in the next round of wage negotiations' through 'sharing in the good times and working harder together in the bad ones'.

He stresses, 'I am not saying that unions are not required to protect workers. To the contrary, we need a strong social component to business operations in South Africa given this is the best way to create value for shareholders in our environment and given our history. Yet if you had a more efficiently driven labour market, it would certainly be much easier to operate.'

This is not the only constraint. 'BEE has been a dismal failure. Attempts to redo it,' says Froneman, 'are not fundamentally investor-friendly.' Equally, efforts to create a state mining entity are problematic. 'Personally I think it will be a failure, not least given that there is no shining example of a state-owned company, and why should this be any different especially in a difficult, highly complex and highly technical business like mining?' he asks. 'If you do this with state money, or state pension money in the form of the Public Investment Corporation, this would simply be irresponsible. Instead of thinking about creating a South African mining entity with the best talent and management, and available sources of capital, we are locked in a paradigm about racial ownership.'

And this relates to what is the most costly aspect of the relationship with government and its partners. 'This is a labour-intensive industry,' reflects Froneman, 'which should be nurtured by government. But it's not. It is despised.'

A winning formula?

This chapter has demonstrated that South Africa has a significant vein of business people who are keen to build world-class firms. By their example, they can provide bridges to the future on how South Africa can compete on the world stage and generate jobs. However, they need an enabling environment, like all entrepreneurs, both to build competitive firms and to overcome some of the challenges posed by South Africa's history and location. While these entrepreneurs by themselves will not solve the unemployment problem, they will be part of the solution and will raise the bar for other industries.

There are, of course, stark realities that have to be faced in order to succeed in being globally competitive South African firms. They include the need to have workers who are skilled and are paid a competitive wage in order to attract and accept the best and brightest skills globally; putting in place a feeder system of high-technology education establishments; creating a productive labour force; and acting on a realisation that being competitive is not a national but rather a global struggle. Sometimes, industrial policy can be another term for picking winners. While there may be some successes when government intervenes, if the Joule's history is a gauge, these will be few and far between. Where there is a role for protectionism, there has to be a plan to graduate from tariffs and quotas, otherwise infant industries become long in the tooth. Instead, policies that push people into a competitive market, rather than shield them from it, is usually best for them and the economy.

South Africa clearly possesses the 'right stuff', people who are capable of discerning the next opportunity. They will not succeed without an enabling environment that allows them to fully utilise their talents for the benefit of themselves and the many they will employ. Given the volume of South Africans who want to be employees, government policy must aim to cultivate more employers.

Conclusion

A Pivot from Confrontation to Competitiveness

> The saying has it: 'To govern is to choose.' Policy is about trade-offs. In these choices, you must be very clear about the costs and benefits of policy.
>
> — Lesetja Kganyago, Governor, South African Reserve Bank

Under apartheid, opportunities were defined by race. Two decades on, wealth and levels of inequality are defined by the employment status of South Africans.

At the moment, therefore, the future of millions of South Africans is bleak because the economy is simply not producing enough jobs. Labour costs are too high and government regulation deters employers from choosing to hire people over using more machines. The unemployment burden will fall on the African youth, who were supposed to benefit from the struggle to upend apartheid. Social grants and informal sector employment will, at most, ameliorate the worst harms of chronic joblessness. But rising levels of government indebtedness highlight that these schemes, worthy as they are, cannot be a long-term solution.

There are other costs and consequences to joblessness beyond simply levels of income and government sustainability. COSATU's Gauteng provincial secretary, Dumisani Dakile, describes the daily corrosive impact of unemployment: 'In the townships, Monday is no different from Friday or Saturday. You see this in attendance at funerals; where attendance in the middle of the week is massive because of unemployment and the promise of a free lunch.'[1] It is imperative that South Africa focuses on generating more jobs as the critical element of reducing poverty and promoting social inclusion and stability. A new sense of policy urgency around jobs is therefore in the interests of the ANC, business, the unions and South Africans at large. As we learnt from the studies of Singapore and Malaysia, it is only with a laser-like focus and sense of urgency that South Africa will be able to transform its economy to the benefit of all of its citizens.

A surplus of uncertainty, a posture of radicalism

The National Development Plan (NDP) was delivered in June 2011 at a moment of low economic and employment growth in South Africa. It offered fresh promise of consensus between government, labour and business around policy that would encourage investment. 'This plan,' it read, 'envisions a South Africa where everyone feels free yet bounded to others; where everyone embraces their full potential, a country where opportunity is determined not by birth, but by ability, education and hard work. Realising such a society will require transformation of the economy and focused efforts to build the country's capabilities. To eliminate poverty and reduce inequality, the economy must grow faster and in ways that benefit all South Africans.'[2]

Yet, for all of the NDP's promise, on economic policy, the South African government has become mired in contradiction and confrontation. For instance, government cannot rationally have both the revision of the Mineral and Petroleum Resources Development Act, which introduces investor uncertainty, alongside the NDP, which aims for a clear diagnosis of the problem and generational policy lucidity as the solution. The NDP cannot recognise the importance of education reform while the government continues to provide blanket support for the dysfunctionality guaranteed by the dominant South African Democratic Teachers' Union. Nor can government insist that it believes in disciplined public sector spending yet condones regular above-inflation wage increases for public sector workers.[3] In contradiction again of the NDP, government cannot signal an intention to seize 50 per cent of land and legislate against foreign ownership, without denting foreign investor confidence.

Why has this happened?

The NDP foundered on the deficits of skills, capital and trust, which have incessantly and corrosively defined South Africa's post-apartheid political economy. South Africa has lacked a convincing 'Big Idea', a far-reaching vision around which society could galvanise itself, along the lines of Archbishop Desmond Tutu's 'Rainbow Nation', or of that provided by President Nelson Mandela's similar brand of racial reconciliation. As a result, its progress has faltered as the economy has stuttered. This is not only due to the high level of unemployment and rising costs, and poor standards of education, infrastructure and public service. It reflects fundamentally a crisis of mistrust and a lack of confidence.

The result has been increasing political radicalism, prompted particularly during the second term of President Jacob Zuma by the theatrics of the Economic Freedom Fighters, their brand of populist politics playing to the gallery of unfulfilled expectations and displaced racial bitterness. Hence, for example, the obstructionist antics in Parliament, and the targeting of colonial-era symbols. How widespread this anger is, however, is uncertain. More certain is that the most effective and sustainable method of assuaging the disaffected does not lie in redistribution.

Of course, any analysis of South Africa's economic challenges has to understand its past history. The systematic, legislated exclusion of black South Africans from sharing the country's wealth has resulted in one of the most highly unequal societies in the world. Hence the early imperative after 1994 to address extreme poverty through a social welfare programme, and to redistribute wealth through BEE and, latterly, BBBEE schemes.

Yet such arrangements have their limits – and their costs. For instance, as a project of elite transformation, as noted, BEE has been successful, but it is more a burden for employers than a transformative agent for the unemployed, less often associated with affirmative action than cronyism in, as former ANC member of Parliament Ben Turok has observed, fostering a class of middle men in the supply chain.[4] Similarly, graduation from social welfare programmes, as important as they have been, has at its core to involve wider-spread employment than today. These circumstances are thus not the blame of government alone. While South Africa is blessed with a highly capable private sector, its effectiveness has been diminished by the extent of fear, suspicion and loathing that is present. As a result, most of the goodwill created in 1994 seems to have disappeared.

As frustrations rise, the twain between business, civil society and government seems to be widening. Rhodes University's vice chancellor, Sizwe Mabizela, is among those who have openly criticised the way in which South Africa's political elite are running the country. 'The noble qualities and values of personal integrity, honesty, humility, compassion, respect for each other, fairness, forgiveness, empathy, selfless dedication and willingness to put others first – that were so beautifully exemplified by President Nelson Mandela – have given way to venality, a complete lack of integrity, moral decadence, profligacy, rampant corruption, deceit and duplicity.'[5] He is not alone. In 2012, the former vice chancellor of the University of South Africa, Barney Pityana, said: 'We must blame nobody but ourselves for the tragedy of our education system, a collapsing healthcare system, a bloated civil service, pervasive crime and corruption that has,' he said, 'become endemic. That is because we have elected a government without any intelligence collectively to understand what must be done ... We have a government trapped in ideological blinkers that believes and behaves like it is unaccountable.'[6]

The answer is to resolve the contradictions between politics and economics, between, for example, the pragmatism of the NDP and radical policy rhetoric, and to do so in favour of those policies that will deliver long-term growth and jobs. And the remedy exists in devising and implementing an agenda for competitiveness to achieve higher rates of growth and inclusion. This requires all parties to play their part and to co-operate: business, government and labour.

Change is in the ANC's best interest

For both itself and for South Africa, it is imperative that the ANC demonstrate the determination to deliver a policy environment that will allow South Africa to create the jobs that it needs.

National political leadership is necessary in setting an overall direction in providing the development story – the abovementioned 'Big Idea' – into which South Africans can buy. Of course, this is not just about a vague vision of prosperity, or of a series of reports, policy papers, clusters or even a commission or panel or three, but an idea of how people must work together and with the world to achieve it. It requires a move beyond patrimonial politics, including cadre deployment, and demands that business and government pivot towards co-operation. It has to be a vision of growth and prosperity.

At the moment, as we saw in Chapter 2, polling evidence suggests that the ANC's support is still shaped by race beyond all else despite the high levels of unemployment, and to the ruling party it may not seem necessary to make these changes. However, while the ANC might not immediately lose power, whatever its short-term performance on economic growth, it would be neglecting its historical mission if it ignores the widening inequality caused by joblessness and low growth.

Moreover, the Tripartite Alliance's poor performance on job creation coupled with voter alienation cannot inspire confidence in its longer-term electoral prospects. The ANC, now increasingly distant from its heroic act of liberating South Africa from apartheid, is called upon to deliver. As journalist Ray Hartley has noted to us, the growth market in South African politics is apathy. Some 31.4 million South Africans were eligible to vote in the 2014 election. Of this number, 25.4 million registered but just 18 million voted, fewer than did so in 1994, despite considerable population growth. Roughly 11 million voted for the ANC, representing 43 per cent of 25 million voters but only about one-third of those who could have voted. In 2009, the ANC majority represented 50 per cent of registered voters, in 2004, 53 per cent, and in 1999, 58 per cent.[7] Further indicating the alienation of the youth, in the 2014 election, the Independent Electoral Commission revealed that only 23 per cent of voters aged 18 or 19 were even registered and only 55 per cent of those between 20 and 29.

There are now a remarkable number of South Africans, many without a job, who are 'up for grabs' in the political marketplace. The ANC's immediate challenge is that they will lose the unemployed to alienation and will continue to win, albeit with reduced margins, at the ballot box. Sooner or later, those who are economically disenfranchised will find someone else to vote for.

In response, however, the ANC has turned inwards, concerned with internal politicking and manoeuvre. The party's own report cards say it has failed to deliver on promised targets for health, energy, water, education and infrastructure, among other sectors; that it has 'messed up'.[8]

This is not unique political behaviour. All kinds of governments adopt policies that are pathological and that will result in eventual and clearly forecasted disaster. Such is much of the history of post-independence Africa. They do so because the immediate political logic that rulers face dictates that for their own (real or perceived) political survival, they go down a path that is bad for the nation. In the light of ramping political radicalism, the temptation might be to attempt to outmanoeuvre a nascent and militant, populist, left-wing critique and threat by increasing the state's interventionism and regulatory role. The case studies in this book highlight the weakness of such an approach.

Still it is in the ANC's interests to act on jobs now. Dakile notes that the current effective unemployment rate close to 40 per cent is not 'just a ticking time bomb but one that could explode any day. There is not a day that comes without [service delivery] protests. We are concerned as COSATU, as organised workers. We can begin to see populists and demagogues exploit this environment, which will create an unimaginable situation, a Hitler for us, who arose in such circumstances, or a Mussolini or an Idi Amin.' This ticking bomb analogy also has been frequently invoked since 2011 by COSATU's former general secretary, Zwelinzima Vavi.[9]

The necessary trust that South Africa desperately needs between government and business will not be developed by feel-good statements. Rather, a change in attitudes will follow from concrete actions that show that government, and business, are taking irrevocable steps to align their interests.

The ANC has not taken the necessary bold moves to improve the job environment in good part because it is afraid of upsetting its coalition partner, COSATU. Yet, as noted above, COSATU is increasingly failing to get out the votes for the ANC – its historic role and one reason why it shares in governing – as more and more South Africans who cannot get a job drop out of the political marketplace. As the drama with the National Union of Metalworkers of South Africa leaving COSATU in 2014 demonstrates, it also is not clear how strong an electoral reed the unions will be in the future for the ANC.

A pivot to competitiveness

Today, to refer to Governor Kganyago's quote at the start of the chapter, choices exist for the South African policy-maker and the public. With current levels of unemployment and related political militancy, coupled with questions about fiscal sustainability, muddling through is not a long-term option.

The ANC has a legacy of being able to transform its policy views when required. In particular, Mandela was committed when he was released from jail to a set of socialist economic policies, which in the 1990s would have proven disastrous to implement. Mandela, as one of the great men of principle, would undoubtedly have tried to implement the policies that he believed in during the 1960s when he left jail after 27 years. Yet, he was persuaded by the evidence that his beliefs would have been terrible for the country and therefore for the ANC. He then heroically switched to a new policy framework that has allowed South Africa to enjoy considerable macroeconomic stability and at least create the jobs that it has. Mandela shifted course radically enough to allow the new South Africa to emerge.

It is not necessary for the ANC's current leadership to make a shift as great as Mandela did in the early 1990s. He upended decades of ANC rhetoric and made real concessions to whites that had not been imagined during the struggle years. Indeed, the change in focus and policies that we suggest are aimed at realising the historic mission of the ANC to deliver both political and economic emancipation.

Moreover, a policy-led change towards a healthier economy and society is also, as is intimated above, good for business, and also for workers. Growth makes it much easier to solve development problems and address historical legacies.

Our in-depth examination of how South Africa really works has convinced us that there are a large number of steps that government, business and labour can take now to address the challenges that South Africa is facing before it is too late. None of these steps is easy and there will always be short-term reasons not to start implementing them. However, the nature of the crisis that South Africa faces requires a comprehensive response from all concerned.

The responsibility of government

The government needs to change rhetorical and administrative tack to focus on employment at all times. The departure point should be: 'Do these actions promote employment?' A pivot to competitiveness requires the following steps:

- New venues should be established to communicate with business, including farmers, that depart from the tired formulas of the past. Instead of set structures that encourage little new thinking, these should be flexible and focus on solving specific problems. Fresh ways must be found to clear the fog of bureaucracy, miscommunication and misperception that exist between government and the captains of industry, which is an impediment to investment.
- A concentrated effort must be made to fix state-run parastatals, starting with Eskom. Government should change its orientation so that the primary goal is for the sector, rather than the state-owned enterprise, to succeed. Thus, liberalisation of electrical supply should be considered. South African Airways should be reoriented so that it brings in the maximum number of tourists at minimum cost to the taxpayer.
- Other state-owned enterprises providing logistical support, notably Transnet and Portnet, should be incentivised to provide cost-effective and efficient service. Government should adhere to global benchmarks in the process when evaluating these companies.
- Minimum wage legislation should be reviewed in order to incentivise firms to hire the maximum number of people. At the same time, small- and medium-sized firms should be exempted from the work of Bargaining Councils or separate agreements should be made that account for the size of firms.
- Labour legislation that makes it overly difficult for firms to manage their work forces should be changed in order to encourage companies to hire more.
- BEE policies should be revised so that they do not discriminate against small firms seeking to sell to the state and, more generally, are not an obstacle to conducting business.

- Far less emphasis should be put on land restitution and much more on infrastructure support for farms.
- Visa policies should be the least restrictive possible in order to encourage tourism and business.
- Subsidies and other forms of business support should have sunset clauses that force firms to graduate to competitiveness. If some ventures are picked by government as potential 'winners', no matter the appeal and importance of this narrow focus, similar sunset clauses must apply.
- Bureaucratic inertia in the taxi industry and elsewhere can be addressed by implementing a system where applications are automatically approved within a certain number of days (21, for example, in Georgia) unless government formally objects, forcing officials to respond within a defined, and short, time frame.[10]
- Far less emphasis should be placed on beneficiation of minerals than mining them. Constraining producers through attempts at imposing 'developmental pricing' are likely to further damage the mining sector's viability.
- Manufacturing could be greatly assisted by trade agreements, especially those with Africa, as a means of supplementing low domestic demand and complementing the more traditional export markets, a point that has been made especially by vehicle manufacturers.
- Manufacturing can also be boosted by procurement policies that depend on price and quality, not solely the race of the intermediary. BEE entrepreneurs should not be allowed to front for foreign purchases over local procurement preferences.
- Encourage the conditions that will enable growth in a venture capital mindset and market.
- Finally, and far from least important, the chronic crisis in South Africa's education system should be addressed as a life-or-death issue for the country.

Business must also change

Highlighting the necessity of the ANC changing does not absolve business in South Africa. Given South Africa's circumstances, business also must respond, just as some of South Africa's best entrepreneurs have, by investing and creating enterprises that can become globally competitive. Business must be conscious that part of its long-term strategy regarding thriving in South Africa should revolve around a calculus that firms, too, can take actions beyond what a short-term reading of the profit sheet demands. We have seen that some employers are able to develop good relations with their employees by paying more and devoting attention to their communities. Other companies have built up trust by investing in their communities. Still others celebrate their job creation. They do so not out of charity but because these actions, if there is an enabling environment, are good business. A better relationship with government and the development of trust with the ANC demands improved confidence so that long-term business actions can be aligned with the national interest. To date, the necessary courage to create this symbiotic relationship is often in short supply.

If established businesses and private sector leaders do not meet the government at least part way, smaller firms will be drawn to an option that threatens everyone: non-compliance, no filling out of forms and episodic adherence to government regulation. However, disappearing under the regulatory radar is a survival and not a growth strategy. Business will not be able to reach its potential in an economy where an increasing number of unemployed are forced to resort to crime and service delivery protest, or to engage in violent strike action.

The important contributions of business should include:

- Consider building constructive relations with government as an extremely high priority and help construct the necessary structures for consistent dialogue.
- The shortage of technical, artisan skills should be addressed by training for these skills by industry itself. Accordingly, the Sector Education Training Authorities should be scrapped as they are failing and the R11 billion in annual levies should be used to subsidise in-house training.
- Business should realise that it has a long-term interest in developing stable workforces whose cultivation may include salaries that are higher than the legal minimum.

- Those industries that are tied to a specific site (for example, farming, mining) must realise that the health of the community and the long-term prospects of business are intertwined. Business should recognise that a reality of current South Africa is that it must occasionally substitute for government in the provision of services. This is not done for charity but for the health of the workforces that are the backbone of companies.
- Business should contribute its expertise to government, as in the case of biometric technology used to distribute the social grant, so that the public sector can be run as efficiently as possible.

The labour dimension

Substituting an environment of confrontation with an agenda for competitiveness also demands labour playing its part. Serious countries intent on transformation and expanding the economic pie through growth do not have five-month-long strikes. Labour has a crucial role to play in fabricating the political consensus around growth and transformation that is lacking in South Africa. To do so, however, labour should recognise:

- Any injury to any business is an injury, in union parlance, to every worker. Unions, while working for their members, must be cognisant of the consequences of their salary demands for the companies that employ them.
- Organised labour has a long-term interest in growing the workforce so that it can have more, younger members.
- Unions should democratise, accepting the secret ballot for strike actions.
- Any rise in real wages should be matched by productivity gains.

We recognise that without racial transformation of the South African economy, political peace is going to become ever-more difficult to maintain. Indeed, 'transformation' has become the label for the extension of the liberation struggle post-apartheid, beyond politics into social and economic change. Transformation should not, however, be defined only by land ownership or business equity. The transformation agenda must be re-imagined to demonstrate that all are encouraged to participate by having a job and the ability to participate in an economy that is growing. This is of particular relevance to labour. Economic transformation is the best route to address the final liberation: freedom from poverty.

Leading change

If South Africa is to break out of the two societies it is building – one rich and employed, the other unemployed and on welfare – and act as an inclusive, high-growth African exemplar, it will need to have a plan matched by priorities and sufficient will to execute it. Such a change is also necessary if the ANC is to survive. This plan has to entail a liberation from the politics of the past, towards economic freedom, reduced dogma, an emphasis on jobs, prosperity and competitiveness, and where the animus to business not only disappears but is replaced by the celebration of business leaders who create jobs and globally competitive firms. With big corporates, private- or state-owned, unlikely to provide the jobs required, an energised job market also needs to support vibrant small- and medium-sized enterprises. This stance, and the specific recommendations we make above will allow the government to avoid the bureaucratic and regulatory strictures of the current conception of the 'developmental state' in favour of creating an environment that promotes growth and job development.[11]

Poignantly we write on the 25th anniversary of State President F.W. de Klerk's groundbreaking announcement to Parliament on 2 February 1990. That speech and the subsequent transition saw all sides make courageous decisions for the benefit of the country despite their previously stated and seemingly entrenched positions. The changes we suggest will similarly require courage to get past today's paralysis, which is induced by distrust and ideology, and for citizens and leadership to each play their part. To change its trajectory to a high economic and employment growth future, South Africa cannot afford to be a country of victims led by indecisive politicians.[12]

The ability to resolve the deadlock thus depends fundamentally on government. Other parties are important, but if the government and the ruling party is not playing its role, the actions of labour and business inevitably will be stunted. If the ANC can assume its critical part, take the necessary steps towards competitiveness, unlock higher levels of growth, and thus change the thrust of the transformation imperative, it will be able to prove that it is not a prisoner of its past, and once again be able to celebrate its mission to liberate all South Africans. If not, an ANC government will doom South Africa to a dismal low-growth and high-unemployment future that is threatening the very fabric of its society.

Notes

Introduction

1 Interview, Empangeni, 22 October 2015.
2 Quoted in South Africa Foundation, 'Growth for All: An Economic Strategy for South Africa', Johannesburg, February 1996.
3 Johannesburg Stock Exchange, 'Black South Africans Hold at Least 23% of the Top 100 Companies Listed on the Johannesburg Stock Exchange', 20 February 2015, https://www.jse.co.za/articles/black-south-africans-top-100-companies-listed-on-the-johannesburg-stock-exchange.
4 Speech made at the Chinese Communist Youth League Conference, July 1962. Quoted in Alison Jones, Stephanie Pickering and Megan Thomson (eds), *Chambers Dictionary of Quotations*. New York: Chambers, 1997, p. 315.
5 This has been a central concern of The Brenthurst Foundation since its inception in 2005. See Barry Desker, Jeffrey Herbst, Greg Mills and Michael Spicer (eds), *Globalisation and Economic Success: Policy Lessons for Developing Countries*. Johannesburg: The Brenthurst Foundation, 2008; Jeffrey Herbst and Greg Mills, *Africa's Third Liberation: The New Search for Prosperity and Jobs*. Johannesburg: Penguin, 2012, second edition, 2014; and Greg Mills, *Why States Recover: Changing Walking Societies into Winning Nations – From Afghanistan to Zimbabwe*. Johannesburg: Picador Africa and London: C. Hurst Co., 2014.
6 See, for example, Alex Boraine, *What's Gone Wrong? On the Brink of a Failed State*. Johannesburg: Jonathan Ball, 2014.

1 South Africa's Development Story

1 Quoted by Andrew Ross Sorkin, 'How Mandela Shifted Views on Freedom of Markets', *New York Times*, 9 December 2013, http://dealbook.nytimes.com/2013/12/09/how-mandela-shifted-views-on-freedom-of-markets.
2 Robin Renwick, 'The Magic of Madiba's Dual Personality', *Mail and Guardian*, 30 January–5 February 2005.
3 See 'Nelson Mandela: Champion of Economic Freedom', *Daily Telegraph*, 6 December 2013, http://www.telegraph.co.uk/news/worldnews/nelson-mandela/10499740/Nelson-Mandela-champion-of-economic-freedom.html.
4 For details, see *Two Decades of Freedom: A 20-Year Review of South Africa*. Johannesburg: Goldman Sachs, 2013.
5 Since 1998, Statistics SA has adopted a 'strict' measure of unemployment as the

official measure for South Africa: to be counted, an unemployed person must have 'taken active steps to look for work or to start some form of self-employment'. The official rate of unemployment, therefore, excludes all individuals who report that they do want to work but have not taken active steps (as specifically defined) to search for work in the previous month, the so-called 'non-searching unemployed' who are included in the broader definition of unemployment. See http://www. politicsweb.co.za/politicsweb/view/politicsweb/en/page71639/page71639?oid=363205 &sn=Detail&pid=71639.

6 The source for the data in Figure 1.1 is South African Institute of Race Relations (SAIRR), *South Africa Survey 2014/2015.* Johannesburg, SAIRR, 2014, p. 212 and p. 255.

7 SAIRR, *South Africa Survey 2014/15*, p. 255.

8 The source for the date in Figure 1.2 is SAIRR, *South Africa Survey 2014/2015*, p. 261.

9 National Planning Commission, *National Development Plan: Vision for 2030.* Johannesburg: NPC, 2011, p. 78 and p. 85.

10 See Ara Go, Jonathan Moyer, Mickey Rafa and Julia Schünemann, 'Population Futures: Revisiting South Africa's National Development Plan 2030', African Futures Paper, http://www.issafrica.org/uploads/AF7_15Oct2013V2.pdf.

11 The cost initially approved by the Eskom board for the construction of Medupi was R69.1 billion and R80.6 billion for the Kusile power stations. The final costs to completion for both the 4 800-megawatt each Medupi and Kusile units are still uncertain, but are currently estimated at R154.2 billion and R172.2 billion respectively. See http://citizen.co.za/281634/medupi-delays-confirmed/.

12 See http://www.southafrica.info/business/economy/debt-140113.htm#. VOhBxo3lqM8.

13 Martin Plaut, 'South Africa: Sinking or Swimming?' *Politicsweb*, 28 September 2014.

14 See http://www.biznews.com/budget/2015/02/26/budget-2015-sas-debtgdp-ratio-scariest-graphic-in-nenes-package/. Figure 1.3 is also drawn from this source.

15 See http://www.dailymaverick.co.za/article/2014-11-12-op-ed-the-role-of-civil-society-in-sustaining-our-constitutional-democracy/?utm_source=Daily+Maver ick+Mailer&utm_medium=email&utm_campaign=First+Thing+with+John+stu part%3A+Tuesday%2C+2+September+2014&utm_term=http%3A%2F%2Fwww. dailymaverick.co.za%2Farticle%2F2014-11-12-op-ed-the-role-of-civil-society-in-sustaining-our-constitutional-democracy%2F#.VHXiU4vF-Sp.

16 See http://data.worldbank.org/indicator/SI.POV.GINI.

17 Mike Schussler, 'The 11th UASA Employment Report', http://www.uasa. co.za/.../2-employment-report?...the...employment-report...11.

18 Discussion, Richard Pike, ADCORP, 16 February 2015.

19 See http://www.enca.com/media/video/more-south-africans-living-poverty.

20 Schussler, 'The 11th UASA Employment Report'.

21 'Mob Frenzy, Hatred Fuel Latest Blast of Xenophobia', *Sunday Times*, 25 January 2015, p. 2.

22 See http://mg.co.za/article/2015-04-16-rights-violation-charge-laid-against-zulu-king.

23 See the article by Stephen Grootes of the same title, http://www.dailymaverick. co.za/article/2015-04-15-op-ed-when-the-economy-suffers-xenophobia-thrives/?utm_source=Daily+Maverick+Mailer&utm_medium=email&utm_camp

aign=First+Thing+with+John+stupart%3A+Tuesday%2C+2+September+2014&u
tm_term=http%3A%2F%2Fwww.dailymaverick.co.za%2Farticle%2F2015-04-15-op-
ed-when-the-economy-suffers-xenophobia-thrives%2F#.VS9kkU3lqM8.

24 Thomas Piketty, *Capital in the Twenty-First Century*. Cambridge, Mass: Harvard
    University Press, 2014.

25 Ricardo Hausmann, *Raising South Africa's 'Speed Limit'*. Johannesburg: Centre for
    Development and Enterprise, 2014, p. 3.

26 See http://www.anc.org.za/show.php?id=3132.

27 African National Congress, 'The Freedom Charter', http://www.anc.org.za/show.
    php?id=72.

28 ANC, 'The Freedom Charter'.

29 Martin Plaut, 'Why Mandela's Communist Party Membership Is Important', *New
    Statesman*, 10 December 2013, http://www.newstatesman.com/world-affairs/2013/12/
    why-mandelas-communist-party-membership-important.

30 Anthony Sampson, *Mandela: The Authorised Biography*. London: HarperCollins,
    1999, p. 435.

31 African National Congress, 'Ready to Govern: ANC Policy Guidelines for a
    Democratic South Africa', 1992, http://www.anc.org.za/show.php?id=227.

32 Ray Hartley, *Ragged Glory: The Rainbow Nation in Black and White*. Johannesburg:
    Jonathan Ball, 2014, p. 34.

33 Hartley, *Ragged Glory*. The RDP has its origins reputedly in the work of COSATU's
    Macro-Economic Research Group.

34 African National Congress, 'The Reconstruction and Development Programme:
    A Policy Framework', 1994, section 4.2.1, http://www.nelsonmandela.org/omalley/
    index.php/site/q/03lv02039/04lv02103/05lv02120/06lv02126.htm.

35 ANC, 'The Reconstruction and Development Programme', sections 4.2.3 and 4.2.4.

36 ANC, 'The Reconstruction and Development Programme', section 1.4.14.

37 Department of Finance, 'Growth, Employment and Redistribution: A
    Macroeconomic Strategy', 1996, http://www.treasury.gov.za/publications/other/gear/
    chapters.pdf.

38 Discussion, anonymous government official, March 2015.

39 Hartley, *Ragged Glory*, p. 85.

40 Hartley, *Ragged Glory*, p. 171.

41 Email correspondence, 23 April 2015.

42 Telephonic discussion, 30 April 2015.

43 See http://new.nedlac.org.za/.

44 Discussion, Johannesburg, 2 April 2015.

45 South Africa Foundation, 'Growth for All: An Economic Strategy for South Africa',
    Johannesburg, February 1996.

46 Discussion, Johannesburg, 2 April 2015.

47 Telephonic discussion, Mike Spicer, 2 April 2015.

48 Figure 1.4 is sourced from the IMF's *World Economic Outlook Database*. The
    2014 figure is based on South African government projections.

49 Stan du Plessis and Ben Smit, 'Economic Growth in South Africa since 1994',
    Stellenbosch Economic Working Papers, 1/2006, Stellenbosch University, 2005,
    www.ber.ac.za/downloads/2006/working_papers/wp-01-2006.pdf, p. 4.

50 'Labour Laws Cut Hiring as South Africa Unemployed Swell: Jobs', *Bloomberg*

Business, 8 August 2012. http://www.bloomberg.com/news/articles/2012-08-08/labor-laws-chill-hiring-as-south-africa-s-unemployed-swell-jobs.

51 Its 34 members comprise Australia, Austria, Belgium, Canada, Chile, the Czech Republic, Denmark, Estonia, Finland, France, Germany, Greece, Hungary, Iceland, Ireland, Israel, Italy, Japan, South Korea, Luxembourg, Mexico, the Netherlands, New Zealand, Norway, Poland, Portugal, the Slovak Republic, Slovenia, Spain, Sweden, Switzerland, Turkey, the United Kingdom and the United States.

52 With thanks to Mike Schussler for this data and Figure 1.5, taken from his '11th USASA Employment Report'.

53 Quoted at http://www.rdm.co.za/business/2015/04/30/actually-south-africa-s-minimum-wage-is -the-best-in-brics.

54 Schussler, '11th USASA Employment Report'.

55 World Economic Forum, 'The Global Competitive Report, 2014–2015', http://reports. weforum.org/global-competitiveness-report-2014-2015/economies/#economy=ZAF.

56 Vivek Arora and Luca Antonio Ricci, 'Unemployment and the Labor Market' in Michael Nowak and Luca Antonio Ricci (eds), *Post-Apartheid South Africa: The First Ten Years*. Washington, D.C.: IMF, 2005. https://www.imf.org/external/pubs/nft/2006/soafrica/eng/pasoafr/.

57 See http://labourguide.co.za/employment-equity/summary-of-the-employment-equity-act-55-of-1998-issued-in-terms-of-section-25-1.

58 See, for example, the arrest of beggars and window-washers in February 2015 in Gauteng, http://www.iol.co.za/news/crime-courts/beggars-window-washers-arrested-1.1818084#.VOIEko3lqM8.

59 http://reports.weforum.org/global-competitiveness-report-2014-2015/economies/#economy=ZAF.

60 Interview, Soweto, 7 February 2015.

61 Hartley, *Ragged Glory*, p. 174.

62 Interview, Dennis George, Federation of Unions of South Africa, Johannesburg, 7 February 2015.

63 Quoted in Hartley, *Ragged Glory*, pp. 175–6.

64 COSATU, 'COSATU's Membership: All the Facts', September 2012, http://www. politicsweb.co.za/politicsweb/view/politicsweb/en/page71656?oid=325136&sn=Detail&pid=7165.

65 See http://www.news24.com/xArchive/News24/The-People-in-Power-20080130.

66 Combined public and private sector capital investment peaked at 30 per cent of GDP in the mid-1970s, falling to 15 per cent in 1995, as a result of the decline in the public share. It rose from 2004 to back over 20 per cent by 2010. Data for Figure 1.6 supplied by the South African Reserve Bank.

67 Discussion, Tana Forum, Bahir Dar, Ethiopia, 18 April 2015.

68 Email correspondence, 19 April 2015.

69 Email correspondence, 23 April 2015.

70 See Loane Sharp, 'Fraying of Business Units is a Real Threat to Growth', *Business Day*, 15 January 2015.

71 This was the critique of Harvard economists who followed up the ASGISA report with a series of studies. See also Hartley, *Ragged Glory*, p. 174.

72 Discussion, Chris Hart, 26 October 2014.

73 Figure 1.7 is sourced from World Bank, 'World Development Indicators', http://

databank.worldbank.org.

74 See http://www.shopriteholdings.co.za/InvestorCentre/SENS/PublishingImages/
    2013/Analyst_Presentation_Feb2014_web.pdf.

75 See http://www.economic.gov.za/communications/publications/
    new-growth- path-series.

76 'Each year the dti launches a revised three-year rolling IPAP with a 10-year outlook
    in a context of rapid economic change and significant global uncertainty.' The first
    was launched in 2007/8. See http://www.thedti.gov.za/industrial_development/
    industrial_development.jsp.

77 See Ann Bernstein and Dave Kaplan, 'Clear Policy Choices are Needed, Not
    Conflicting Plans', *Business Day*, 30 October 2013, http://www.bdlive.co.za/
    opinion/2013/10/30/clear-policy-choices-are-needed-not-conflicting-plans.

78 NPC, *National Development Plan*, pp. 3–4.

79 NPC, *National Development Plan*, p. 270.

80 Interview, Dumisani Dakile, COSATU provincial secretary, Jabavu, Soweto,
    7 February 2015.

81 NPC, *National Development Plan*, p. 111.

82 Interview, Trevor Manuel, 25 October 2014.

83 The rankings for Table 1.1 are sourced from Transparency International, Corruption
    Perception Index, http://www.transparency.org/research/cpi/overview; Heritage
    Foundation, Index of Economic Freedom, http://www.heritage.org/index/; World
    Economic Forum, Global Competitiveness Report, http://www.weforum.org/
    reports/global-competitiveness-report-2014-2015; Fraser Institute, Freedom of the
    World, http://www.freetheworld.com/.

84 SAIRR, *South Africa Survey 2014/15*, p. 225.

85 Carol Paton, 'Overpaid Public Servants Now Part of "Richest 30%"', *Rand
    Daily Mail*, 26 February 2015, http://www.rdm.co.za/business/2015/02/26/
    overpaid-public-servants-now-part-of-richest-30.

86 Schussler, 'The 11th UASA Employment Report'. Figure 1.8 is reproduced from the
    same report.

87 See http://led.co.za/story/2012/01/23/public-service-employment-growing-four
    -times-faster-total-employment.

88 See the statement by the South African Chamber of Commerce and Industry, 6 May
    2013.

89 For a discussion on this term see, for example, http://www.iol.co.za/news/politics/
    zille-warns-against-state-capture-1.1591459#.VS0Abk3lqM8.

90 Interview, Johannesburg, 11 February 2015.

91 Discussion, Roger Baxter, 26 October 2014.

92 See http://www.afrobarometer.org/publicationsbp110-perceptions-and-realities-
    corruption -south-africa

93 C.W. de Kiewiet, *A History of South Africa*. Oxford: Clarendon Press, 1941, p. 89

2 Expectations of a New Country

1 Telephonic interview, 20 February 2015.

2 All data on per capita income in this chapter (including Table 2.1) is from the World

Bank, 'World Development Indicators', http://databank.worldbank.org.

3 This is drawn from several interviews and discussions with former President Nathan, including in December 2013 and September 2014. A more fulsome account appears in Greg Mills, *Why States Recover: Changing Walking Societies into Winning Nations – From Afghanistan to Zimbabwe*. Johannesburg: Picador Africa and London: C. Hurst & Co., 2014, especially pp. 464–6.

4 This section is based in part on a visit to the Intel plant in Penang in September 2014, and various subsequent email exchanges with Intel. See also http://info.worldbank.org/etools/docs/library/251665/Yeow%20Teck%20Chai%20and%20Ooi%20Chooi%20Im%20-%20The%20Development%20of%20Free%20Industrial%20Zones%96The%20Malaysian%20Experience.pdf.

5 Interview, Penang Development Corporation, September 2014.

6 Email correspondence, Intel, September 2014.

7 This section is based on visits to Singapore and Malaysia in August and September 2014.

8 Hilary Joffe, 'Zuma Revisionism Does Not Explain SA Power Crisis', http://www.bdlive.co.za/opinion/columnists/2015/01/14/zumas-revisionism-does-not-explain-sa-power-crisis.

9 Telephonic interview, 5 January 2015.

10 Email correspondence, Tony Ehrenreich, 15 February 2015.

11 Discussion, Richard Pike, 16 February 2015.

12 With thanks to Tim Harris for these figures. See also http://www.politicsweb.co.za/politicsweb/view/politicsweb/en/page71656?oid=325136&sn=Detail&pid=71656.

13 See http://www.economist.com/node/16248621.

14 As cited in Robin Renwick, *Mission to South Africa: Diary of a Revolution*. Johannesburg: Jonathan Ball, 2015, p. 176.

15 Interview, Cape Town, 6 January 2015.

16 See http://www.bbc.com/news/world-africa-22478916.

3 Agriculture

1 Carol Paton, 'New Minimum Wage "Will Spur Overhaul of Farming"', http://www.bdlive.co.za/business/agriculture/2013/02/05/new-minimum-wage-will-spur-overhaul-of-farming.

2 Paton, 'New Minimum Wage'.

3 See Frikkie Liebenberg and Philip Pardey, 'South African Agricultural Production and Productivity Patterns' in Julian M. Alston, Bruce A. Babcock and Philip G. Pardey (eds), *The Shifting Patterns of Agricultural Production and Productivity Worldwide*. Ames, IA: Midwest Agribusiness Trade Research and Information Center, Iowa State University, 2010.

4 South African Institute of Race Relations, *South Africa Survey 2014/15*. Johannesburg: SAIRR, 2015, p. 251.

5 See https://www.facebook.com/max.dupreez.3/posts/815486305181354.

6 Sol Plaatje, *Native Life in South Africa, Before and Since the European War and the Boer Rebellion*, 1916, http://hsf.org.za/resource-centre/focus/focus-70-on-focus/focus-70-oct-politicsweb.pdf/download.

7 Cited in Martin Meredith, *Diamonds, Gold and War: The British, the Boers, and the Making of South Africa*. New York: Public Affairs, 2008, p. 523.

8 See http://hsf.org.za/resource-centre/focus/focus-70-on-focus/focus-70-oct-politicsweb.pdf/download.

9 *Hansard*, 15 May 1913, http://hsf.org.za/resource-centre/focus/focus-70-on-focus/focus-70-oct-politicsweb.pdf/download.

10 Harvey M. Feinberg, 'The 1913 Natives Land Act in South Africa: Politics, Race, and Segregation in the Early 20th Century', *International Journal of African Historical Studies* 26, 1993, p. 70.

11 See http://www.news24.com/SouthAfrica/Politics/Land-laws-are-biased-Zuma-20140227.

12 Telephonic interview, 28 November 2014.

13 See http://www.politicsweb.co.za/politicsweb/view/politicsweb/en/page71619?oid=403340&sn=Detail&pid=71619.

14 Unless otherwise indicated, the figures in this section were provided by AgriSA.

15 See http://www.politicsweb.co.za/politicsweb/view/politicsweb/en/page71619/page71639?oid=282525&sn=Detail&pid=71639.

16 See http://www.politicsweb.co.za/politicsweb/view/politicsweb/en/page71619/page71639?oid=282525&sn=Detail&pid=71639.

17 Figures supplied by AgriSA, November 2014.

18 Telephonic interview, Hans van der Merwe, 28 November 2014.

19 Mari Harris, '0% of South Africans Regard Land as Most Important Issue to them Personally', 11 February 2015. Quoted in *Politicsweb*, http://www.politicsweb.co.za/politicsweb/view/politicsweb/en/page71619?oid=950245&sn=Detail&pid=71616.

20 Based on a trip to Makhathini Flats in Vryheid in the company of Malcolm Ferguson, Hans van der Merwe and Leila Jack, 30 January 2015.

21 This is based on a trip to Just Veggies in Vryheid, 30 January 2015.

22 Discussion, Just Veggies, 30 January 2015.

23 Visit to Paul Cluver Wines, 22 December 2014.

24 Telephonic discussion, 23 December 2014.

25 Material from a visit to Kakamas, 7 January 2015, and a meeting with Roy Fine in Cape Town, 22 December 2014.

26 See http://www.fbreporter.com/component/content/article?id=25284:huge-new-eastern-cape-tomato-project; and http://www.mediaclubsouthafrica.com/component/content/article?id=2556:east.

27 Discussion, 29 December 2014.

28 Correspondence with Mark Harris, 6 March 2015.

29 This section is based on a series of telephonic interviews during December 2014, and a visit to Kidd's Beach and Bathurst in January 2015. Gauteng had the highest employment rate at 70%, followed by the Western Cape at 67.9%, with a drop-off after that to 56.9% in the Free State. The Eastern Cape had the lowest employment rate at 43.4%. See http://www.bdlive.co.za/economy/2012/10/30/census-sas-population-of-51.8m-is-still-young.

30 Global production is around 20 million tonnes. Since 1960, pineapple production worldwide has risen by 400%. Fresh pineapple exports worldwide are around one million tonnes.

31 Telephonic discussion, 27 December 2014.

32 See https://www.facebook.com/max.dupreez.3/posts/815486305181354.

33 Email communication, 31 January 2015.

4 Selling Forever?

1 Special Economic Zones Act, No. 16 of 2014, 19 May 2014.
2 Discussion, St James, 4 February 2015.
3 Discussion, Atlantis, 3 February 2015.
4 Figure 4.1 is sourced from Ejaz Ghani and Stephen D. O'Connell, 'Can Services be a Growth Escalator in Low Income Countries?', Policy Research Working Paper 6871, World Bank, July 2014, http://www-wds.worldbank.org/external/default/WDSContentServer/WDSP/IB/2014/07/22/000158349_20140722093642/Rendered/PDF/WPS6971.pdf, p. 10.
5 See http://www.worldbank.org/depweb/beyond/beyondco/beg_09.pdf.
6 Figure 4.2 is sourced from World Bank, World Development Data, and include World Bank national accounts data and OECD National Accounts data files.
7 Discussion, Pretoria, 1 December 2014.
8 The figures on tourist trends are sourced from data supplied by the South African Department of Tourism, December 2014.
9 'Killing the Golden Goose', *The Economist*, 14 February 2015, p. 43.
10 The visa issue goes beyond tourism. The increasingly strict work permit and 'business visitor' measures taken by the Department of Home Affairs run counter to the operation of a modern economy. In particular they will hinder the developmental role that South Africa has professed to in Africa.
11 See http://www.ibtimes.com/2014-soccer-world-cup-brazil-predicts-revenue-20-times-over-south-africas-2010-experts-skeptical.
12 See the Statistics SA report of 2010, http://www.statssa.gov.za/publications/Report-03-51-02/Report-03-51-022010.pdf.
13 See http://jae.oxfordjournals.org/content/23/2/290.full#xref-corresp-1-1.
14 Stan du Plessis and Wolfgang Maennig, 'The 2010 World Cup High-Frequency Data Economics: Effects on International Awareness and (Self-Defeating) Tourism', 2010, http://ideas.repec.org/p/hce/wpaper/037.html.
15 Stan du Plessis and Cobus Venter, 'The Home Team Scores! First Assessment of the Economic Impact of World Cup 2010', Stellenbosch Economic Working Papers 21/10, Department of Economics, Stellenbosch University.
16 See http://www.telegraph.co.uk/finance/newsbysector/retailandconsumer/leisure/8192484/South-Africa-recoups-just-a-tenth-of-the-3bn-cost-of-staging-World-Cup-2010.html.
17 See http://www.forbes.com/sites/mikeozanian/2014/06/05/the-billion-dollar-business-of-the-world-cup/.
18 Interview, Patricia de Lille, Mayor of Cape Town, 15 October 2014.
19 See http://www.iol.co.za/capetimes/city-back-to-square-one-over-stadium-1.1797507#.VJhGZA7UIB.
20 See Binyamin Applebaum, 'Does Hosting the Olympics Actually Pay Off?' *New York Times Magazine*, 5 August 2014, http://www.nytimes.com/2014/08/10/magazine/does-hosting-the-olympics-actually-pay-off.html?_r=0.
21 Applebaum, 'Does Hosting the Olympics Actually Pay Off?' The trade impact is

taken from a 2009 study by Andrew K. Rose and Mark M. Spiegel, http://www.imf.
org/external/pubs/ft/fandd/2010/03/pdf/rose.pdf; and http://faculty.haas.berkeley.
edu/arose/SAIS.pdf.

22 Interview, Cape Town, 3 December 2014.

23 See Dave Mullany, 'The Flying Springbok' in Herman Potgieter, *Aviation in South
Africa*. Cape Town: Struik, 1986, especially pp. 14–15.

24 In 1996, SAA employed 11 100 people, of whom 3 100 were engineers, and
owned and operated 48 aircraft. See 'SAA in the World Airline Directory',
Flight International, 3–9 April 1996. By 2013 the state-owned company had
11 044 employees, just over 500 licensed engineers and 52 aircraft. See http://
www.bdlive.co.za/business/transport/2013/02/17/saa-staff-plane-ratio-slammed;
and http://www.staralliance.com/en/about/airlines/south-africa_airlines/#.

25 See http://www.da.org.za/2013/04/is-saa-getting-another-bailout/.

26 See http://www.engineeringnews.co.za/article/
saa-launches-90-day-action-plan-to-stabilise-itself-2014-12-09/rep_id:3182.

27 See http://www.engineeringnews.co.za/article/saa-gets-billions-more
-financial-guarantees-from-state-2015-01-22/rep_id:3182.

28 See http://www.iol.co.za/business/companies/saa-revenue-jumps-12-percent-1.1811577.

29 This section is based on discussions with several South African-based aviation
experts.

30 See http://www.engineeringnews.co.za/article/saa-to-halt-direct-flights-to
-india-2015-02-04/rep_id:3182.

31 Telephonic interview, SAA employee, 19 December 2014.

32 *South Africa's Yesterdays*. Cape Town: Reader's Digest, 1981, p. 283. This is also based
on a discussion with Gareth Ackerman in Cape Town, 16 December 2014.

33 Based on a discussion with Simon Susman, Steenberg, Cape Town, 13 January 2015.

34 Based on email correspondence, 6 and 7 February 2015.

35 Discussion, Sandton, January 2015.

36 The taxi drivers only wanted to be identified by their first names, and then
reluctantly so.

37 Discussion, Midrand, 21 January 2015. We are grateful to Murray Bridgman for
highlighting the role of the taxi industry in entrepreneurship. The drivers were
interviewed at the Rosebank, Wanderers and Bree Street ranks in Johannesburg in
January 2015.

38 See http://www.reuters.com/article/2014/03/10/safrica-taxis
-idUSL6N0LQ3BL20140310.

39 The total number of road deaths worldwide is calculated at 1.2 million. The
International Transport Forum's 2013 Road Safety Annual Report ranked South
Africa the worst, out of 36 others, when it came to the number of road fatalities.
South Africa's road fatalities per 100 000 was at 27.6 deaths in 2011 – compared to
developed countries such as the US with 10.4 or Australia with 5.6. Argentina and
Colombia were around 12, while Malaysia came off second worst with 23.8. On other
statistics (World Health Organization and United Nations), Eritrea is home to the
highest concentration of road deaths (48.4 per 100 000 people), the Cook Islands
are next (45.0 road deaths per 100 000 people), followed by Libya (34.7), South
Africa (33.2) and Iran (32.2). See http://www.theguardian.com/global-development/
poverty-matters/2011/may/11/most-dangerous-roads.

40 See http://mg.co.za/article/2013-10-04-00-the-state-of-sas-public-transport.

5 The Manufacturing Basics

1 On the history of the Ngagane plant, see http://heritage.eskom.co.za/heritage/ingagane.htm.

2 Figure 5.1 is drawn from http://www.nda.agric.za/publications/publications.asp?category=Statistical+information.

3 These were Lethabo (3 708 megawatts; building started 1980, final plant commissioning 1990); Tutuka (3 654 megawatts; 1985 and 1990); Matimba (3 990 megawatts; 1981 and 1993); Kendal (4 116 megawatts; 1982 and 1993); and Majuba (4 110 megawatts; 1983 and 2001).

4 'Thirty Years of Mistakes at Eskom', http://www.bdlive.co.za/businesstimes/2014/12/14/thirty-years-of-mistakes-at-eskom.

5 See Anton Eberhard, 'The Political Economy of Power Sector Reform in South Africa', http://www.gsb.uct.ac.za/files/StanfordCUPBookChapterp215-253_6.pdf.

6 See the article 'Eskom Over the Last 30 Years: Why It Has Crashed', *Engineering News*, 8 February 2008, http://www.engineeringnews.co.za/article.php?a_id=125510.

7 'Eskom Over the Last 30 Years'.

8 'Eskom Over the Last 30 Years'.

9 Peak household usage is at 35 per cent of generating capacity.

10 See http://www.huffingtonpost.ca/david-himbara/south-africa-electricity-shortage_b_6305412.html.

11 'Electricity Woes to Lock SA into Low-Growth Path, Bank Warns', *Engineering News*, 10 February 2015, http://www.engineeringnews.co.za/article/electricity-woes-to-lock-sa-into-low-growth-path-bank-warns-2015-02-10/rep_id:3182.

12 Cited in *Popular Mechanics*, January 2015, p. 56.

13 See, for example, http://www.timeslive.co.za/businesstimes/2015/02/08/black-coal-backfires-on-eskom.

14 See *South Africa's Yesterday's*. Cape Town: Reader's Digest Association, 1981, especially pp. 270–1.

15 See http://www.bdlive.co.za/economy/2014/10/30/little-change-in-jobless-rate. Figure 5.2 is drawn, between 2000–7, from Statistics SA's Labour Force Survey, and between 2008–14 from Quarterly Labour Force Survey.

16 This section is based on an interview with Premier David Makhura and his senior colleagues, Johannesburg, 26 January 2015.

17 Telephonic interview, 5 January 2015. Figure 5.3 is drawn from South African Reserve Bank data.

18 Discussion, Midrand, 22 January 2015.

19 See the unpublished report by Thabiti Consultants, 11 December 2014.

20 See http://www.doingbusiness.org/rankings.

21 Telephonic interview, Minister of Small Business Development, Lindiwe Zulu, 9 February 2015.

22 Interview, Richard Pike, ADCORP, 16 February 2015.

23 Figure 5.4 is calculated from Department of Labour statistics. See http://www.

politicsweb.co.za/politicsweb/view/politicsweb/en/page71656?oid=257156&s
n=Detail&pid=71616. See also http://businesstech.co.za/news/general/65348/
r6-7-billion-in-wages-lost-to-sa-strikes/.

24 See http://www.miningweekly.com/article/
sa-one-of-the-worlds-most-violent-strike-prone-countries-2014-08-06.

25 Cited in ibid.

26 See http://africacheck.org/reports/are-most-estimates-of-what-strikes-cost-the-sa-
economy-accurate-probably-not-take-them-with-a-big-pinch-of-salt/.

27 Interview, Dennis George, 7 February 2015.

28 Discussions, March 2015.

29 For the background to this, see Tang Xiaoyang, 'The Impact of Asian Investment on
Africa's Textile Industries', Carnegie-Tsinghua Center for Global Policy, 27 August
2014, http://carnegietsinghua.org/publications/?fa=56320.

30 The visit to Newcastle and Ladysmith was conducted in November 2014.

31 *South Africa's Yesterday's*, p. 15.

32 See, for example, http://www.bee-scorecard.co.za/bee_information.html.

33 See Urban-Econ Development Economists, 'Detailed Analysis of the Furniture
Manufacturing Sector in KwaZulu-Natal', Final Report, 2014; see also the
Department of Trade and Industry's 'Strategy for the Development of the Furniture
Industry', October 2011.

34 Communication from National Liaison Office, Furniture Manufacturing,
23 February 2015.

35 Not their real names, though the companies exist.

36 See http://www.financialmail.co.za/moneyinvesting/2014/11/20/
furniture-retail-removal-trucks-pull-in.

37 See, for example, David Kaplan, Mike Morris and Lucy Martin, 'Identifying and
Developing Sustainable Interventions to Promote Non-Automotive Industries in the
Eastern Cape'. Report prepared for the (South African) National Treasury, 13 January
2014.

38 These impressions were gained in a roundtable with the Border Industries
Employers Association, 28 January 2015.

39 Roundtable, 28 January 2015.

40 Cited at http://en.wikipedia.org/wiki/Television_in_South_Africa.

41 Visit to Vektronix, 28 January 2015.

42 Interview, Pretoria, 2 December 2014.

43 Discussion with Premier David Makhura and colleagues, Gauteng Legislature,
Simmonds Street, Johannesburg, 26 January 2015.

44 Discussion, Coenraad Bezuidenhout, Manufacturing Circle, 19 November 2014.

45 Ibid.

46 See, for example, Dan Senor and Paul Singer, *Start-Up Nation: The Story of Israel's
Economic Miracle*. Boston: Twelve, 2009, p. 86.

6 Mining

1 Conversation, Croft's, Parkview, 18 November 2014.
2 The data in Figure 6.1 is supplied by the Chamber of Mines.
3 This is based on a visit to Driefontein's Number 5 shaft in March 2015.
4 See http://uk.reuters.com/article/2011/02/04/uk-south-africa-mining
   -idUKLNE713003020110204.
5 This section is partly drawn from a telephonic discussion with Roger Baxter,
   23 September 2011, then chief economist of the South African Chamber of Mines.
6 Mike Schussler, 'The 11th USASA Employment Report', http://www.miningmx.
   com/news/markets/SA-richest-country-in-the-world.htm.
7 Discussion, Woodmead, Johannesburg, 2 February 2015.
8 See http://www.mining.com/south-africas-attractiveness-for-mining
   -investment-plummets/.
9 See the MPRDA, http://www.dmr.gov.za/publications/summary/109-mineral-and-
   petroleum-resources-development-act-2002/225-mineraland-petroleum-resources-
   development-actmprda.html.
10 See http://www.miningmx.com/page/special_reports/mining-yearbook/mining-
   yearbook-2014/1644177-SA-miners-may-be-stung-by-BEE#.VGsu_U3lqM8.
11 Discussion, Johannesburg, 19 November 2014.
12 See https://www.facebook.com/notes/chamber-of-mines-supports-the-mprda-
   amendment-bill/601544369919751.
13 Discussion, Cape Town, 4 February 2015.
14 The report of the committee, delivered in 2012, proposed significant state
   involvement in the mining sector. One recommendation is that government
   introduces a 50 per cent Resource Rent Tax on mining 'super profits', defined as a
   rate in excess of Treasury Long Bond Rate plus 7 per cent (currently about 15 per
   cent). The proceeds would be ring-fenced in a Sovereign Wealth Fund and used to
   finance a Fiscal Stabilisation Fund, a Regional Development Fund and a Minerals
   Development Fund. Overall, however, the report confirms that nationalisation
   would be too expensive if it occurred with compensation (R1 trillion-plus) and too
   damaging to foreign investment if it occurred without. For an overview, see Jasson
   Urbach, 'State Intervention in Mining is Not Good for South Africa', http://www.
   ngopulse.org/article/state-intervention-mining-not-good-south-africa.
15 See http://www.moneyweb.co.za/moneyweb-the-burning-question/
   how-sas-businesses-keep-the-country-poor.
16 See http://www.dailymaverick.co.za/article/2015-02-12-lord-renwick-on-mining-
   indaba-its-not-about-the-numbers-its-about-the-real-deals/#.VOcWyo3lqM8.
17 Justice Malala, 'The Marikana Action is a Strike by the Poor against the State and the
   Haves', *The Guardian*, 17 August 2012.
18 This section is based on a discussion with a South African legal expert, 2 February
   2015.
19 Marikana Commission of Inquiry, Preliminary Report: Phase 2, 15 August 2014,
   p. 48.
20 The data in Figure 6.2 is supplied by the Chamber of Mines.
21 Discussion, Angloplats, 21 November 2014.
22 See Ray Hartley, 'The Brave New World of Mining Puts Machines the Rock at
   Machines at the Rock Face', *Business Times*, 21 September 2014,

http://www.bdlive.co.za/businesstimes/2014/09/21/
the-brave-new-world-of-mining-puts-machines-at-the-rock-face.
23 Discussion, Johannesburg, 27 November 2014.
24 This is based partly on a visit to Venetia on 25 November 2014.
25 See http://mg.co.za/article/2013-10-22-zuma-mining-has-a-bright-future-in-sa.
26 See http://www.southafrica.net/za/en/articles/entry/article-a-brief-history
-of-mining-in-south-africa.
27 See the excellent report, 'Coal 2014: A Review of South Africa's Coal Sector Research
Report', *Engineering News*, November 2014.
28 See http://www.bdlive.co.za/business/mining/2014/04/17/coal-reserves-study-gives
-lie-to-eskom-supply-scare.
29 The data in Figure 6.3 is supplied by the Chamber of Mines.
30 'Coal 2014', p. 12.
31 See http://www.financialmail.co.za/coverstory/2014/03/27/mining-new-territory
-waterberg-coal-field.
32 'Coal 2014', pp. 13–14.
33 Telephonic interview, 20 February 2015.
34 This is based on a visit to Anglo Platinum's School of Mines at Siphumelele Mine
in Rustenburg, 26 November 2014, and various interviews at their Johannesburg
headquarters, 21 November 2014.
35 Ibid.
36 Discussion, Johannesburg, 27 November 2014.
37 Discussion, Johannesburg, 2 February 2015.

7 The Social Wage and Education

1 See http://www.financialmail.co.za/features/2013/12/12/unemployment-set-to
-threaten-sa-s-welfare-system.
2 See http://www.bloomberg.com/news/2014-04-03/south-african-poverty-rate-
drops-as-government-expands-welfare.html.
3 Rob Rose, 'The Last Word', *Sunday Times Business Times*, 11 January 2015. See also
Jonathan Jansen and Molly Blank, *How to Fix South Africa's Schools: Lessons from
Schools that Work*. Johannesburg: Bookstorm, 2014.
4 African National Congress, 'The Freedom Charter', http://www.anc.org.za/show.
php?id=72.
5 African National Congress, 'Ready to Govern: ANC Policy Guidelines for a
Democratic South Africa', 1992, http://www.anc.org.za/show.php?id=227.
6 ANC, 'Ready to Govern'.
7 African National Congress, 'The Reconstruction and Development Programme',
1994, section 2.13.5, https://www.nelsonmandela.org/omalley/index.php/site/q/03lvo
2039/04lvo2103/05lvo2120/06lvo2126.htm.
8 ANC, 'The Reconstruction and Development Programme', section 2.13.11.
9 ANC, 'The Reconstruction and Development Programme', section 2.3.3.
10 Department of Finance, 'Growth, Employment and Redistribution: A
Macroeconomic Strategy', 1996, http://www.treasury.gov.za/publications/other/gear/
chapters.pdf, p. 15.

11 Department of Finance, 'Growth, Employment and Redistribution', p. 10.
12 Michael Samson, Kenneth MacQuene and Ingrid van Niekerk, 'Social Grants: South Africa', Policy Brief 1, Overseas Development Institute, February 2006, pp. 3–4, http://www.odi.org/sites/odi.org.uk/files/odi-assets/publications-opinion-files/1688.pdf.
13 Discussion, Pretoria, 23 January 2015.
14 Haroon Bhorat and Aalia Cassim, 'South Africa's Welfare Success Story II: Poverty-Reducing Social Grants', *Brookings Brief*, 27 January 2014, http://www.brookings.edu/blogs/africa-in-focus/posts/2014/01/27-south-africa-welfare-poverty-bhorat. Table 7.1 is sourced from http://www.treasury.gov.za/documents/national%20budget/2014/guides/2014%20People's%20Guide%20English.pdf.
15 See his 2007 budget speech at http://www.dfa.gov.za/docs/speeches/2007/manu0221.htm.
16 'Africa Check: Separating Myth from Reality – A Guide to Social Grants in South Africa', http://www.dailymaverick.co.za.
17 Murray Leibbrandt, Ingrid Woolard, Arden Finn and Jonathan Argent, 'Trends in South African Income Distribution and Poverty since the Fall of Apartheid', OECD Social, Employment and Migration Working Papers, No. 101, 2010.
18 For his biographical details see http://www.kznonline.gov.za/index.php?option=com_content&view=article&id=116&Itemid=170.
19 Discussion, Empangeni, 22 October 2015.
20 See http://www.citypress.co.za/news/social-grants-cant-be-sustained-zuma-20111124/.
21 See http://www.cde.org.za/rethinking-the-welfare-state-2/
22 See http://www.financialmail.co.za/features/2013/12/12/unemployment-set-to-threaten-sa-s-welfare-system.
23 See http://www.financialmail.co.za/opinion/editorial/2014/10/09/editorial-sa-is-headed-for-a-fiscal-cliff.
24 See http://www.economist.com/news/international/21638127-developing-countries-are-cutting-fraud-and-waste-anti-poverty-schemes-deciding-who?frsc=dg%7Ca.
25 Telephonic discussion and email correspondence, 26 and 27 January 2015.
26 See http://www.ipea.gov.br/portal/.
27 See http://veja.abril.com.br/idade/exclusivo/bolsa_familia/08.html.
28 See http://www.bnb.gov.br/content/aplicacao/Eventos/ForumBNB2007/docs/impactos-do-programa.pdf.
29 Figure 7.1 is drawn from World Bank data, http://data.worldbank.org/indicator/SI.POV.GINI.
30 See http://www.dw.de/ten-years-on-brazils-bolsa-familia-still-going-strong/av-17241829.
31 See http://www.theguardian.com/global-development/2013/dec/19/brazil-bolsa-familia-political-tool-social-welfare.
32 Based on Fernando de Holanda Barbosa's 2014 presentation to students at the Gordon Institute of Business Science, University of Pretoria.
33 Ibid.
34 See http://www.oportunidades.gob.mx:8010/index1.php.
35 See http://www.pbs.org/newshour/bb/health-july-dec09-mexico_12-29/.
36 For a review of the programme, see http://www.ids.ac.uk/publication/equal-opportunities-for-all-a-critical-analysis-of-mexico-s-oportunidades.

37 Telephonic discussion, 29 December 2014.

38 Rose, 'The Last Word'.

39 See http://mg.co.za/article/2014-12-30-ieb-matric-results-9838-percent-pass-rate-and-14-900-distinctions. See also 'SA's "real" matric pass rate: 42%', at http://businesstech.co.za/news/general/76561/sas-real-matric-pass-rate-41/.

40 With thanks to Nel Marais for this point.

41 See http://www.citypress.co.za/news/sas-maths-science-teaching-worst-world/. Figure 7.2 is sourced from the World Economic Forum and World Bank data.

42 See a 2014 study by Nic Spaull and Hansa Venkatakrishnan, http://www.iol.co.za/news/south-africa/kwazulu-natal/dire-state-of-sa-s-grade-6-maths-teachers-1.1731759.

43 Ibid.

44 Cited in Jansen and Blank, *How to Fix South Africa's Schools*, p. 31.

45 Interview, Dumisani Dakile, COSATU provincial secretary, Soweto, 7 January 2015. See also http://www.iol.co.za/news/south-africa/kwazulu-natal/teachers-deserve-longer-holidays-sadtu-1.1725123.

46 Discussion, Richard Pike, 16 February 2015.

47 There are large differences in the unemployment rates for white and black graduates, as there are across different society groups. Black graduates were, in 2012, almost three times as likely to be unemployed than their white counterparts, though then broad unemployment rate for black graduates was low against the *aggregate* unemployment rate amongst the black population, which exceeded 41 per cent. (The aggregate unemployment rate amongst the white population was below 8 per cent.) The number of black graduates has grown considerably as part of this pool – in 1995 there were some 1.7 white graduates for every black graduate; by 2012 this ratio had decreased to 0.9. And black graduate employment grew, on average, by 6 per cent per annum between 1995 and 2012, from 145 000 to 454 000, the majority employed in the public sector. The number of black graduates employed in the public sector more than doubled between 1995 and 2012, while the number employed in the private sector increased more than fourfold. See http://www.econ3x3.org/article/how-high-graduate-unemployment-south-africa-much-needed-update.

48 This data on the economically active population is obtained from Statistics SA's Quarterly Labour Force Survey, September 2009, the analysis of which can be found at http://www.workinfo.com/Articles/EAP.htm.

49 'Until the mid-1990s Zimbabwe was recognised as relatively successful in providing quality education for all. It had achieved universal primary education and innovative secondary education for the majority (65 per cent) by the late 1980s. This was a remarkable achievement, given that at independence in 1980 only a third of Zimbabwe's children had access to primary education, and only four per cent attended secondary school.' See http://www.bwpi.manchester.ac.uk/medialibrary/research/ResearchAreaProjects/Zimbabwe/Moving_forward_in_Zimbabwe_h_Chapter_06.pdf. According to reports, Zimbabwe leads the literacy rate in Africa, with 91 per cent. See http://www.sabc.co.za/news/a/5c11890044581c8fbd02fd744a7933f3/Zimbabwe-leads-literacy-rate-in-Africa-20140612.

50 Discussion, Paul Cluver Jnr, Grabouw, 5 January 2015.

8 A Bridge to the Future?

1 Launched in 2000, 21 SETAs were set up to reverse the country's skills crisis and thereby address the plight of the 3.4 million 18- to 24-year-olds who are not in employment, education or training. Their 2014–15 allocation is nearly R11 billion, money collected from private companies through the skills levies. See http://mg.co.za/article/2014-08-20-only-a-few-setas-fail-audits-the-rest-do-good-work.

2 See http://mg.co.za/article/2014-08-07-billions-wasted-on-setas-funding-as-skills-crisis-worsens.

3 The visit to the plant was conducted on 10 February 2015. Jeff Nemeth was interviewed in Johannesburg on 12 November 2014.

4 Samcor was created in 1985 through the merger of Ford's local subsidiary and Anglo-American Motor Corporation. In 1988, Ford divested from South Africa and sold its stake in Samcor. In 1994, Ford purchased 45 per cent of Samcor, and in 1998 bought the remaining stake, renaming the company Ford Motor Company of Southern Africa.

5 See http://www.mercedes-benzsa.co.za/uploadedFiles/mbsa/Corporate_Profile/MBSA%20Sustainability%20Report%202012%20.pdf.

6 Interview, Johannesburg, 7 November 2014.

7 See 'Car Industry Must Gear Down Change', *Business Report*, 1 December 2014.

8 Interview, Johannesburg, 22 January 2015.

9 Automotive Industry Export Council (AIEC), *MIDP: The Track Record, 1995–2012*. Arcadia, AIEC, 2013.

10 AIEC, *MIDP*.

11 See 'Car Industry Must Gear Down Change'.

12 We are grateful to Mike Schussler for this insight. See also South African Treasury, *Budget Review*, 23 February 2011.

13 Joe Studwell, *How Asia Works: Success and Failure in the World's Most Dynamic Region*. London: Profile, 2013.

14 See McKinsey's 'Recharging China's Electric-Vehicle Aspirations', July 2012, http://www.mckinsey.com/insights/energy_resources_materials/recharging_chinas_electric-vehicle_aspirations.

15 For his version of the history of the project, see http://issuu.com/kobusmeiring/docs/the_joule.

16 See http://www.carmag.co.za/news/a-joule-of-a-plan/.

17 See http://issuu.com/kobusmeiring/docs/the_joule.

18 Interview, Jimmy Price, and visit to High-Tech Auto's factory, Port Elizabeth, 21 October 2013, and subsequent email communication, 12 January 2015.

19 Interview, Pretoria, 2 December 2014.

20 See http://issuu.com/kobusmeiring/docs/the_joule.

21 Telephonic discussion, Cape Town, 4 February 2015.

22 See http://www.itweb.co.za/index.php?option=com_content&view=article&id=53923.

23 This is based on an interview with Dr Paul Potgieter, 12 November 2014, and several visits to Aerosud.

24 This is based on email correspondence with Stephen Saad, 6 February 2015. See also Ray Hartley, 'How a Small Factory in Port Elizabeth Conquered the World', *Business Day*, 16 June 2013, http://www.bdlive.co.za/business/healthcare/2013/06/16/how-a-small-factory-in-port-elizabeth-conquered-the-world.

25 This is based on a meeting with Eric Goldblum, Johannesburg, 31 October 2014, and a visit to Ladysmith, 5 November 2014.
26 This is based on a discussion with Neal Froneman at Sibanye's Corporate Headquarters, Westonaria, 13 February 2015.

Conclusion

1 Discussion, Dumisani Dakile, Soweto, 7 February 2015.
2 See http://www.gov.za/sites/www.gov.za/files/devplan_2.pdf.
3 See Linda Ensor, 'Industrial Plan, National Development Plan "in Conflict", Says DA', *Business Day*, http://www.bdlive.co.za/economy/2013/04/23/industrial-plan-national-development-plan-in-conflict-says-da.
4 Cited in *Financial Mail*, 9–15 April 2015, p. 22.
5 Cited in 'Ruling Elite "Rotten"', *The Times*, 10 April 2015.
6 'Ruling Elite "Rotten"'.
7 With thanks to Ray Hartley for this insight.
8 See, for example, 'Report on Implementation of ANC Commitments' tabled by the Presidential Infrastructure Co-ordinating Committee at the ANC's January 2015 Lekgotla, as reported in 'We Messed Up, Says ANC', *Mail and Guardian*, 6–12 February 2015.
9 See, for example, http://www.bdlive.co.za/articles/2011/06/07/jobless-youth-a-ticking-time-bomb-for-sa-vavi-warns1;jsessionid=6E03153EC368AADB7DAEA4B59 4D2C383.present1.bdfm.
10 Discussion, Georgian President Mikheil Saakashvili, London, 11 February 2010.
11 See Songezo Zibi, *Raising the Bar: Hope and Renewal in South Africa*. Johannesburg: Picador Africa, 2014, especially pp. 278–9 and pp. 187–93, concerning the need for robust institutions and better leadership.
12 In the words of Gareth van Onselen on the situation of leadership over the removal of the Rhodes statue from the University of Cape Town, see http://www.bdlive.co.za/opinion/columnists/2015/04/15/the-rhodes-statue-of-mad-panics-and-permanence.

Index

Note: Page numbers in italics refer to tables and figures.

Acknowledgements

This book is based on interviews with a large number of government officials, entrepreneurs, economists and other analysts, and media in South Africa and farther afield, most of which were conducted in the last quarter of 2014 and the beginning of 2015. Interviewees gave generously of their often hard-pressed time, for which we are most grateful. We hope that we have done their insights justice, and salute their commitment to the country.

A number of the suggestions about the book from a dialogue held at Tswalu Kalahari Reserve in March 2015 were able to be included, and thanks are expressed to the participants for their valuable observations.

No one should ever believe that the task of economic reform is easy, especially where the majority of constituents have been systematically discriminated against over many centuries by the political system, and where their expectations are heightened by radical political change, as occurred in South Africa in 1994. We have gained much respect for South Africa's political and business leadership as it struggles to balance the tensions between redistribution and growth, equality and prosperity, and efficiency and inclusion.

We have been enthusiastically supported in our task by The Brenthurst Foundation, and thank the Oppenheimer family in particular for their continued commitment to the cause of strengthening Africa's economic performance.

The Pan Macmillan team has done a tremendous job in seeing this publication to fruition in a short time. Wendy Trott and Leungo Motlhabane were a great help in digging out facts and assembling graphs, while Ray Hartley, Mike Spicer, David MacGregor, Dickie Davis, Sharon Polansky and several other reviewers offered important leads and comment on the drafts. Malcolm Ferguson, Roy Fine and Hans van der Merwe were most helpful in hosting a trip to various agriculture projects in January 2015. The Wesgro team kindly arranged a visit to facilities up the Cape West Coast in February 2015, while Martha Ngoma offered useful translation and facilitation skills, especially with Johannesburg's taxi drivers. Ghairoon Hajad and Leila Jack, as ever, provided critical logistical support at The Brenthurst Foundation.

We are most grateful to Nicky Oppenheimer and to the musical icon Johnny Clegg for offering their thoughtful insights and reflections on South Africa's developmental status quo in the forewords. This book, too, has an accompanying ballad, 'This is How it Works', the lyrics of which follow, written jointly with Cape Town's Robin Auld, and available at www. thebrenthurstfoundation.org and www.robinauld.co.za.

Thanks are also expressed to Professor Barry Desker, then Dean of the S. Rajaratnam School of International Studies in Singapore, where Dr Mills enjoyed a stint between August and October 2014 as a Visiting Senior Fellow. This occasion provided comparative Southeast Asian insights, which appear here, especially on the manufacturing and services sectors.

All errors and omissions, of course, are ours alone.

Finally, this book is dedicated to our brothers and sisters: Shelley Sandell and Roddy Mills; and Steven Herbst and Susan Herbst. We have benefited from their wonderful support throughout our lives.

'This is How it Works'

(Lyrics Robin Auld/Greg Mills)

21 years along the road
for some the streets are paved with gold
The rich get it all
the poor get the blame
the more things change they stay the same

From apartheid to democracy
Madiba's dream is getting harder to see
Sushi for wabenz
Payola stands tall
All pay don't pay for much at all

Chorus:
This is how it works
Isebenza ngoluhlobo
This is how it works
E bereka Jaana
This is how it works
Isebenza kanje
This is how it works
E Sebetsa tjena

For some the power is running out
for some the lights well they never go out
Send you a letter to tell you what you're owing
you pay 5 times just to get where you are going
The culture of the land don't count for a thing
we got the vuvuzela where we used to sing

VIPs in darkened limousines
in parliament they are a'fighting

Before divided by white and black
now it's jobs and hope that we lack
can't fiddle any longer to build our nation
too many still waiting for their liberation
This beautiful land we have to share
done so much we're only halfway there
if we are to move beyond 21
it has to work for everyone

This is how it works
From Kakamas to Cape Town
This is how it works
De Aar to Botshabelo
This is how it works
in the foundries of Dimbaza
This is how it works
The machines of Madadeni
This is how it works
On the boats of St Helena
This is how it works
The taxis of Mthata
This is how it works
In the mines of Tshikondeni
This is how it works
the factories of Jozi
This is how it works
Isebenza ngoluhlobo
This is how it works
E bereka Jaana
This is how it works
Isebenza kanje
This is how it works
E Sebetesa tjena